Shandilya Bhakti Sutra

Aphorisms for Devotion to God and

The Principles of the Philosophy of Love for Him

[Roman Transliteration of Verses, English Exposition, Elaborate Notes]

Ajai Kumar Chhawchharia

ISBN: 9781982980122

DEDICATION

I dedicate this Book to Lord Sri Ram who is my dearest of dear, most beloved, the essence of my life and being, and for whom, and for whose pleasure, and on whose behest, and on whose divine mission, this book is dedicated.

Nothing that I write is of my own creation. It is the Lord who is getting it done. So I deserve no credit. However, being an ordinary man like the rest of us, I may have committed errors, and for those I beg forgiveness. I hope this book will help to continue the great tradition of singing the glories of the different aspects of same indivisible one Divinity in order to meet diverse needs of the Soul, the Spirit, one such being to find peace and happiness amidst the surrounding turmoil of the world by being able to spend some time in the thoughts of the Divine Being, the same 'Parmatma', the same Lord known by different names in different tongues.

No creature is perfect; it's foolhardy to claim so. The best of paintings cannot replace the original; the best of words cannot express the original emotions and sentiments. Even the Lord was not satisfied by one flower or one butterfly—he went on endlessly evolving and designing newer forms. So, I have done my best, I have poured out my being in these books. Honestly, I am totally incompetent—it was the Lord who had done the actual writing and had moved my fingers as if they were merely an instrument in his divine hands. But nonetheless, it's a tribute to the Lord's glory that he does not take the credit himself, but bestows it to them whom he loves as his very own. And to be 'his very own' is indeed an unmatched honour. However, I still beg forgiveness for all omissions, commissions and transgressions on my part that I may have inadvertently made. It's the Lord's glories that I sing, rejoice in, write on and think of to the best of my ability. I hope my readers will also absorb the divine fragrance effusing from the flowers representing the Lord's books, enjoy the ambrosia pouring out of them and marvel at the Lord's stupendous glories.

I submit this effort at holy feet of my beloved Lord Ram whom even Lord Shiva had revered and worshipped. And surely of course to Lord Hanuman who was a manifestation of Shiva himself. Finding no words to express my profound gratitude to Ram, I just wish to remain quiet, and let my silence do the speaking and praying on my behalf.

I hope the reader will find my book useful and interesting. Since English is an international language, this book will help the English speaking world to access this masterpiece of classical Indian scriptural text.

"He leadeth me! O blessed tho't!
O words with heav'nly comfort fraught!
What-e'er I do, wher-e'er I be,
Still 'tis God's hand that leadeth me!" [A Hymn by: Joseph Henry Gilmore in 1862.]

Ajai Kumar Chhawchharia

Author

CONTENTS

SPACE FOR READER'S NOTES

(1) PREFACE

The book "Shandilya Bhakti Sutra" is a Book of 100 Aphorisms that explains what 'Bhakti', the spiritual philosophy dedicated to devotion and love for Lord God, actually is, and how to attain success in developing this eclectic spiritual virtue. It also points out the finer nuances of Bhakti and deals with this subject from the perspective of the philosophy as expounded in the scriptures such as the Upanishads, the ancient Purans such as the Vishnu Puran, the Geeta of Lord Krishna, and the Srimad Bhagvat Mahapuran. Hence, the 'Shandilya Bhakti Sutra' is an intelligent assessment and analysis of the esoteric spiritual concept of Bhakti that would convince a person of its immense importance and unmatched value as a unique and singularly effective path to God-realisation with its attendent bliss and beatitude.

This book can also be called "Shandilya Bhakti Shatak" as it has 100 verses. ["Shatak" = 100]

The 'Shandilya Bhakti Sutra' is named after sage Shandilya. We come across this name in different scriptural texts, right from the Vedic and the Upanishad period till the period of the epic Mahabharat which coincides with Lord Krishna's Geeta period.

A quick look at these sages as they are mentioned in these

ancient scriptures: (a) One sage named Shandilya is mentioned several times in the Shatapath Brahmn (9/4/4/17; 10/1/4/10). He was a great authority on the ritual of the fire sacrifice. He is said to be a disciple of sage Kushri and a teacher of sage Vaatsya. (b) Another Shandilya appears in the Sama Veda tradition's Chandogya Upanishad, 3/14. (c) The name of sage Shandilya is mentioned in the Shukla Yajur Veda's Brihadaranyka Upanishad at three places, i.e. 4/6/1, 4/6/3 and 6/5/4. (d) An Upanishad named 'Shandilya Upanishad' is also attributed to him, and it is the 14th Upanishad of the Atharva Veda tradition. This Upanishad presents the metaphysical philosophy behind the concept of Yoga and is comparable to Patanjali's Yoga Sutra which essentially deals with the physical aspect of Yoga. (e) One Shandilya is mentioned as a sage in the court of king Yudisthir in the epic Mahabharat, Sabhaaparva, 4/17.

However, sage Shandilya who penned his philosophical thoughts on Bhakti in his book 'Bhakti Sutra' most probably belongs to the post-Krishna's Geeta period as he has cited the philosophy of many scriptures that existed at that time, such as the Geeta itself, the Purans such as the Srimad Bhagvat Mahapuran, the Vishnu Puran, the Nrisingh Puran, the epic Mahabharat, as well as the Upanishads, all of which are referred to by him, either directly or indirectly by inference.

Some such instances where these scriptures have been freely used by sage Shandilya to support his logic and arguments in favour of the supremacy of Bhakti over all other means of God-realisation are the following:

(a) He has directly quoted from Krishna's Geeta in Sutra no. 14 where he refers to the Gopis, Sutra no. 23 where Chapter 12 of Geeta is referred to, and Sutra no. 83 where a direct mention of the Geeta is done (as this Sutra refers to Geeta's verse nos. 6/30, 9/22, 9/34, 11/55, and 12/6).

(b) At numerous other places he has cited the Geeta to support his philosophy, e.g. in Sutra nos. 6, 9, 17, 22, 41, 46, 47, 50, 52, 54, 56,

57, 58, 66, 70, 76, 81, 83, 84). (c) He has also cited the Srimad Bhagvat Mahapuran (Sutra nos. 14, 52), the Vishnu Puran (Sutra nos. 52, 74, 75), and the Nrisingh Puran (Sutra no. 67).

(d) At other places, he has cited the Upanishads, for example the Chandogya Upanishad (Sutra nos. 3, 11, 31), the Taitteriya Upanishad (Sutra no. 6), the Shwetashwatar Upanishad (Sutra no. 18), the Brahm Sutras (Sutra nos. 30, 91), the Mahabharat (Sutra nos. 53, 79).

The question arises: was the teacher named Shandilya who enunciated the 'Bhakti Sutras' the same as the ones appearing in the scriptural texts as mentioned herein above? Though the physical time frame covered in these scriptures extends over several eras, yet it is quite possible that all these names refer to the same person. It is because some of the ancient sages had mastered and perfected the art and science of controlling their life forces, known as their Prans or their vital winds, so much so that they could live for extended periods of time, much beyond the average lifespan of an ordinary human being. This is expected especially with Shandilya as he was an expert on Yoga, the branch of knowledge that deals, among other things, with the control of the vital winds through different methods. This is clear when we read Shandilya Upanishad cited above.

He was a great and renowned teacher and philosopher par excellence. People from far and wide used to come to the hermitages of such enlightened teachers in those times to gain knowledge. Shandilya used to preach them on various aspects of metaphysical and theological knowledge pertaining to the Vedas, the Upanishads and the Purans. Later on he must have realized that he did not get internal peace inspite of expounding on the scriptures for the better part of his life. He contemplated upon this dilemma to determine the reason why he was not at peace with himself, and came to the conclusion that true peace does not come with mere knowledge, even of the Supreme Lord, but it comes only when the creature develops true love, affection and devotion for the Lord.

He thought over the matter and saw that if this was the case with him then it would also be the case with the countless disciples he had taught, who had graduated from his hermitage and went on to become established teacher in their own right. So he wondered that, after all, what is the use of having a deep knowledge of metaphysics and theology and studying the numerous scriptures, of being an expert in these scriptures and the knowledge they grant, if a person can't obtain that object for which he acquires this knowledge? What is the use of his life as a teacher and advisor if the generations that depend upon his teachings and advices can't actually gain something worthwhile, if they continue to suffer in the endless cycle of birth and death inspite of having the best person as their teacher? So he should change track from merely preaching about the scriptures and do something about the question concerning peace of the soul.

Upon intense deliberation he concluded that true peace, bliss, beatitude and blessedness of the soul comes only by having devotion and love for the Lord God, for ultimately the teachings of all the scriptures is meant to bring the living being closer to the Supreme Lord, and if this objective is not met then the whole exercise is wasted. All the methods prescribed in the scriptures for this purpose are true, correct and effective, but they are difficult to implement and the chances of failure are higher than that of success. Everyone cannot reach his spiritual goal by pursuing the many methods advised by the scriptures.

So, what was the solution? Being an enlightened teacher, this question perennially disturbed him, especially because others looked up to him for guidance. Upon intense contemplation and delving deep into this matter he determined that the solution lies in 'Bhakti'—the path of devotion and love for the Lord God. Hence he decided to preach on Bhakti henceforth, and utilize his expertise on the scriptures to prove the supremacy and effectiveness of Bhakti as a far better spiritual pursuit as compared to other methods to attain God-realisation with its attendent eternal peace, blessedness, bliss, beatitude and felicity. Bhakti was the easiest way to find liberation and deliverance from the cycle of miseries and torments associated with this mortal and gross world of transmigration.

This is very clear in the first verse (Sutra) itself of this book, wherein sage Shandilya opens his discussion by saying "Now we shall enquire about Bhakti". It clearly means that he had been teaching or preaching about other topics, and finally decided to dwell upon Bhakti because whatever he taught or preached was not sufficient in fulfilling his desires to help himself as well as disciples to attain the goal of life, which is to attain eternal internal peace for the soul as well as find liberation and deliverance from the cycle of transmigration. This objective can be fulfilled only by attaining God-realisation, i.e. being able to establish oneness between the individual and the supreme Lord, to merge one's own 'self' known as the pure consciousness with the 'Supreme Self' known as Brahm who is the cosmic Consciousness personified.

Now, let us examine the title of this book 'Bhakti Sutra' more closely. The word 'Sutra' means a 'key', a 'code', an 'aphorism', a 'formula', a 'principle'. A 'Sutra' when applied to any body of knowledge refers to a basic formula or the key principle by understanding which one can easily grasp the wider body of knowledge. Here that knowledge pertains to how 'Bhakti' (devotion and love) for the Lord God can be practiced, what its many variants are, what are the pitfalls to be guarded against, and what its spiritual rewards are. A 'Sutra' is an indicator of something of profound importance and great significance. A wise man's effort should be to understand what that indication is; he must look for the spiritual goal that Bhakti points to and leads to.

The word 'Sutra' also means a 'thread'. So, 'Shandilya Bhakti Sutra' is like a garland of salutary spiritual wisdom consisting of the many beads symbolized by the excellent practical advice given by sage Shandilya to all spiritual aspirants who seek the nectar of eternal happiness, joy, peace, bliss and beatitude, and these beads of spiritual wisdom have been threaded together using an easy medium of having the purest and the truest form of 'love' for Lord God, a method that everyone can access and easily practice. The additional bonus that the spiritual seeker gets is attainment of liberation, deliverance, emancipation and salvation for his soul. This is achieved by following the path of Bhakti, i.e. the path of submission, devotion, love and faith in Lord God, the path that requires no formalities and rituals, a path that is absolutely easy to follow, and a path that grants the fruit that is difficult for even great sages and ascetics to obtain by practicing other spiritual methods advised in the scriptures.

All learners need an easy to read and understand guide-book to help them grasp the essentials of the subject of their interest. Similarly on the spiritual path too an aspirant would need guidelines and a road map to show him the correct way forward, to tell him what to do in order to achieve success in his spiritual endeavours and warn him against the various pitfalls and how to avoid them, to provide him with some benchmarks against which he can judge his success, and at the same time tell him the wonderful reward that awaits him if he follows the instructions properly.

In the spiritual realm, Bhakti (devotion and love) for Lord God is of tremendous and singular importance. There are scriptures that deal with this eclectic spiritual theme, but they are so many of them, so vastly scattered and voluminous, and so varied in their contents and different in their prescriptions that a devotee is more likely to get confused and lost in the maze of advices given by them than actually be able to benefit from reading them. The present book 'Shandilya Bhakti Sutra' fulfils this necessity—as it presents the guidelines of Bhakti in a very precise and concise form in a language that is easy to understand.

This book contains gems of spiritual wisdom and is certain to inspire any person who is seeking spiritual guidance as to how to please his beloved Lord God in the easiest and the best possible way. This path would also lead him to the true goal of human life, which is to attain eternal bliss and beatitude as well as to find liberation and deliverance for the soul from the endless miseries associated with the cycle of birth and death in this mortal, delusory and gross world, which is attained by God-realisation and becoming one with the cosmic Soul.

'Bhakti Sutra' fulfils the six basic characteristic qualities for any formula to be excellent and practicable—viz, it is easy to understand and remember as it is clear and unambiguous, it gives complete information on Bhakti, it is succinct, concise and aphoristic, it contains the essence of the matter presented in a beautiful manner, it has a universal application and covers the entire theme by not leaving anything out of its ambit, and it is irrefutable in as much as its veracity and effectiveness cannot be challenged.

Bhakti is a spiritual practice that helps the seeker to establish a direct link with the Supreme Lord in a very easy manner. This path is free from the strenuous efforts needed for other paths such as Yoga (meditation), Dhyan (contemplation), Karma (doing deeds righteously and dispassionately offering all its rewards to the Lord God), Dharma (living a righteous life in accordance with the many principles of right living and right conduct as expounded in the scriptures) etc.

Bhakti is something that is natural and effortless as it basically consists of the virtues of 'love and devotion' for the Lord God whom the devotee begins to love and be sincerely devoted to from the core of his heart. This will come automatically once the devotee realises that the Lord whom he loves is the one who is his best friend and companion, who will take care of all his temporal as well as spiritual welfare and needs in a selfless manner like no other Lord or Master would ever do. Bhakti comes spontaneously, and like a spring of nectar sprouting forth from the bowls of the earth, Bhakti would provide eternal blessedness, blissfulness and beatitude to the devotee, it would provide profound solace and succour to his soul in a world full of endless miseries and torments. Not only this, the devotee is assured of emancipation and salvation by the virtue of having Bhakti by his side.

The "Sutras" are so short in their primary form that they seem too difficult to be understood without the help of an explanatory commentary in an easy language which would bring out the profound spiritual truths that they refer to. Hence, many learned souls have tried their best to explain them in the way they had interpreted them. Obviously this gives way to variations in the way the Sutras are explained by different people because each person has his own unique style of writing and explaining things in the way he has understood it.

There is another excellent book of 'Bhakti Sutras', and it is called 'Narad Bhakti Sutra'. These two books compliment each other as they deal with the same subject from two angles. A student of Bhakti will be best advised to read both these books, i.e. the Narad Bhakti Sutra and the Shandilya Bhakti Sutra, to get a comprehensive knowledge of what Bhakti consists of.

Though both Narad and Shandilya have dealt with this theme of Bhakti in a systematic manner, but they differ in their approach to it—for whereas Narad has dealt with Bhakti at an emotional level linked to the heart, sage Shandilya has tackled Bhakti from the intellectual and philosophical level. This is expected—because whereas Narad was a devotee par-excellence of Lord Vishnu who had chosen the easy to follow and practical path of pure love and devotion for the Lord as the only means of attaining beatitude and bliss as well as liberation and deliverance from the world of transmigration, sage Shandilya was more contemplative and intellectual by nature as he was a learned sage who was more knowledge oriented and wished to first study the different scriptures to understand the philosophy and the logic behind the supremacy of Bhakti over other spiritual paths to God-realisation as expounded in these ancient scriptures before actually accepting it. So naturally therefore, his exposition on Bhakti is based on logical reasoning and citing of instances from the scriptures to prove and establish the effectiveness of Bhakti as a spiritual path leading to attainment of bliss, beatitude and oneness with the Lord God.

Hence, whereas Narad's prescription of Bhakti are simple to understand and would appeal to a person who is driven by the emotions of his heart, sage Shandilya exposition on Bhakti would attract those who need an intellectual basis to be convinced of anything, and these Sutras need a bit of explanation as well as they are too abstract to be comprehended easily.

One crucial point is to be noted here. If a wise person wishes to reach a goal in life, he will first research on the goal itself, then on the various options available to him to fulfill his desire, and finally decide for himself which path is best for him. Once he is convinced that a particular path or mean is the best way he can use to reach his desired goal in life, he will then be able to follow the selected path faithfully, free from distractions arising out of confusions and doubts; he will follow the path with zeal and commitment. This will ensure his success. On the other hand, if he merely goes on a path because someone has said it is good, then the chances of falling on the way and getting fidgety and confused are pretty high.

To wit, in the realm of spiritualism, this method also applies to a devotee who wishes to reach his Lord God and attain eternal bliss and beatitude. A wise devotee is one who first convinces himself in no uncertain terms that Bhakti is the best way to attain his God. The Shandilya Bhakti Sutra would help in this basic step of convincing him of the supremacy of Bhakti over all other paths of God-realisation in a logical way by citing the proof and the authority of the scriptures to establish the reputation of Bhakti as the supreme path to God.

Once convinced and determined that he would follow Bhakti to realize his spiritual goal, the devotee can now rely on sage Narad's advice given in the Narad Bhakti Sutra as a practical guide to move ahead.

That is why sage Shandilya is very particular in giving proofs (known as Pramaan) of what he proposes because he wants to be logical and likes to present his concepts in a rationale way by eliminating arguments and doubts that contradict the basic truth he is putting forth in the Sutras. Narad, on the other hand, is not interested in any intellectual discussions but goes straight to the practical aspects of Bhakti, so his approach is to the point and straightforward as it is based on his personal practical experiences regarding Bhakti.

A spiritual aspirant would really benefit if he studies both the Sutras of Shandilya and Narad to reach his goal of God-realisation.

One salient feature of 'Shandilya Bhakti Sutra' is that it freely draws from the philosophy of the Upanishads and other scriptures to establish the fundamental principles that govern Bhakti, the spiritual path of devotion and love for the Lord God that leads to Go-realisation with its attendent bliss and beatitude as well as final liberation from the cycle of transmigration which traps an ordinary soul. This is naturally expected because sage Shandilya was a great exponent of the Upanishads. He has liberally utilized his deep understanding of metaphysics and theology as enunciated in the Upanishads, and has used this knowledge to establish the supremacy of Bhakti over all other spiritual paths. During his discourse he cautions us that the object of this Bhakti is only one Lord, and he is the Supreme Being whom the Upanishads call Brahm, the personified form of the cosmic Consciousness, and that the realization of this Brahm is the real aim of Gyan, spiritual wisdom and enlightenment. Bhakti aims to bring about a union between an individual's 'self', i.e. his Atma, with this supreme Brahm who is the Supreme Atma or the Parmatma, also known as the Lord God of creation.

Now let us examine the basic formula employed by sage Shandilya in Bhakti Sutra. The Sutras can be classified under the following four headings—(a) The "Pramaans" or the proof of any given knowledge, here that knowledge is concerned with Bhakti; (b) The "Prameya" or the object that is to known through these proofs, and the object here is the Supreme Lord that is the ultimate object of Bhakti; (c) The "Saadhans" or the practical way or mean to be adopted to attain that object and fulfill one's objective, which here is attainment of God-realisation; and (d) "Mukti" or final liberation and deliverance from the mundane existence for those aspirants who have followed the prescribed spiritual path of Bhakti diligently; it is synonymous with being one with the Supreme Being, the Lord God of the world; it is also synonymous with the merger of the individual's Atma or soul with the cosmic Atma or the Supreme Soul of creation.

The "Pramaans" are of three kinds—(i) one that is actually witnessed by the sense organs of perception such as the eye which sees it, ears which hear it, skin which touches it, tongue which tastes it, and nose which smells it; (ii) one that is imagined by applying the mind and logic, and it is based on inference; and (iii) one that is based on the words of the scriptures which are authentic in their nature. Out of these three, the proof based on the scriptures is the best as they always speak about the Universal Truth.

The "Prameya", the object sought through this knowledge and proof, is also three—viz. (i) God or the Supreme Being, also known as Brahm in the Upanishads; (ii) The Jiva or the living being; and (iii) The physical world, both the animate and the inanimate. Out of these three, the knowledge of Brahm is the best because he represents the cosmic Consciousness that is eternal and the only spiritual truth in this creation. The other two entities, i.e. the Jiva and the world, are manifestations of Brahm, hence subsidiary to the Supreme Being.

The "Saadhan" are the means by which one can attain his selected objective, which here is to attain God-realisation. These Saadhans, are many and varied. Some of them are like Yoga (meditation), Dhyan (contemplation), Tapa (austerity and penances), Yagya (religious sacrifices), and so on and so forth. But the best means is called Bhakti, or having devotion for the Lord God. Shandilya proves it by citing the philosophy of the different scriptures.

The "Mukti" is the ultimate aim of all spiritual practices. It is to attain liberation and deliverance from the cycle of birth and death; it is to attain emancipation and salvation for the soul. Gyan or knowledge, Karma or doing deeds, and Bhakti or devotion are the three main ways by which this Mukti can be achieved. Out of these three paths ("Saadhanas") Bhakti is said to be the easiest and the best as it is loved by the Lord (the "Prameya") himself. And what is the proof ("Pramaan") of it? Spontaneous attainment of an extreme level of ecstasy, bliss and joy is the proof of the effectiveness of Bhakti vis-à-vis other methods. Shandilya gives signs that would indicate that a spiritual aspirant has attained maturity in Bhakti (verse no. 44).

Sage Shandilya has graded 'Bhakti' into two categories (and so has sage Narad). One is called 'Paraa Bhakti' which is the supreme form of Bhakti; it is the primary form of Bhakti. The other is called 'Gauna Bhakti' which is secondary kind of Bhakti; or it is subsidiary to the primary Bhakti. We shall read about them in the text. The Paraa Bhakti is primarily related to the inner-self and is directly concerned with the heart and the soul which are intensely and sincerely in love with the Lord God so much so that one loses awareness of one's self as well as of his surrounding, while the Gauna Bhakti is an external form of devotion that relies on doing of deeds such as offering of worship, chanting the Lord's holy name, singing the glories of the Lord, doing Yoga (meditative exercises), participating in community religious services as making charities, doing sacrifices, fasting, keeping of vows etc.

Both these two types of Bhaktis lead to God-realisation, but while Paraa Bhakti or the supreme form of devotion for the Lord God establishes oneness with God immediately as it is a self-kindled fire that springs up spontaneously, the Gauna Bhakti takes a long time to mature as it is step-by-step method that one takes to start the same fire.

Further, the 'Paraa Bhakti', the primary and the principle kind of Bhakti, the best form of Bhakti, is to have true, undiluted and selfless form of love, affection and devotion for the Lord God. The 'Gaun Bhakti', the secondary or the subsidiary form of Bhakti, are the various ways that a devotee adopts to attain the Lord God; they aid a person to obtain success in Bhakti.

Bhakti has also been classified into three different categories as follows: 'Gyan Bhakti' (one develops devotion for the Supreme Being when he becomes wise and enlightened, when he understands the Truth and the truthful path to God-realisation—verse nos. 2-11), 'Yoga Bhakti' (using meditation and contemplation as a tool for devotion and God-realisation—verse no. 19), and 'Gaun Bhakti' (devotion for the Lord God that is obtained in a subtle manner by practicing different spiritual paths—verse nos. 20-71). This last, i.e. the Gaun Bhakti, has been further classified into three categories (verse no. 72)—viz. 'Aarta Bhakti' (when one is extremely distressed he takes refuge with the Lord God in order to overcome his sufferings and adverse circumstances), 'Jigyasaa Bhakti' (when one has heard about the Lord and wishes to explore more about him and to know what the spiritual rewards of Bhakti are, and so he follows this path more with an intention to examine it than for the sake of love for Lord God), 'Arthaarthi Bhakti' (when one expects any worldly reward from doing Bhakti and offering worship to the Lord).

The wonderful thing about sage Shandilya's Bhakti Sutra is that it clearly states that every human being has an equal right to attain the Supreme Being through the path of Bhakti, irrespective of his caste, birth and race—verse no. 78.

Since the Bhakti Sutras of Shandilya are quite esoteric in nature, they need to be told and explained in a simple and day-to-day language so that even a common man can easily understand them. That is why I have adopted a "minimalist approach" in my own book—that is to say, I have explained the meaning of the verses in simple terms with the main emphasis on brining out their intent and purpose, and have also given references to other scriptural texts when they are referred to in a particular verse, but have desisted from either delving too much and too deeply into each verse or quoting the cited references from the scriptures in detail so that brevity and simplicity in my narration can be maintained.

My effort is to make these wonderful Sutras on Bhakti easily understandable by all so that at least some who read them may be motivated or inspired by this reading to adopt this excellent path of Bhakti and develop devotion for the Lord God, and not to prove any scholarship or expertise of any kind whatsoever. So it is vital for me to keep my version of "Shandilya Bhakti Sutra" simple, straightforward and uncomplicated. I do not want my reader to get mentally overwhelmed by too high a philosophical and intellectual discussion on a subject that actually should be appealing and motivating instead of being something of a sort of a burden on the mind. After all, Bhakti is a subject that is expected to be exceptionally attractive and nourishing for the soul; it is expected to be succulent and fresh as pure nectar for the Spirit, and not something that would instead put one off.

We shall observe during our reading of this excellent work on the spiritual theme of Bhakti that sage Shandilya has covered all its important aspects as he takes a broad sweep at it. For instance, we read about Saguna Bhakti as well as Nirguna Bhakti—i.e. devotion for the formless, invisible and cosmic form of the Supreme Being known as Brahm as well as the Lord's manifested that has a name and the details of which is easily understood and well documented, such as Lord Krishna or Lord Vasudeo and Lord Ram (verse nos. 27-28, and 46-48 respectively).

Then we read about the different ways the Supreme Being is attained by Bhakti depending upon the spiritual evolvement and the level of enlightenment of the aspirant, i.e. about Brahm-realisation (verse nos. 28-29), about self-realisation (verse no. 30), and about God-realisation (verse nos. 46-49).

There are many ways by which Bhakti can be practiced

successfully. For instance, there is the path of Prem (undiluted love for the Lord God—verse nos. 2 and 83); Gyan (acquisition of knowledge that leads to development of devotion for the Lord God—verse nos. 16-17, 26-27); Yoga (which teaches how to bring about a union between the individual soul with the supreme Soul—verse no. 32); proper application of the mind, wisdom and enlightenment that helps removal of delusions and confusions (verse nos. 33-42); Bhajan (worshipping the Lord God at a personal level—verse nos. 56, 76); Kirtan (singing the Lord's glories aloud in a group—verse nos. 57, 76); many other forms of worship such as Sacrifices (verse no. 66); Daan (charity—verse nos. 68, 70); Dhyan (contemplation and remembrance of the Lord God and his glories—verse no. 65), Japa (repetition of the Lord's holy name—verse no. 61), Karma (doing righteous deeds and offering everything to the Lord God—verse nos. 64, 71), formal services such as offerings of oblations and libations that are made to the Lord God (verse nos. 67-68, 70), even the humblest form of offering such as a mere leaf or a flower that is offered to the Lord God with due love and devotion (verse no. 70), and so on and so forth.

The signs of success in Bhakti as exemplified by the characters exhibited by acclaimed devotees of the Lord God have also been outlined in brief (verse nos. 43-44). It is also acknowledged that some inadvertent errors may be made by a person in the path of Bhakti, but then he need not lose hope as he is advised to neutralize their negative affects by taking remedial steps (verse nos. 69, 74-75).

A word of caution here: When the phrase "Lord God" is used anywhere in the text it refers to the 'Supreme Being' whom the devotee worships. This Supreme Being is the Lord as well as the God for the devotee. A person may have other Lords and Masters in this world to whom he is obliged to pay his respects to and be obedient to because of exigencies of life in the world; and similarly there are hosts of other Gods in this creation too before whom a creature is obliged to bow and keep them in good humour. But the person does so only because he is under obligation to honour them and obey them for practical reasons even if he does not want to do so, for antagonising such Gods, Lords or Masters would create unnecessary problems for him which he can easily avoid by simply keeping them happy and pleased. But the 'Lord God' is someone for whom love, respect and adoration comes spontaneously from within the heart of the person, for this 'Lord God' represents the Supreme Being who is the person's loving Father and Redeemer, his true Friend and his spiritual Destiny. This 'Lord God' is the one whom Jesus Christ referred to as "My Father", and who is called "Brahm" by the Upanishads and the Vedas. Therefore, when the term "Lord God" is used in our text, the reader must clearly understand that it is referring to the Supreme Being who has manifested in the particular form that is loved, adored, revered and worshipped by the individual devotee. It may be the Lord's visible form with attributes (such as those of Lord Ram or Lord Krishna), or the Lord's invisible cosmic form that is known as pure Consciousness that has no attributes or discernible forms (such as Brahm). It is the devotee's choice as to how he would prefer to worship and love the Lord God who is the Almighty Supreme Being and whose primary form is nothing but 'pure cosmic Consciousness'. It is only the Supreme Being who is worthy of having devotion for, who is worthy for offering worship and saying prayer to; it is only the Supreme Being who can provide ultimate bliss and beatitude to the creature; it is only the Supreme Being who can grant liberation, deliverance, emancipation and salvation to the living being. Hence, 'He', the Supreme Being, is not merely a 'God' or a 'Lord', but the "Lord God"!

I finally wish to say that by writing this book I am only trying to selflessly serve my beloved Lord God and obey his divine command in the best possible way I can think of, as through these books I try to spread the 'good word of the Lord' and make the pitcher of excellent nectar of spiritualism contained in the ancient Indian scriptural texts for which they are so famed, but unfortunately this nectar was restricted due the language barrier, available to the world in the English language so that they can be easily accessed by even the common man. I will feel happy if even a few souls benefit from my book.

It is a service that I am rendering to my beloved Lord Sri Ram. And I pray to the Lord to bless me as well as my esteemed reader with his divine grace and mercy!

I also express my thanks to Sri Somil Bharti ji who was kind to provide the Roman Transliteration of the Sanskrit verses to me. I pray to the Lord God to bless him.

Date: 21st May, 2018

Author: Ajai Kumar Chhawchharia.

(2) SHANDILYA BHAKTI SUTRA

Aphorisms for Devotion to God and

The Principles of the Philosophy of Love for Him

[Roman Transliteration of Text, English Exposition, Elaborate Notes]

Chapter 1, Part 1:

Verse nos. 1-9

|| शाण्डिल्य भक्ति सूत्रम् ||

प्रथमोऽध्यायः

प्रथममाह्निकम्

|| śāṇḍilya bhakti sūtram ||

prathamō 'dhyāyaḥ

prathamamāhnikam

१ / १/ १ अथातो भक्तिजिज्ञासा ॥ १ ॥

1/ 1 / 1 athātō bhaktijijñāsā || 1||

(1/1/1) Now we shall discuss (contemplate and deliberate upon; to enquire) about the doctrine (the principles or the philosophy) of 'Bhakti'. [Or, 'now let us examine and analyse in detail what Bhakti actually consists of'.] (1)

['Bhakti' means to have devotion and love for the Lord God. So sage Shandilya says that now he shall discuss about this subject in detail.

Shandilya says that he wants to 'inquire' into Bhakti; he wants to analyse it and determine why and how it is the best and the supreme path to God-realisation. He wants to do it to remove all doubts and confusions about Bhakti.

The opening words of this verse clearly indicate that sage Shandilya had been expounding upon other philosophical and metaphysical topics and discussing the numerous scriptures before he finally decided to dwell upon the subject of Bhakti. He was an illustrious and enlightened sage, one who was well-versed in all the scriptural texts such as the Vedas, the Upanishads and the Purans. He had been preaching on them for a lifetime, but unfortunately he did not find the sort of deep internal peace and bliss that this knowledge is supposed to grant to a person.

Contemplating upon the matter and wondering how to get internal peace and bliss for the soul he concluded that though it is true that the knowledge of the scriptures is necessary for one's wisdom and enlightenment, but that true peace and beatitude does not come merely with this knowledge. The true purpose of all the scriptures is to show the creature the path to God-realisation, to advise him how to find liberation and deliverance from the cycle of transmigration with its attendent chain of miseries and torments, to guide him so that he can find true peace, bliss and happiness in life. But if this aim is not easily achieved, then the entire exercise would fail.

Shandilya discovered that except for a few spiritual aspirants and seekers of God, the majority failed to reach their spiritual goal by trying to follow the various paths advised in the scriptures. So therefore he decided to teach his disciples the path of 'Bhakti', i.e. the path of undiluted love, affection and devotion for the Lord God as a means to attain one's spiritual objectives very easily and without any hassles associated with the other paths.

Being a learned sage he also knew that in the final analysis it was 'Bhakti' that would grant his soul an eternal sense of peace and bliss and contentedness. This is because while all other topics are related to the mind, Bhakti is directly related to the heart where the soul resides. Besides this, Bhakti is also very dear to the Lord God, and being in touch with Bhakti is like being in direct touch with the Lord himself. Since the Lord God is an embodiment of eternal bliss and beatitude, and since Bhakti is directly related to the Lord, therefore it follows that a person who adopts Bhakti as a means to reach God has accessed a pitcher of endless spiritual peace, joy and bliss for himself.

So therefore, the illustrious sage Shandilya, who had thoroughly dealt with all the branches of the Vedas, the Upanishads, the Purans etc., who was a repository of all secular knowledge and spiritual wisdom, after having expounded upon and discussing all the other branches of the scriptures, had finally turned his attention to the doctrine of Bhakti because he could not find anything anywhere that was more suitable for the attainment of his desired goal of having eternal bliss and beatitude for his soul, of finding eternal peace and rest for his soul by being one with the supreme Soul known as the Parmatma, than the path of Bhakti.

This conclusion is very clear in this verse (Sutra) itself when sage Shandilya opens his discussion by saying "Now we shall enquire about Bhakti". It clearly means that he had been teaching or preaching about other topics, and finally decided to dwell upon Bhakti because whatever he taught or preached was not sufficient in fulfilling his desires to help himself as well as disciples to attain the goal of life, which is to attain eternal internal peace for the soul as well as find liberation and deliverance from the cycle of transmigration. This objective can be fulfilled only by attaining God-realisation, i.e. being able to establish oneness between the individual and the supreme Lord, to merge one's own 'self' known as the pure consciousness with the 'Supreme Self' known as Brahm who is the cosmic Consciousness personified.]

१ /१ /२ सा पराऽनुरक्तिरीश्वरे ॥ २॥

1 /1 /2 sā parā'nuraktirīśvarē || 2||

(1/1/2) That (i.e. Bhakti) is to have supreme, true, undiluted and untainted love and attachment (parā 'nurakti) for the Supreme Being, the Lord God of creation (rīśvarē). (2)

[To have true, undiluted and untainted love and devotion for the Lord God is the 'primary' form of Bhakti. All other forms by which Bhakti is practiced, and about which we shall read in due course in this book, are 'secondary' types of Bhakti; they are subsidiaries to Bhakti. This is because they aid in fulfilment of Bhakti; their aim is to give the devotee success in his Bhakti for the Lord God.

To wit, having love, affection and devotion for the Lord God is the 'primary' or the 'principal' way Bhakti is practiced, while all other ways are 'secondary' or 'subsidiary' in nature.

Why is love the primary form of Bhakti? It is because it is favoured by the Lord God himself; it is because it creates an unbreakable bond between the devotee and his Lord; it is because all other things become secondary and inconsequential once love and devotion for the Lord God takes a firm root in the heart and the mind of the devotee. When this actually happens, nothing in the world would ever distract him from his goal of attaining his beloved Lord; nothing would come in the way of his determination to attain oneness with his object of adoration, i.e. to become one with the Lord, or attaining 'God-realisation'. Bliss, beatitude, eternity, liberation, deliverance, emancipation, salvation etc.—all become irrelevant to a devotee and he is not worried about them at all. They come to him without asking.

The importance of 'love' for the Lord God as the paramount requirement of Bhakti has been endorsed in verse no. 83 also.

This form of Bhakti is called 'Paraa Bhakti', the best form of devotion for the Lord God, or the primary form of Bhakti. There are many ways one can express his devotion for the Lord God, such as offering of worship to the Lord, praying to him, reciting his holy name, singing his glories, reading scriptures related to him, etc. But if one does not love the Lord God, if one does not have affection for him, then he cannot be said to have reached maturity in his devotion for the Lord.

One thing is to be kept in mind here. The 'love and longing and attachment' that are being endorsed in this verse relate to the Supreme Lord, and not to the world and anything related to it. That is why this kind of love is called "Paraa"—'supreme'.

This 'attachment' for the Lord is different from the attachment that one has for the world and its material objects, for while attachment with the Lord leads to final liberation and deliverance from this world, attachment with the world leads to further entanglement with it.

It is observed in the world that a person derives immense pleasure when he thinks of an object to which he is emotionally attached and which he intensely loves. That is why emphasis is given on having 'love and attachment' to God in the realm of Bhakti. Since the main objective of Bhakti is to establish oneness between the devotee and the Lord God, this sort of undiluted and untainted 'love and attachment' is of paramount importance because it helps in bringing this oneness to fruition.

When one truly loves the Lord God and develops an intense affection for him, then all other things become irrelevant. Remembering the Lord and remaining lost in his thoughts, which would be equivalent to doing meditation and contemplation on the Lord, at all times of life would be a natural thing when a person begins to love him. This is observed even in the secular world when a lover appears to be lost in the memory of his beloved if the love between the two is true and intense.

When this eclectic and spiritually evolved stage is reached, then no other formalities are needed between the devotee and the Lord. To wit, the development of love and affection for the Lord God in the heart of his devotee is the ultimate aim of Bhakti, because this establishes an inviolable relationship between the devotee and the Lord God; it's a bond that cannot be broken. This love for the Lord is equivalent to creating oneness between the devotee and his Lord God—which is also the aim of other spiritual practices.

Bhakti, with its special emphasis on love, is a spontaneous emotion sprouting from the deep recesses of the heart of the devotee that makes him long for his beloved Lord God and be attached to him like no other spiritual practice would ever do.

The importance of love for the Lord God is stressed in the Vishnu Puran, 1/20/18, where Prahalad, one of the greatest devotees of Lord Vishnu, says: "Let a steady flow of love for the Lord not cease from my heart in any of the births that I may have to take."

Similarly, in Vishnu Puran, 1/20/19, he says: "Oh Lord! Let a steady flow of love for you not cease from my heart in the same way as attachment for the world and worldly things do not cease from the heart of ordinary mortals."

In Srimad Bhagvat Mahapuran, 11/14/21, the Lord declares: "I, who am the beloved Self of a holy soul, can be captivated only through Bhakti. Devotion to me absolves even the lowly person of the stigma that is attached to his low birth".

In Srimad Bhagvad Geeta, 10/9-10, Lord Krishna says: "My devotee who knows me as his only object of adoration and love, who is attached to me with a single-minded devotion and faith, who has his mind and senses focused on me, who is completely absorbed in me, is able to purify his heart and enliven his inner self by nurturing my thoughts and remembering my divine glories, my holy name, my forms etc. at all times. To wit, he lives for me, he breathes for me, he eats and drinks for me, and he lives in me to the extent that without me he would have no independent existence. Verily indeed, he lives solely for my sake; his life is to serve me and give pleasure to me. For him even a moment's separation from me is unbearable. He carries on with his worldly duties and responsibilities, but only because these activities please me, and not because any of his own interests are served by them. I alone am enshrined in such a devotee's glorious heart (i.e. there is no other God whom he worships and loves except me). To wit, I am a darling of this devotee (and by extension, he is a darling of mine). To him who has devotion for me in the aforesaid manner, I eliminate the darkness and the gloom of delusions and ignorance from his heart, and at the same time I am responsible to lighten his path leading to the final liberation and deliverance that grants eternal bliss and beatitude."

The love of God is an infinite and absolute feeling of spiritual ecstasy and joy which grants immense bliss and beatitude to the blessed devotee. It is something to be experienced personally, and not something that can be explained to others by the use of words. 'Bhakti' therefore is longing for the Lord God that is so intense and deep down in the heart of the devotee that he thinks of nothing else but the Lord. Bhakti is a unique feeling that overcomes all other emotions; it is a desire for love of God that negates all other desires. It fills the heart of the blessed devotee with extreme ecstasy and profound bliss like it was a pitcher overflowing with pristine pure and freshly produced nectar.

A person who has once experienced love for God would never think of anything else.]

१ /१ /3 तत्संस्थस्यामृतत्वोपदेशात् ॥ ३ ॥

1 /1 /3 tatsaṁsthasyāmṛtatvōpadēśāt || 3||

(1/1/3) It is because he who has established himself in 'it' (i.e. who has established his own 'self' in the supreme 'Self' known as Ishwar or Brahm, the Supreme Lord, by being one with him; he who has attained God-realisation by following the path of Bhakti) is deemed to have found the eternal nectar of immortality and bliss unbound. Verily indeed, this is the universal and unequivocal declaration of the scriptures. (3)

[The first word 'it' establishes a link between what is being said in this verse with the previous verse no. 1/1/1 and what is said in it.

In the previous verse we have read that having love and attachment for Lord God is the best form of Bhakti or devotion for the Lord. Now this verse tells us the reward of having such love and attachment for the Lord God. What is this reward? It is the symbolic pitcher of nectar of immortality, beatitude and eternal bliss that a devotee gets for his Bhakti for the Lord.

To wit, if a person develops truly intense love for Lord God, then he is able to experience ecstasy and bliss that has no parallel.

This idea is also expressed in the Chandogya Upanishad, 2/3/2 wherein it is essentially said that: "A person who develops devotion for Brahm is able to attain immortality."

In the Chandogya Upanishad, 2/23/1 it is said that all other rites and rituals may lead a person to their respective results, but it is devotion to the Supreme Lord alone that would help him to attain immortality.

It is said in the Katha Upanishad, 2/3/17-18 that: "By having undiluted and purest form of devotion for the Lord God, one is able to transcend the mundane world of mortal existence, and attain eternal bliss and final beatitude.

Sage Shandilya says: Some may say that for developing Bhakti or devotion for the Lord God, philosophical knowledge known as Gyan is indispensable. To wit, without metaphysical and theological knowledge of the Supreme Being, it is not possible to develop devotion and love for him. But it is an erroneous proposition. Because an atheist may have studied the scriptures and therefore has all the theoretical knowledge required about Brahm or the Supreme Being, but he will not have a trace of love and devotion for the Lord either in his heart, nor will his mind ever believe in the universal and irrefutable existence of the Lord. So therefore, merely having 'knowledge' does not mean that one would have 'love and devotion' for the Lord God.

Again, though a person who has studied the scriptures may have access to all the metaphysical and theological knowledge they contain, but he never has eternal bliss and a tremendous feeling of beatitude and blessedness that a devotee experiences.

Hence, sage Shandilya says that it is crucial for a wise person to learn what Bhakti consists of; he says that it is the primary reason for his teaching of the Sutras on Bhakti.]

१ /१ /४ ज्ञानमिति चेन्न द्विषतोऽपि ज्ञानस्य तदसंस्थितेः ॥ ४॥

1 /1 /4 jñānamiti cēnna dviṣatō 'pi jñānasya tadasaṁsthitēḥ || 4||

(1/1/4) Now, to be firmly established in the supreme Brahm is made possible only by attainment of wisdom and enlightenment about the 'self' (because the 'self' of a devotee is pure consciousness known also as the Atma, and Brahm is also the same consciousness known as the Parmatma operating at the universal level of existence).

So therefore, does it mean that Gyan (knowledge; gnosis) is equivalent to Bhakti (devotion)? Is it correct to say that Bhakti is another aspect of Gyan? [This doubt arises because both Gyan and Bhakti help a seeker to be established in the Supreme Being; both help him to attain oneness with the Lord God.]

No, it is not so. For instance, a person may have full 'knowledge' about his enemy, he may know everything worth knowing about the enemy, but this knowledge does not mean that he 'loves' his enemy who is inherently antagonised against him, who hates him. How can a person be affectionately attached with an enemy even if he tried to do so; it's incredulous to even think of it! (4)

[The verse has the word "saṁsthitēḥ"; it means to be firmly

established.

In the realm of metaphysics, being Brahm-realised is usually treated to be equivalent to being self-realised. This comes with the supreme knowledge about the truth of the 'self'—that the person's true identity and his true 'self' is not his gross physical body but the Atma, that this Atma is pure consciousness which is the same as the cosmic Consciousness embodied in the form of the Parmatma, the Supreme Lord and God of creation. Hence, there is no distinction between the individual's 'self' and the supreme Self (i.e. the Parmatma or the Lord God) whom the devotee loves and worships.

So it may be argued that the 'Gyan' or the knowledge of the self which leads to self-realisation and makes a wise and enlightened person be firmly established in the Truth that there is no distinction between his 'own self' and the 'supreme Self' known as the Parmatma (Lord God; Brahm) because both are the same universal and cosmic entity known as pure Consciousness, is the same as 'Bhakti' which also aims to establish the same oneness or uniformity between the devotee and his Lord God.

Sage Shandilya refutes this line of argument by giving the example of an enemy. A wise person would gather all information he can lay his hand upon about his enemy, but that does not mean that this knowledge would make him love his enemy. A person is so worried about his enemy that he would always remember him, not this remembrance is not out of love and affection for him. On the contrary, the mere thought of the enemy would make him angry and irritated. So there is no question of a person loving an enemy simply because he remembers him day and night, that his mind and heart are occupied by the thoughts of that enemy, or because he has acquired all possible knowledge that is required of that enemy.

Similarly in the spiritual field, simply having 'Gyan' (knowledge) of who the Supreme Being is does not mean that the devotee would develop 'Bhakti' (love and devotion) for him. It is obvious, because whereas 'Gyan' is an activity of the mind and the intellect which usually works rationally, 'Bhakti' is the activity related to the heart with its emotions and sentiments which are usually immune to all other considerations.

The principle expounded in this verse can be understood by another example. In a king's court there are many ministers and councillors who are extremely wise and experts in their fields. Then there are others who are ordinary in their knowledge but are very faithful to the king and devoted to him; some may even love their king more than their own families. Now in this scenario, though the king would give the wise and skilled members of his court great respect, but at the personal level his heart would be more inclined towards those ministers who are totally devoted to him and would willingly lay down their lives for his sake. The king knows that when bad times fall upon him, or he stares at ruin due to some unfortunate situation, then there are fair chances that his wise ministers may abandon him because they see no future in supporting him any longer, but those who are totally devoted to him would prefer to die but not betray their beloved king.

Similarly, the Lord God prefers to show his grace upon his devotees who love him unconditionally as opposed to those persons who are experts in the knowledge of the scriptures which also teach about the same Lord God. The reason is that the Lord knows that his poor devotees are totally dependant upon him as they have no where else to go to seek solace and succour, while the learned persons have other resources at their disposal by which they can obtain liberation from their miseries.

It is said in the Srimad Bhagvat Mahapuran, 10/14/4, that: "Those who abandon the path of undiluted and untainted love and devotion for the lotus-like holy feet of the Lord God who is the source of true well-being, and instead labour to acquire knowledge that is dry and abstract just for its own sake, such persons toil in vain like those who pound empty husks of paddy in an attempt to extract grain from it."

In Srimad Bhagvad Geeta, 12/5, Lord Krishna says: "My devotee alone is on the real path to attain the highest state of blessedness, whereas the path of Gyan is beset with dangers and results in a sorrowful wreck of its adherents.

A similar view has been expressed by Lord Ram in Ram Charit Manas, Chaupai line nos. 1-5 that precede Doha no. 45 when he says: "Gyan is a difficult path full of pitfalls, and is also not favoured by me as compared to the path of Bhakti. Hence, wise ones prefer Bhakti over Gyan."]

१ /१ /५ तयोपक्षयाच्च ॥ ५॥

1 /1 /5 tayōpakṣayācca || 5||

(1/1/5) Besides this (as said in the previous verse no. 1/1/4), it is also observed that with the rise of Bhakti in a person's heart, Gyan is proportionately reduced (till a time comes when Bhakti is at its zenith best and Gyan is completely eliminated). [This is another reason why Bhakti is superior to Gyan.] (5)

[When one begins to love someone dearly, when this element of love between the lover and the beloved become steady and deep-rooted, then all other matters take a back seat and are rendered irrelevant.

In the realm of spiritualism, when the devotee begins to love and have devotion for his beloved Lord God, then all other spiritual practices become useless and redundant for him. After all, the main purpose of Gyan (knowledge; gnosis) is to make a person become aware of the true purpose of his life and understand the truth concerning his own self as well as the Supreme Lord. Gyan enlightens him about the real goal of his life—which is to find freedom from the cycle of birth and death with its accompanying miseries and torments, to attain emancipation and salvation for his soul, to find liberation and deliverance for himself by merging his own 'self' known as the Atma with the supreme Self known as the Parmatma, the Lord God, and thereby find eternal peace, rest, bliss, beatitude and felicity.

A devotee is easily able to attain this spiritual goal by following the path of Bhakti, with the added benefit of getting first-hand help and support from his beloved Lord God who would virtually hand-hold him to success. In the case of Gyan though the goal is the same but the path would be tedious and full of risks, and the seeker would have to make all efforts himself.

The devotee who pursues the path of Bhakti is like an infant in the care of its parent who is very concerned that the child remains safe and happy, while the devotee who pursues the path of Gyan is like an adult who has to take care of himself. This has been expressly made clear by Lord Ram in Ram Charit Manas, Aranya Kand, Chaupai line nos. 4-10 that precedes Doha no. 43.

When a devotee can easily attain his beloved Lord God and experience a sense of eternal bliss, peace, joy and blessedness by following the path of Bhakti, then there is no need for him to look elsewhere for this purpose. So he stops pursuing the path of Gyan which would have also made it possible for him to reach this final spiritual goal of his life, but with a lot of difficulties encountered on the way, besides the constant risk of failure—refer Ram Charit Manas, Uttar Kand, Chaupai line nos. 2-4 that precedes Doha no. 45.

As it has already been said in verse no. 2 herein above, Bhakti is nothing but undiluted and untainted love and devotion for Lord God that is of the purest kind. It needs no intellectual efforts associated with Gyan, thereby making it accessible even to an ordinary person of an intellect that may not be up to the mark.

Srimad Bhagvat Mahapuran, 7/7/52, says: "Attaining Gyan leading to Brahm-realisation, Godhood and an exalted stature equivalent to that of a wise and enlightened sage or seer, or doing numerous meritorious deeds such as austerity, penance and charity, or acquiring the best of knowledge and wisdom, or observance of sacred vows and sacraments etc.—nothing pleases the Lord like having pure and undiluted devotion for him does."

In Srimad Bhagvad Geeta, 7/23, Lord Krishna says: "All sorts of offerings (made in the sacred fire and other rituals) go to respective Gods, but (offering made by a devotee in the form of his) devotion comes straight to me."

Similarly, in Srimad Bhagvad Geeta, 12/7, Lord Krishna says: "I quickly provide deliverance from the ocean of transmigration to him whose mind is fixed on me (i.e. who has deep devotion for me)."

In Vishnu Puran, 1/20/20, 28, the Lord told Prahalad: "Since your mind remains steady in having devotion for me, since you are steadfast in it, surely emancipation and salvation will come to you. And I bless you that your devotion and love for me will never diminish."

A devotee exults and is ecstatic when he becomes one with his beloved Lord God, and then he exclaims as said in the Shvetashvatara Upanishad, 3/8: "I have realised the transcendental Brahm who shines brilliantly like the sun that is beyond the reach of darkness. Only by realising him one attains freedom from the cycle of birth and death in this mundane life characterised by transmigration. There is absolutely no other way of God-realisation and its attendent blessedness."

So therefore, when Bhakti dawns on the mental horizon of a person, Gyan loses all its charms and fades away. To wit, as soon as Bhakti appears, Gyan disappears automatically. Hence, Bhakti is preferred by those who are wise and intelligent.]

१ /१ /६ द्वेषप्रतिपक्षभावाद्रसशब्दाच्च रागः ॥ ६ ॥

1 /1 /6 dvēṣapratipakṣabhāvādrasaśabdācca rāgaḥ || 6||

(1/1/6) Such negative emotions as hatred, antagonism, bitterness, suspicion, opposition and malice are not the characters associated with Bhakti because it is related to sweetness of emotions that provide extreme bliss and eternal joy that are derived by a person when he tastes the sweetness of unadulterated nectar. (6)

[Bhakti is nectar-like in its sweetness and blissfulness. There should be no trace of antagonism, bitterness, suspicion, opposition and ill-will between the devotee and his beloved Lord God. Even from the standpoint of the mundane world it is observed that love between two individuals is sustainable only when they trust each other completely, and there is no iota of bitterness, malice or hate between them. Both individuals derive immense pleasure in each other's company, and this pleasure compares with nothing as far as they are concerned. True love matures when even sitting silently with one's lover gives bliss and happiness to the beloved that would even surpass the joy of drinking nectar.

So is the case with Bhakti. A devotee revels in his Lord God; he derives profound joy and immense bliss by merely remembering the Lord. Bhakti sprouts only in a heart that has been thoroughly cleansed of the negativities mentioned herein above. Both can't coexist.

This fact has been endorsed in Taitteriya Upanishad, 2/7, which says: "The fortunate ones are able to taste the bliss of Brahm-realisation as well as of self-realisation which is far sweeter than any other taste".

The Taitteriya Upanishad, 11/7, says: "Supreme Brahm is an embodiment of ecstasy and bliss. If one devotes himself to him (i.e. if one thinks of nothing but Brahm), one is able to enjoy the taste of this nectar (of ecstasy and bliss)."

In Srimad Bhagvad Geeta, 2/59, Lord Krishna says: "Those who have attained stability of the mind turn away from enjoyment of the sense objects of this world; they find no enjoyment in their taste if they have tasted the bliss of Brahm-realisation."

In Srimad Bhagvad Geeta, 16/18-20, Lord Krishna says: "Those who are ignorant are not only filled with negative qualities such as egoism, arrogance, haughtiness, lust, anger and malice for everyone, but they hate me too (for no rhyme or reason inspite of the fact that I am their best friend and well-wisher, and I live in their own body as their true 'self'). I send such malicious fools to take an ignominious birth (literally go to a demonic womb) in the world of transmigration. Birth after birth they keep sinking down in the vast ocean of transmigration (because they are incompetent to attain me and find deliverance for themselves, for these stupid fools don't know that their salvation lies in having devotion for me)."

Bhakti is in the form of deep love and attachment for Lord God who is the beloved of the devotee. This love is similar to the love that the Gopis (the milkmaids and other female householders of Vrindavan) had for Lord Krishna. Refer: Narad Bhakti Sutra, verse nos. 21-23.

Earlier, verse no. 1/1/2 has already said that Bhakti takes the form of 'deep attachment for the Lord God'. Now, this 'attachment' for the Lord is different from the attachment that one has for the world and its material objects, for while attachment with the Lord leads to final liberation and deliverance from this world, attachment with the world leads to further entanglement with it.

Sage Shandilya's ideal of true Bhakti is that the individual's soul should be fully saturated with love, affection and attachment for the

Lord God, for otherwise he will not get his due share of bliss and ecstasy even if he has attained self-realisation by way of having Gyan (gnosis; metaphysical and theological knowledge). To wit, the path to God is Bhakti and not Gyan.]

१ /१ /७ न क्रिया कृत्यनपेक्षणाज्ज्ञानवत् ॥ ७॥

1 /1 /7 na kriyā kṛtyanapēkṣaṇājjñānavat || 7||

(1/1/7) Bhakti is not dependent upon any action to fructify or become effective (na kriyā) as is the case with Gyan which requires diligent efforts in order to mature and bear fruits (to yield the desired result). (7)

[Since Gyan is an intellectual activity requiring an active participation of the mind and the intellect with their different components, it would need concerted effort to bear fruit. For instance, one would be required to study the scriptures thoroughly, practice their various doctrines and test their efficacy, be able to focus the mind on the work at hand, be contemplative and analytic in approach, be able to maintain balance of the mind in the face of constant distraction from the external world, be consciously able to renounce all temptations arising from the sense objects of this world, and so on and so forth.

Even practicing the many spiritual paths to liberation and deliverance as advised in the scriptures need effort—such as doing meditation, penances, austerities, sacrifices, keeping of vows, charities, self-control over the sense organs, renunciation of the world etc. Without diligent and concerted efforts, success eludes the spiritual aspirant.

But this is not the case with Bhakti. It is because Bhakti relates to the emotions of love, affection and attachment with the Lord Gods that originate in the heart of the devotee, and are natural and effortless by their very nature. No one has to make an effort to love someone. We say 'I have fallen in love with such and such person'. Now, the word "fallen" itself indicates that no effort is involved, because effort is made to go uphill and not while falling down from a cliff. It does not mean that Bhakti is the downfall of the soul; not at all. This phrase is cited just to show how no effort is needed 'to be in love with anybody', for it is a spontaneous emotion that sprouts on its own accord. No one has to make an effort to love someone even though effort has to be made to reach the place where the beloved lives. Remember: we are dealing with love for the Supreme Being, hence misinterpretation of the phrase "to fall in love" is absolutely not called for here.

In the case of Bhakti which entails having undiluted and untainted love and affection for the Lord God, the unique situation is that there is no need to go anywhere to find the Lord who is the object of this love. So while initiating the process of Bhakti the devotee does not have to make any kind of 'effort' as it purely consists of having love and affection that have a spontaneous origin in his heart, even attainment of the object of his love, i.e. the Lord God, needs no effort on his part because the Lord is present everywhere as he is omnipresent and all-pervading, even residing within the devotee's own heart so that he need not go anywhere to search for his beloved Lord. Refer verse nos. 82 and 85 also in this context.

So we conclude that no physical effort is needed in Bhakti from its beginning till its fruition. It is an effortless exercise as opposed to Gyan which is based on efforts, and its success also depends of the ability to make efforts properly.

This fact is endorsed by Lord Ram in Ram Charit Manas, Uttar Kand, Chaupai line no. 1 that precedes Doha no. 46 where he says: "Say, what effort is needed for success in Bhakti, for it does not depend on any kind of exercises which are necessary for other spiritual practices such as meditation, contemplation, fire sacrifices, austerities, penances, keeping of vows etc. To wit, Bhakti is indeed an effortless path to God-realisation."

In the same breath, Lord Ram says in Ram Charit Manas, Uttar Kand, Chaupai line nos. 3-4 that precede Doha no. 45: "Gyan is a very difficult proposition. It has difficult requirements, and the mind finds it difficult to remain focused on this path. Only a few can obtain success in it even after enduring the greatest of difficulties. To wit, the path of Gyan is full of hassles and pitfalls."

Like the flame of the lamp which not only illuminates its own self but also its surrounding effortlessly, Bhakti fills the devotee's inner self with bliss and ecstasy along with spreading this joy seamlessly and effortlessly to others who come in contact with him.

Why does 'Bhakti' need no effort while 'Gyan' needs it? It is because Bhakti is of the form of selfless love that does not have any desire for results, hence a devotee need not strive to attain success in Bhakti because if it this Bhakti is true in him success in the form of God-realisation with its attendent bliss and beatitude will come to him automatically. On the other hand, Gyan expects results; there are benchmarks for progress in the path of Gyan and set objectives that are to be achieved. So the aspirant is always on his toes to be vigilant in the path of Gyan, as even a slight carelessness on his part would undermine his success, even neutralising all previous successes, and lead to his ultimate downfall and ruin.]

१ /१ /८ अत एव फलानन्त्यम् ॥ ८॥

1 /1 /8 ata ēva phalānantyam || 8||

(1/1/8) This is why the spiritual rewards of Bhakti are profound and infinite. (8)

[The discussion in the previous verses has established the supremacy of Bhakti over all other spiritual practices that lead to God-realisation. Since Bhakti provides eternity and beatitude to the soul, since it brings about oneness between the soul of the devotee and supreme Soul represented by the Lord God whom the devotee loves, Bhakti leads to final liberation, deliverance, emancipation and salvation of its practitioners. So its effects and results are beyond measure.

All other meritorious deeds and actions provide heaven and its pleasures and comforts to the creature, but in due course of time when these good effects of his good deeds wear out the creature has to return to this world to do more deeds and take more actions to re-achieve that heavenly pleasure and comfort that he had been enjoying earlier. This is clearly mentioned in the Chandogya Upanishad, 8/1/6 which says: "Meritorious deeds and actions helps the creature to gain sovereignty of this world, but when their good effects end so does this sovereignty. Similarly, good deeds give the creature sovereignty of the heaven, but when these good effects wear off the sovereignty too ends."

This is why it is said in the Srimad Bhagvat Mahapuran, 6/11/52 that "A devotee who has tasted the blissful nectar of Bhakti for the Lord does not crave or covets anything else. So he says—'Oh Lord, I do not want the upper heaven known as the Brahma-Loka, nor do I want to go to the heaven known as the Indra-Loka where other Gods live, or the sovereignty of the upper worlds nor of the lower worlds, and I do not want success in the different forms of Yoga as well, and neither do I want salvation. I want nothing but love and devotion for your holy lotus-like feet.' " Surely this declaration clearly indicates that a person who known the pleasure that comes by tasting the nectar of bliss, joy, beatitude and felicity that comes with Bhakti would not like any other kind of pleasure. To wit, Bhakti has unique rewards.

Similarly, it is said in Srimad Bhagvat Mahapuran, 10/16/1/37 that: "Those who have found for themselves the pollen of bliss represented by the Lord's holy lotus-like feet would neither covet the realm of Brahma, nor the sovereignty of the whole earth, nor the dominion over the nether worlds, nor acquisition of mystical powers that are obtainable by Yoga, and not even liberation and deliverance that is the aim of enlightened and self-realised ascetics. They want nothing but pure love for the Lord and service of his holy feet."

An exactly identical idea is expressed by sage Sutikshan when he met Lord Ram. He told the Lord: "Oh Lord! I have only one wish, and it is that you reside in my heart eternally as if it was your own dwelling place. I wish that I feel proud that I am a humble servant of the Lord, and he is my Lord and Master!" Refer: Ram Charit Manas, Aranya Kand, Chaupai line nos. 20-21 that precede Doha no. 11.

When king Manu and his wife Satarupa did Tapa (penance) to have a divine vision of Lord Vishnu, the Supreme Being, the Lord revealed himself before them and asked them to request him for any boon that they wanted to be granted. The couple asked the Lord that they want nothing but pure and undiluted love and devotion for his holy feet. Hearing this wise request from his devotees, Lord Vishnu was very pleased and amused because he did not expect that after doing such hard penance the couple will not want any worldly rewards. Of course the Lord granted this wish. This is narrated in Ram Charit Manas, Baal Kand, Chaupai line no. 8 that precedes Doha no. 150 –to—Chaupai line no. 3 that precedes Doha no. 151.

All the joys and pleasures of the world and heaven taken together are like the shallow water of a stream, while the spiritual bliss and ecstasy obtained by Bhakti is like the ocean of nectar.

It is said in the Srimad Bhagvat Mahapuran, 1/2/28-29 that: "The ultimate aim of the Vedas is realisation of Lord Vasudeva (the Supreme Being); the various sacrifices also have this aim of attainment of Vasudeva; the different forms of Yoga also lead to this Vasudeva; all sorts of rituals have their end in Vasudeva; and all wisdom has its culmination in Vasudeva; all austerities and penances have Vasudeva as their goal; all spiritual virtues aim at the realisation of this Vasudeva; and all destinies end in Vasudeva."]

१ /१ /९ तद्वतः प्रपत्तिशब्दाच्च न ज्ञानमितरप्रपत्तिवत् ॥ ९॥

1 /1 /9 tadvataḥ prapattiśabdācca na jñānamitaraprapattivat || 9||

(1/1/9) Even a person who has Gyan (i.e. who is an expert in metaphysics and theology; who is wise, learned and enlightened; who is self-realised and Brahm-realised) may surrender or submit (prapatti) himself before the Lord God (in order to fulfil certain of his spiritual objectives) like a devotee who surrenders himself before his beloved Lord in order to attain oneness with him[1].

But simply surrendering or submitting oneself before the Lord God does not mean that a person has Bhakti for him[2]. (9)

[[1]Both types of persons derive bliss and beatitude with this self-surrender, albeit with a difference. What is the difference? Surrendering to the Lord God in Bhakti by a devotee is different from surrendering to him in Gyan by a person who is an expert in the knowledge of the scriptures and metaphysics. This is because a person who surrenders himself in Bhakti does not expect anything from his beloved Lord; he surrenders before the Lord just because he loves his Lord God very dearly and more than anything else, while a person who knows the rewards of Brahm-realisation would surrender to the Lord because he expects some of the spiritual rewards that come with it. So therefore, while the 'Bhakta', i.e. a devotee, surrenders himself before the Lord just for the sake of his love for the Lord, the 'Gyani', i.e. a person who is learned in the scriptures, would surrender before the same Lord God but he does so as he expects some reward by doing this. To wit, the 'devotee' surrenders himself before the Lord for the sake of his love for him as he expects nothing in return, but a 'learned person' surrenders himself before the same Lord with some sort of expectation from him.

Though it is true that Bhakti is selfless because the devotee does not want any reward for his devotion and love for the Lord God, but it is also true that it is not without any reward, albeit these rewards come on their own accord and unasked for. Gyan also has rewards, but they are sought after and attained consciously by the learned person.

So we see that in both the cases of Bhakti and Gyan the spiritual aspirant has to surrender his own self before the Lord, but in the case of Bhakti it is done in a selfless manner that is driven by pure love and affection for the Lord God because Bhakti itself is based on the premise that it is love for the Lord God for the sake of love only, while in the case of Gyan it is done with one's spiritual interest and welfare in mind, hence it is not selfless.

[2]A man may surrender himself before a deity in the belief that this deity would fulfil his wishes. So there is some worldly desire in this relationship. If the objective of this surrendering is achieved, the person who surrenders would continue to worship that deity, otherwise he would certainly look to some other deity who would fulfil his needs. So this sort of surrender or submission is definitely not Bhakti. It may be driven by Gyan—i.e. the knowledge that a particular deity is

empowered to fulfil a particular wish of the worshipper, but there is no element of love, affection or devotion involved for the deity. It can be said that it is like a business proposal—the deity fulfils the worshipper's wishes, and the worshipper continues to offer his reverence to the deity. This is surely and certainly this type of surrender or submission before the Lord is neither Bhakti nor Gyan at all!

It is not 'Bhakti' because there is no trace of love, affection and devotion for the deity involved, and this surrender before the deity has not come from the heart but it is a selfish wish for certain worldly fulfilment of desire. It is not 'Gyan' either because the reward expected by surrendering before a deity is not attainment of eternity, nor bliss and beatitude that comes with liberation, deliverance, emancipation and salvation of the soul, but some kind of worldly gain. A person who has true Gyan would know that the world is transient and it is worthless to ask for anything related to it, and surely therefore he would never surrender or submit himself before any God for fulfilment of worldly wishes.

Therefore it is conclusively proved that merely surrendering or submitting before the Lord God (prapatti) is neither the way of Bhakti nor the way of Gyan!

There is another way we can interpret this verse. It has been said that even those who have Gyan, i.e. those who are wise and learned, too surrender themselves before someone in order to fulfil their desires. For instance, even a learned person who has some desire that needs to be fulfilled will be inclined to surrender himself to any junior god or deity if he thinks that his desires can be fulfilled by doing so even though he knows fully well that such fulfilment would be transient in its nature as the world itself is transient, that such surrender and its expectant fruit would not grant him any kind of eternal peace and fulfilment as is obtainable by being contented, by having renunciation and by obtaining the bliss of self and Brahm realisation. Nevertheless, desires for some gain may force even a wise and learned person to surrender and show affection to some junior deity in the hope of fulfilling his wishes.

Refer: Srimad Bhagvad Geeta, 7/19-23, where Lord Krishna says: ""A truly enlightened soul is one who worships me with the realisation that there is no other God but me. But such souls are rare. Those who think that they are wise and learned are often carried away by many desires so much so that they begin worship other deities in the hope of fulfilment of these desires. Whatever form the devotee chooses to worship me with a craving for fulfilment of some worldly desire, I establish his faith in that particular form he has chosen to worship. This enables the devotee to fulfil his worldly desires. But these so-called wise, learned and enlightened men are actually of low understanding as they forget that everything in this mortal world is perishable. Such people do not find eternity. On the other hand, my devotees have no worldly desires, nor are they attached to subsidiary form of mine. So they find me, they come to me, and they become eternal like me. To wit, Gyan does not ensure that a devotee would find eternity and bliss."

Hence, to surrender before any deity does not automatically mean that the person is wise, learned and enlightened, because such surrender to fulfil worldly desire only indicate that the person is totally ignorant of the essence of the knowledge of the scriptures (Gyan) that he claims to have.

But surrendering before the Lord God in Bhakti is different from the above surrendering because in the case of Bhakti it is selfless, it is driven by pure love and affection for the Lord, and there is no desire or expectation involved in it.]

----------******----------

(3) SHANDILYA BHAKTI SUTRA

Aphorisms for Devotion to God and

The Principles of the Philosophy of Love for Him

[Roman Transliteration of Text, English Exposition, Elaborate Notes]

Chapter 1, Part 2:

Verse nos. 10-26

॥ शाण्डिल्य भक्ति सूत्रम् ॥

प्रथमोऽध्यायः

द्वितीयमाह्निकम्

|| śāṇḍilya bhakti sūtram ||

prathamō 'dhyāyaḥ

dvitīyamāhnikam

१ /२ /१ सा सुख्येतरापेक्षितत्वात् ॥ १० ॥

1 /2 /1 sā sukhyētarāpēkṣitatvāt || 10||

(1/2/1) Amongst all the spiritual practices (that lead to attainment of God-realisation, to attaining eternity of the soul, and attaining bliss and beatitude by having liberation and deliverance from this mundane existence), Bhakti is the chief one. This is because other practices (such as Gyan or self and Brahm realisation) depend upon Bhakti for bearing fruits.

To wit, Bhakti is the primary and fundamental means of God-realisation, and all other means are subsidiary to it. (10)

['Bhakti' stands for total commitment and devotion towards the Lord God, total surrender to him, to have undiluted and untainted love, faith and belief in him, to pursue the path leading to God-realisation without having any doubt, confusion and distraction, to be steady and unwavering on the way, and to feel extremely ecstatic and blissful.

Since the primary requirement for Bhakti is to have deep love and affection for the Lord God, it follows that a devotee would be totally focused on his path, and think of nothing else but his beloved Lord just like the case of a person who falls in love with another in this world. For a lover it does not matter if his object of love, the beloved, 'the darling of his heart', loves him or not, or what good qualities, if any, the beloved may have, or the geographical distance between the lover and the beloved, and all such related matters. A true lover would be lost in the thoughts of the beloved so much so that time comes to a standstill for him, and the surrounding world cease to exist.

In Bhakti the 'heart' is involved, while in other spiritual practices such as Yoga, Tapa, Japa Yagya, Karma, Dharma etc. the 'mind and the intellect' are involved. When the heart gets involved in any pursuit, the person becomes fully committed to his object because he becomes emotionally and sentimentally attached to it. If only the mind is involved then the chances are that he would have to cope with distractions. This is also observed in day-to-day life. When a person is in love with someone, then he would find it hard to focus his mind on the job at hand, for the heart would keep tugging at him and every now and then his mind would turn away from the work and start thinking of the beloved, the 'darling of the heart'. To wit, the heart would succeed in overpowering the orders of the mind.

So is the case also with Bhakti vis-à-vis other spiritual paths to God-realisation. One may feel distracted in a lesser or greater degree while doing meditation (Yoga), contemplation (Dhyan), repetition of the Lord's holy name (Japa), doing righteous deeds (Karma), living a meritorious life (Dharma), doing sacrifices (Yagya), renunciation and dispassion (Vairagya), going on pilgrimage (Tirtha) etc. if the heart does not agree fully with these practices, for it would keep nagging at the aspirant and pull his mind away from what it wants to do or is doing towards that object which the 'heart loves to do or wants to do'. To wit, all other spiritual endeavours would succeed only when they rely on the virtues of Bhakti—i.e. to love and be totally devoted to the Lord God, be unwavering in one's spiritual pursuit and be fully committed to God-realisation by overcoming all hurdles.

So in effect this verse implies that the sort of devotion, sincerity and commitment and other unique characteristics that Bhakti possesses are also to be practiced by the followers of other spiritual paths. Or, it can be said that all other spiritual paths are subsidiaries of Bhakti. To wit, if there is no Bhakti (love, affection and devotion for the Lord God) in the heart of the spiritual aspirant, then no other path would lead him to true God-realisation. He may get a taste of this eclectic spiritual transcendental state of God-realisation with its bliss and ecstasy, but it would be fleeting as he will not get it permanently, nor would he be able to taste this divine nectar in its purest form.

If one does not possess the unique virtues characteristic of Bhakti, then no matter which spiritual path he has chosen for himself for God-realisation he will find that his spiritual journey is full of problems and cumbersome, and the chances of failure are great. One of the primary reasons for this is that in the case of Bhakti the Lord God himself takes care of the spiritual seeker's future, whereas in all other paths he has to fend for himself.

This fact is reiterated in Ram Charit Manas, Uttar Kand, Chaupai line nos. 3-8 that precede Doha no. 116 where it is said that Maya (worldly delusions) and Bhakti are both close to Lord Ram (the personified form of the Supreme Being), but while Maya is like a dancer in a royal court who has to dance in accordance to the pleasure of the king, Bhakti is a maid who serves the king directly and is his favourite. So Maya is always afraid of Bhakti and subservient to it because it fears that if Bhakti gets annoyed then the Lord would also get annoyed.

To wit, other spiritual practices such as Yoga, Tapa, Karma, Gyan etc. will not be able to help the aspirant to attain true and sustainable bliss, beatitude and spiritual peace that comes with God-realisation if Bhakti is not invoked.

Say, what purpose will be served if one merely discusses about the quality, taste and benefit of certain kind of food at the intellectual level without actually eating and enjoying it. Can anyone get nourishment by merely analysing the food's nutritional value or discussing about it, if he is not able to actually eat it? So it is with Bhakti—say, what is the use of Gyan (knowledge of the scriptures and of the Supreme Being) and all other spiritual practices if one is not able to drench oneself in the cool and refreshing water of bliss and joy and feel blessed that comes by loving and endearing the Lord God, something that Bhakti teaches him. So therefore, Bhakti is the best method to enjoy the bliss and blessedness that comes with God-realisation. There is no doubt about it.]

१ /२ /२ प्रकरणाच्च ॥ ११ ॥

1 /2 /2 prakaraṇācca || 11||

(1/2/2) There are references in the scriptures with regard to this (i.e. to what has been said in the previous verse). (11)

[One such reference is found in Ram Charit Manas, Uttar Kand, Chaupai line nos. 3-8 that precede Doha no. 116. It has already been quoted herein above in the note appended to the previous verse no. 10.

Some of the other references are the following:

Chandogya Upanishad, 7/23/1 says: "'That Supreme Being is the pinnacle of the knowledge contained in the scriptures, and is the final goal of all religious and philosophical concepts. It is only from him that bliss is derived, and it only possible by completely surrendering to him and having devotion for him alone."

Similarly, Chandogya Upanishad, 7/25/2 says: "All this is nothing but the supreme Self known as Brahm or the cosmic Consciousness. He who knows this, he who is convinced of this, he who sees this truth, he indeed develops deep affection and devotion for this Truth in the form of the Self, he always thinks of this Truth, he finds pleasure in this Truth, he pursues this Truth, and finally he attains this Truth to become one with it. This transcendental state is achieved if one has saturated himself with this Truth (i.e. when one is deeply in love with the Lord

God who represents this spiritual Truth)."

To wit, even the Upanishads endorse the importance of having complete faith, devotion and surrender to the Lord God as well as to have deep love exclusively for him if one wishes to attain eternal bliss and beatitude in life.]

१ /२ /३ दर्शनफलमिति चेन्न तेन व्यवधानात् ॥ १२॥

1 /2 /3 darśanaphalamiti cēnna tēna vyavadhānāt || 12||

(1/2/3) Some may say that to 'see God' is the ultimate reward of Bhakti. But it is not so, for there are obvious objections to and discrepancies in this theory. (12)

[Bhakti does not want any reward; it is a selfless service to the Lord God that revolves around undiluted and untainted pure love for him from the depth of the heart. The true devotee does not say, 'Oh Lord, I want to see you.' This is like ordering the Lord which no humble servant would ever think of doing.

The term 'seeing' can be interpreted at two levels of consciousness: one is at that a person actually sees someone at the physical level of existence with his physical eyes, and the second is that a person experiences the presence of the other person at a subtle level even without actually seeing him with his eyes.

The former way of 'seeing' relates to the gross world and the gross organ of sight known as the eye. This organ of the body can see only gross things of the material world, and not those things that are actually there but have a subtle presence. This is evident from the following example: we can actually see the flower with our eyes, but can we see the scent of that flower? A blind man does not actually see the flower, but he will immediately know that a flower is near because he can perceive its presence by the virtue of the flower's subtle quality represented by its scent. Similarly, we can't see air, but does that mean that air is not present around us?

In the spiritual field a devotee does not have to actually 'see his beloved Lord God in physical terms with his own eyes' to derive the profundity of ecstasy, joy, blissfulness and blessedness that comes with God-realisation. God is not a physical thing to be seen or perceived by any of the gross sense organs of the creature's body. He is pure Consciousness that is too sublime and subtle for this to happen at the gross level of mundane existence. God is experienced and perceived only at a subtle level of consciousness, a level that transcends the mundane and the gross.

So a devotee deeply in love with his beloved Lord God lives in a perpetual state of bliss and blessedness as he 'sees' his darling Lord with the subtle eyes of his consciousness; he experiences the presence of his beloved Lord right inside his own being so much so that he feels his entire self has been possessed by the Lord. The ecstasy and bliss then becomes natural and inherent to him because God is bliss and joy personified! There is no separate entity now like a devotee and his Lord God—for they have become one and unified.

For others who do not have that level of enlightenment or spiritual attainment to understand what 'seeing of God' actually means, the claim that the devotee is so ecstatic and blissful because he is seeing his Lord right in his front would seem sheer madness and nonsense. It is because they only know one level of seeing anything—the level at which gross things of the world can be seen. They have no knowledge of seeing things at the subtle level of consciousness.

The Supreme Being's primary form is pure cosmic Consciousness that it is subtle and sublime, and it is so all-pervading that it is present in the form of all that exists in this creation. So in a sense we can 'see' the Lord God in every creature and every unit of creation if we have the 'eye' of wisdom.

It often times happens that the same invisible Lord who is an embodiment of cosmic Consciousness sometimes reveals himself in a physical form for the pleasure of his devotees. When this happens, the concerned devotee is able to 'see' the Lord in physical terms also in this world—as happens during the various incarnations of the Lord. But that does not mean that a devotee who has reached a transcendental state of consciousness when he can experience the presence of God inside his own self, resulting in his being in an extremely ecstatic and blissful state is deceiving others simply because the Lord God is not there in physical terms that can be verified.

Therefore, it cannot be said that 'seeing God' in physical form is the only criterion for success in Bhakti or its culmination. The objection to this proposition has been explained herein above in clear terms.]

१ /२ /३ दृष्टत्वाच्च ॥ १३॥

1 /2 /3 dṛṣṭatvācca || 13||

(1/2/3) This (i.e. what has been said in verse no. 12 herein above) is also observed in the world[1].

[There is another way of interpreting this verse as follows:] It is also observed in the world that when one sees something it is easy for him to develop love and affection for it. So therefore, when a devotee sees a form of the Lord God or witnesses the blissful state of others who have experienced God first hand (i.e. have attained God-realisation), it ignites a longing in his heart for the Lord, he also wants to witness the Lord and derive bliss and beatitude experienced by others[2]. (13)

[[1]It is observed in the physical world that the sun, however brilliant it may be, can be seen only through a transparent material such as glass, and not through anything that is opaque and hard such as wood or stone. But not being able to see the sun does not mean that the sun is not there.

Likewise, the Lord God reveals himself only to a devotee whose heart is softened by love and devotion for the Lord, and not to others, including those who have Gyan. But not being able to see or experience the Lord in this way by Gyan (gnosis) and other spiritual practices does not mean that he has no existence.

We have already read about the example of the 'flower' and the 'air' in the note appended to verse no. 12. So, not seeing God in physical terms by a devotee is no proof that Bhakti has no effect. Surely it has, but its effect is seen and felt and experienced at a subtle and sublime level that transcends the grossness of the world because the subject it deals with, i.e. the 'self' and the 'supreme Self', is also subtle and sublime as it is 'pure consciousness' and *not* like the gross things of the world and the equally gross organs of the physical body of the living being whose presence can be ascertained only by physically seeing them.

[2]This interpretation refers to the devotee beginning to have love for the Lord God when he reads and hears about the Lord's glories as narrated in the scriptures and glorified by the saints. The devotee realises that the Lord is his best friend and well-wisher, that the Lord would selflessly help and protect him, and that the Lord is the only one who can mend his future and provide him with peace and happiness that he so much

longs for. So the devotee begins to love and be devoted to the Lord.

Hence, Gyan or knowledge of something helps a person to develop love and affection for that object because he 'sees' something good for himself.

In this situation too, the reward of Gyan is Bhakti, and vice versa also. To wit, first there is the knowledge ("Gyan") of the existence of the divinity known as God, then there is the knowledge of the benefits that would accrue by being devoted to this God and surrendering before him, and this finally results in development of love and affection ("Bhakti") for the Lord. So, Gyan leads to Bhakti.

On the other hand, when one begins to love the Lord God, one would be too happy to know more about him as this knowledge would only cement his bond of love for the Lord, make his commitment and devotion for the Lord more robust as it would be based on conscious decision that relies on strong evidence and truth rather than on hearsay and imaginations.

It is said in Ram Charit Manas, Uttar Kand, Chaupai line nos. 5-8 that precede Doha no. 89 that: "The life's torments do not go away without worshipping Lord Ram. But without the grace of the Lord one is not able to know the Lord's greatness, divinity, majesty, glories and truth. Without this knowledge or awareness it is difficult to be steady in one's commitment and faith in the Lord, and without it Bhakti or devotion and love for the Lord will not be steadfast and deep-rooted."

And how does one come to know about the Lord? It is by the grace of the Lord himself—refer: Ram Charit Manas, Ayodhya Kand, Chaupai line nos. 3 that precedes Doha no. 127 that says: "Oh Lord! One comes to know about you only by your grace, and once that happens the spiritual seeker becomes one with you." Obviously this is also the aim of Bhakti—to be one with the Lord God, to establish oneness between the devotee and the Lord he worships.

From an intelligent and collated the reading of the verses it becomes clear that though Bhakti is independent and self-sustaining yet it is also true that knowledge (Gyan) and devotion (Bhakti) are complementary and supplementary to each other.]

१ /२ /४ अत एव तदभावाद्वल्लवीनाम् ॥ १४॥

1 /2 /4 ata ēva tadabhāvādvallavīnām || 14||

(1/2/4) That is why the Gopis (the milkmaids or female cowherds of Vrindavan; "vallavīnām") attained liberation and deliverance by merely having deep love and affection for Lord Krishna and being devoted to him in their love inspite of their not having access to any whit of metaphysical or theological knowledge of the scriptures, or being able to see the Lord in physical terms (after he left Vrindavan and moved to Mathura and onwards to Dwarka). (14)

[In this context, refer to Narad Bhakti Sutra, verse nos. 18-22 which directly relate to this verse.

The Gopis of Vrindavan were ordinary householders. They had never studied any scripture. Their life revolved around mundane existence and humdrum affairs of daily life. Yet they were praised by the Gods and lauded in the scriptures, and they found liberation and deliverance from the cycle of birth and death by just having something as plain and simple as love for Lord Krishna. This is being cited here to stress that for emancipation and salvation of the soul nothing is needed, except to have love and devotion for the Lord God. Gyan has no role to play here.

The Gopis loved and adored Lord Krishna from the core of their hearts. But the Lord had to move on with other duties of his life, so he had to leave then for good. Though he was not visible to them in physical terms but his image was permanently etched in the Gopis' hearts so much so that this heart itself became a shrine dedicated to the Lord. Whenever they closed their eyes they could 'see' Krishna. The Lord knew it and he kept contact with them at a transcendental plane, even remaining lost in their memory as much as they were lost in his. This eclectic form of Bhakti was not comprehendible to his companion named Uddhav who could not understand why the Lord was absent minded most of the time. So the Lord sent him to Vrindavan to test the Gopis' love for him. What transpired changed the life of Uddhav and the entire concept of Bhakti for the Lord that he had before this. Uddhav found the Gopis living like someone who is drunk and intoxicated. They had no care of their homes or household chores, or even of their own selves, tears gushed forth by the mere mention of the Lord, and they lived like walking corpses—so lost they were in the thoughts of Krishna. Refer to Srimad Bhagvat Mahapuran, 10/82/45.

These Gopis attained emancipation and salvation because they remained ever engrossed in the thoughts of Lord Krishna, a personified form of the Supreme Being; they revelled in this thought, they remained ecstatic and eternally blissful in it, and they were drowned in it so much so that their mind stopped from wandering elsewhere as it remained submerged in the thoughts of the Lord, their past sins wasted away and no deeds accrued to them in the future as their inner-self was not engaged in doing any worldly deeds because it remained totally fixed on the Lord with no time or inclination for anything else. Thus being the case, the Gopis attained the fruit of their lives; they attained Mukti—final dissolution that leads to beatitude and eternity.

It is said in Vishnu Puran, 5/13/19-22 that these Gopis were so ecstatic by the remembrance of Lord Krishna that "some of them danced and sang, some sat motionless as in a trance, some even fainted and died so that they found instant liberation and deliverance because their mind was focused on Lord Krishna at that moment."

A similar situation is described in Ram Charit Manas at two places. The first instance is when Lord Ram and his younger brother Laxman had gone out for sigh-seeing in the city of Janakpur where they had gone with their Guru sage Vishwamitra to attend the marriage ceremony of Sita, the daughter of the king of that place. All the citizens, males, females and children of all ages, were mesmerised by the sight of the Lord. They forgot about their household affairs and rushed out to see the Lord up close. All throughout the visit it appeared that the entire city had poured out on the streets with people milling around the Lord and following him wherever he went. The balconies and lofts of the houses were overcrowded by ladies craning out their heads to have a glimpse of the Lord; the men-folk pushed and shoved to be near him; and the children vied with each others to hold the Lord's hand and pull him in this and that direction. Refer: Ram Charit Manas, Baal Kand, from Chaupai line no. 1 that precedes Doha no. 220—to Doha no. 225.

The second instance of this sort of undiluted affection for Lord Ram is described when he was on the way to the forest. All the innocent and simple-hearted people of the villages and hamlets that fell on the way of the Lord's journey to the forest were extremely exhilarated, thrilled and ecstatic when they came to know that the Lord had come their way. The mere sight of the Lord made them exuberant and fulfilled in the same way as an ascetic feels when he attains self-realisation and Brahm-realisation. Some offered the Lord a seat to take rest, some brought refreshments, some talked with him and others just stood dumbfounded, some smiled and some had tears in their eyes, some offered their own homes to the Lord to stay while others wanted to accompany him, some stayed where they were and some followed him for as long as they could go, some who could not come at that time rushed after him to meet him a long way ahead. And when the Lord moved ahead on his journey, he left all the village folks numbed with grief and overwhelmed with love and affection for him which they harboured for the rest of their lives. This has been elaborately described in Ram Charit Manas, Ayodhya Kand, (i) from Chaupai line no. 7 that precedes Doha no. 109—to Chaupai line no. 6 that precedes Doha no.

110; (ii) from Chaupai line no. 3 that precedes Doha no. 112—to Doha no. 122.

The important point to note here is that none of them—the Gopis of Vrindavan, the citizens of Janakpur or the villagers whom Lord Ram met en-route to the forest—were 'Gyanis', i.e. none had studied the scriptures, theology and metaphysics. Yet they attained the level of bliss and blessedness and found ecstasy and joy that is attained by ascetics and sages when they become Brahm-realised and self-realised. These humble people did not even know that they were seeing the Supreme Being in a human form right in front of their eyes. They fell in love with the Lord for the sake of love alone. The idea is that Bhakti is a spontaneous emotion of love and affection for the Lord God that has its origin in the heart and not the mind as is the case with Gyan.]

१ /२ /५ भक्त्या जानातीति चेन्नाभिज्ञप्त्या साहाय्यात् ॥ १५॥

1 /2 /5 bhaktyā jānātīti cēnnābhijñaptyā sāhāyyāt || 15||

(1/2/5) [The Lord says:] "One becomes God-realised with the help of Bhakti." One comes to know the Lord God fully and in totality with the help of Bhakti. To wit, Bhakti helps in attaining Gyan or knowledge of God; Bhakti leads to God-realisation. (15)

[There are two ways in which this verse can be read and understood. Let us see them.

(a) The first interpretation is that this verse establishes the supremacy of Bhakti over Gyan though the aim of both spiritual paths is the same—i.e. God-realisation.

We have read in the note of verse no. 14 herein above that prior knowledge of the Lord God is not necessary to develop love and affection for him as was the case with Gopis of Vrindavan with respect to their love for Lord Krishna, or the citizens of Janakpur and the villagers who fell in love with Lord Ram when they met him.

Though it is true that prior knowledge of the greatness and glories of someone one begins to love surely helps to reinforce one's love and affection for that person, but it is not absolutely necessary. It is a common observation in this world that when a person falls in love with someone, usually it is a spontaneous emotional urge that does not at all depend upon any prior knowledge of the virtues and goodness of the object of one's affection. This knowledge may come later on when one comes closer to the beloved and keeps constant company with him or her.

Similarly, Bhakti brings the devotee close to his beloved Lord God in a natural and spontaneous manner, and it is later on that he comes to know about the majesty, the greatness, the glories and the divinities of the Lord when he begins to feel the ecstasy, the blissfulness and the beatitude that comes automatically with his association with the Lord God. He then experiences the blessedness of God-realisation that would have come to him if he had pursued the path of Gyan—the path of knowledge and gnosis, the path of acquiring wisdom and enlightenment through the study of the scriptures and practicing its many spiritual doctrines that lead to self and God realisation.

But at the same time it ought to be noted that the statement "one comes to have knowledge of the Lord God by the path of Bhakti" also means that 'Gyan', or the knowledge of God or God-realisation, is the aim of Bhakti. Establishing oneness of the individual soul with the Supreme Soul is the aim of Bhakti as is also the aim of Gyan. But Bhakti is independent while Gyan is dependent upon many factors. So therefore Bhakti is superior to Gyan. Refer verse no. 10.

(b) There is another way this verse can be interpreted. Since Bhakti (devotion) leads to God-realisation, it is a "tool" of Gyan (knowledge of God; self-realisation; gnosis; spiritual wisdom and enlightenment).

Now, this statement is true as well as not so true. It is true because both Bhakti and Gyan complement and supplement each other as they both help the spiritual aspirant to realise God. It is not so true because we have already read that Bhakti is superior to Gyan as the latter is dependent upon many factors while Bhakti is independent. Refer verse no. 10.

But it must be remembered that Gyan has its own importance and should not be undermined with respect to its ability to provide God-realisation. This fact will also be endorsed in the next verse no. 16 herein below.

So, what is the relationship between Bhakti and Gyan? It is made clear in Srimad Bhagvad Geeta, 18/55 which explicitly explains: "Through having supreme devotion for me (the Lord God) the devotee comes to know me in reality, of who I am, and how great, majestic, holy and divine I am. By this knowledge he forthwith enters into my supreme form to become one with me—i.e. he becomes God-realised, and attains emancipation and salvation for his soul."

Similarly we read in Ram Charit Manas, Uttar Kand, Chaupai line nos. 5-8 that precede Doha no. 89 that says: "The life's torments do not go away without worshipping and having devotion for Lord Ram. But without the grace of the Lord one is not able to know the Lord's greatness, divinity, majesty, glories and truth—i.e. have Gyan or knowledge of the Lord. Without this knowledge or awareness it is difficult to be steady in one's commitment to the Lord and have unwavering faith in him, and without this, Bhakti or devotion and love for the Lord will not be steadfast and deep-rooted."

Again in Ram Charit Manas, Ayodhya Kand, Chaupai line nos. 3 that precedes Doha no. 127 it is said that: "Oh Lord! One comes to know about you only by your grace, and once that happens the spiritual seeker becomes one with you." Obviously this is also the aim of Bhakti—to be one with the Lord God, to establish oneness between the devotee and the Lord he worships.

The implied meaning is that one should not discard Gyan altogether even if one has Bhakti for the Lord God, for Gyan is needed to reinforce one's commitment and faith in God. So therefore, whatever doubts that may linger in the mind of the devotee with respect to Bhakti and its spiritual goal will be taken care of by Gyan.

We conclude that Gyan is an aid to Bhakti; it tells us how to have devotion for the Lord God and how to attain success in it. It plays a 'secondary' role because there may be an instance when one can spontaneously develop natural love for the Lord God. However, Gyan enlightens a person about the true nature and form of the Lord God for whom he must have Bhakti, because otherwise he may go astray and offer his services to some secondary or junior god in the mistaken belief that he is serving the Supreme Being.]

१ /२ /६ प्रागुक्तं च ॥ १६॥

1 /2 /6 prāguktaṁ ca || 16||

(1/2/6) These principles have already been mentioned before. (16)

[A quick reading of the previous verses would clearly indicate that the discussion is about Gyan and Bhakti as means to God-realisation, and which of the two is more important than the other.

The first argument is that one must first have Gyan or knowledge of God, and then Bhakti or devotion and love for him follows naturally. This is endorsed in Srimad Bhagvad Geeta, 18/54 which says: "The Brahm-realised soul is always cheerful; he never grieves nor feels happy or craves for anything (i.e. he practices exemplary equanimity, dispassion, detachment and renunciation). For him all the creatures are the same and he interacts with them equally. Such an exalted and enlightened soul surely attains me, the Supreme Being, by having supreme devotion (Bhakti) for me." Refer also to note (b) appended to the previous verse no. 15.

When one is certain of the goal and its prime benefits, one would strive to reach that goal with full commitment of the mind and the heart, and with full zeal. Prior knowledge of who the Lord God is, what are his greatness and glories, would help the spiritual aspirant to be steady in his path of devotion. One cannot reach a goal if the goal itself is not clear. This clarity about one's spiritual goal and how to reach it comes from Gyan. Then Bhakti is a natural outcome because Gyan also tells the spiritual aspirant that Bhakti is the easiest and the best path to God-realisation.

To wit, true Gyan not only enlightens the devotee about his spiritual goal in life, but it also recommends the path of Bhakti to him.

But the other argument is also equally true and holds equally good. It is that Bhakti is superior to Gyan. This is the obviously main theme of this book. In Srimad Bhagvad Geeta, 18/55, Lord Krishna explicitly says: "Through having supreme devotion for me (the Lord God) the devotee comes to know me in reality, of who I am, and how great, majestic, holy and divine I am. By this knowledge he forthwith enters into my supreme form to become one with me—i.e. he becomes God-realised, and attains emancipation and salvation for his soul."

Similar idea is expressed at many places in Ram Charit Manas. For instance, we read about it in its Uttar Kand's following verses: (i) Chaupai line nos. 2-4 that precede Doha no. 45; (ii) Chaupai line nos. 5-6 that precede Doha no. 84; (iii) Chaupai line nos. 1-4 that precede Doha no. 115; (iv) Chaupai line nos. 4-8 that precede Doha no. 116; and (v) from Chaupai line no. 1 that precedes Doha no. 119—to Chaupai line no. 15 that precedes Doha no. 120.

We shall now cite only one example from these aforesaid verses of Ram Charit Manas to see how Bhakti is said to be superior to Gyan. In Uttar Kand, Chaupai line nos. 1-4 that precede Doha no. 115 it is said that: "A person who abandons Bhakti, which is like the all wish fulfilling cow known as Kamdhenu, and goes out in search of the acacia plant in order to find its sap to quench his thirst (instead of quenching it by drinking the milk of this cow)—is indeed a very stupid fellow. So likewise, a person who wishes to find happiness, bliss and beatitude by some other path except Bhakti is like a stupid fellow who wants to cross a huge ocean symbolised by this world of transmigration by trying to swim across it instead of boarding a strong ship that would easily take him across."

Briefly it can be said that a person who has become Brahm-realised (or God-realised) by the means of Bhakti has no need for Gyan again, albeit Gyan may help him in this path at some stage.]

१ /२ /७ एतेन विकल्पोऽपि प्रत्युक्तः ॥ १७॥

1 /2 /7 ētēna vikalpō 'pi pratyuktaḥ || 17||

(1/2/7) This fundamental knowledge (about Bhakti and Gyan, that both of them have one single objective—which is to bring about God-realisation) removes all disputes, debates, paradoxes, contradictions and oppositions (with respect to Bhakti and Gyan, and their objectives). (17)

[To wit, Bhakti and Gyan do not oppose each other, but they aid each other. They are complimentary and supplementary to each other. No one of them is either superior or inferior to the other. They equally help the aspirant to reach his spiritual goal which is the same in both the cases.

This verse is intended to settle all disputation about the importance and significance of these two noble paths to God-realisation—the path of Bhakti and the path of Gyan. It settles that both are equal and effective. The hidden idea is that the spiritual aspirant has to choose for himself which path would suit him best. As has already been said earlier, if the spiritual aspirant is inclined to learn about his goals first and apply his mind to everything he does, then Gyan is the path for him. On the other hand, if he is driven by the call of his heart more than the mind, then Bhakti is the path best suited for him.]

१ /२ /८ देवभक्तिरितरस्मिन् साहचर्यात् ॥ १८॥

1 /2 /8 dēvabhaktiritarasmin sāhacaryāt || 18||

(1/2/8) If Bhakti is applied to or understood to mean devotion to any other entity except the Supreme Being, then it is a degraded or inferior kind of Bhakti. To wit, offering worship to any sundry god or goddess or any ordinary deity except the Supreme Being (Brahm) is not the true form or purpose of Bhakti. (18)

[Bhakti means 'devotion, surrender and love for the Lord God', but this verse clarifies that the object of this devotion and love should be the 'Supreme Being', the Lord of this world, the God who is supreme and there is no other God superior to him.

To wit, Bhakti does not mean devotion for and surrendering of oneself before any random deity or god or goddess. Worshipping any random god or goddess or deity is not Bhakti even if it is done with due reverence and faith. Such Bhakti is not true spiritual practice as it would never provide the sort of spiritual reward one expects from it. This kind of Bhakti will not give eternal peace, bliss or beatitude; it will not grant liberation, deliverance, emancipation or salvation for the soul.

Lord Ram has said in Ram Charit Manas, Uttar Kand, Chaupai line nos. 3-4 that precede Doha no. 46 that: "If one calls one's self my true devotee ("daasa"—literally meaning a servant but actually the meaning is a faithful devotee) but expects anything from others, then say what right does he have to claim this privileged status (of being my devotee). What more can I say except that this is the principle I follow."

Then once again in Ram Charit Manas, Uttar Kand, Chaupai line no. 6 that precedes Doha no. 41 the Lord says that: "Thus, those who are wise and erudite worship me alone because they know that all other kinds of worship result in delusions and countless miseries."

There is another instance when Lord Ram reiterates this fact. It is when he tells sage Narad in Ram Charit Manas, Aranya Kand, Chaupai line no. 10 that precedes Doha no. 43 that: "Therefore, taking everything into consideration and weighing all the pros and the cons, those who are experts and wise in their knowledge of the scriptures prefer to have Bhakti for me (and worship me alone) even if they have access to Gyan (gnosis; metaphysics and theology)."

To wit, Lord Ram clearly and unequivocally says here that a true devotee is one who does not worship any other god or goddess, or any deity for that matter, except the Supreme Lord himself.

Refer: Shvetashvatara Upanishad, 6/23 which says: "Bhakti should be offered only to the Supreme Being, and not to even one's Guru (teacher) or other Gods." At the most, some worldly desires would be fulfilled by this inferior kind of Bhakti; nothing more.

Srimad Bhagvad Geeta, 9/23-25, says: "Those who have Bhakti inside them (i.e. in their heart) but use this virtue to worship gods other than the Supreme Being (in the hope of fulfilment of certain desires), then though it is true that they are worshipping me in these forms yet this kind of worship is not the proper way to worship me. Since such worshippers are deluded under the influence of Maya because they do not recognise who I am (as they worship other Gods instead of directly worshipping me), they fall back into the cycle of transmigration instead of breaking free from it and attaining deliverance. This is because those who worship other Gods go to them (and all these Gods are said to preside over different aspects of creation that are assigned to them, but surely not the supreme state of beatitude and blessedness that is the sole realm of Brahm). Only those who worship me (the Supreme Being) come to me to get final deliverance."

To wit, true Bhakti is direct devotion for the Supreme Lord, and not to his many other forms—because this latter kind of Bhakti may fulfil the worshipper's worldly desires, but it will not give him emancipation and salvation.

We come across countless instances in the world when people propitiate sundry gods and goddesses or worship this or that deity for fulfilment of so many of their desires because they believe that the particular deity is empowered to fulfil his wishes. Some want wealth, some wish to have children, some yearn for success in career, some long for fame, some want to overcome adversities that dog them, and so on and so forth. All such people do whatever they can, with full faith and conviction, to please the gods or the goddesses who have the power to fulfil their worldly wishes. Such people make vows that if their wishes are fulfilled then they will make certain special offerings to these gods and goddesses. This is pure and simple business. This is not the purpose of Bhakti, and this is not how it should be practiced. This verse warns us against this situation.

True Bhakti is deep and selfless love and devotion for the Supreme Lord, and not anyone else; true Bhakti is to seek nothing in return from the Lord, and not ask for this and that. A true devotee leaves himself in the care of his Lord God, but it must be remembered that the Lord is very obliging, graceful and merciful, so he will not let the devotee's surrender go unrewarded. The quality and the quantum of any reward are in according with the status and dignity of the person who gives the reward. An emperor's reward for services rendered unto him will surely be far superior to the reward given by a small king of a small kingdom. Hence, the reward that the Supreme Lord of world gives to his devotee is the best he can expect. And what is it? Herein comes handy the true understanding of the word 'Gyan'. Gyan or spiritual wisdom and enlightenment that comes with deep study of the scriptures tells us that the best and the ultimate reward for a creature is to attain freedom from worldly miseries and torments associated with the endless cycle of birth and death in this mundane gross world, and have eternal peace and bliss for himself. How does this happen? It happens when the devotee realises that the world is false, that his true identity is not his gross physical body but his Atma which is pure consciousness, and that final liberation from the cycle of transmigration with its attendent horrors comes when this Atma of his merges with the cosmic Atma or the cosmic Consciousness represented by Brahm, the Supreme Being. This is known as 'self and God realisation'. Bhakti leads to this, and hence eternal bliss, peace, beatitude and felicity as well as freedom from the cycle of birth and death are the reward of Bhakti. To wit, seeking wealth, prosperity, children, fame, career and other successes is not Bhakti at all. These attainments only drag the person further down in the pit of problems and they fortify his attachments with a world that is inherently entangling, horrifyingly gross and troubling, so how can he ever have peace and happiness for which he wants any of the things of this material world in the first place? Surely he has no 'Gyan' or true knowledge in him; he is deluded and ignorant.

Another significant point is to be noted here. In a subtle way this verse also points towards the importance of 'Gyan'. The verse says that only service rendered to the Supreme Being is true form of Bhakti, and not that rendered to any other subordinate forms of the Lord. How do we know who is the Supreme Being who is to be worshipped? We come to understand this only when we learn about him by studying the scriptures, analysing their doctrines and discussions with other senior and learned people who have this knowledge. This is how Gyan is acquired. So therefore, Gyan plays a crucial role in the fulfilment of Bhakti. To wit, devoid of true Gyan, true Bhakti cannot be practiced.

Gyan is like an academic counsellor in a great college who advises the student on the course he should select for himself after taking into consideration the student's aptitude, interests and abilities. In this example, Bhakti is the course that the Gyan-counsellor advises the student, the spiritual aspirant, to take up in order to reach his goal, which is to attain God-realisation in this case.

Refer verse no. 24 herein below which says 'merely having faith or belief in a deity or worshipping that deity with reverence is not true Bhakti though these virtues do constitute an important part of Bhakti like love, affection and devotion do'.]

१ /२ /९ योगस्तूभयार्थमपेक्षणात् प्रयाजवत् ॥ १९॥

1 /2 /9 yōgastūbhayārthamapēkṣaṇāt prayājavat || 19||

(1/2/9) 'Yoga' (meditation; concentration of the mind; focusing one's attention on some carefully chosen objective) is equally important for attainment of success in Gyan as well as in Bhakti as it helps the spiritual aspirant to concentrate his mind and focus his various faculties on the spiritual path and the objective he has chosen for himself. [This objective is God-realisation and attainment of spiritual bliss. Success in this spiritual endeavour gives liberation from the grossness associated with this mundane existence. The aspirant is able to have emancipation and salvation for his soul that gives him final beatitude and eternal peace.]

Though it is true that Yoga is a branch of Gyan (gnosis; metaphysics), but since Gyan itself is a means to Bhakti (which is the objective or aim of Gyan), it follows that Yoga too is a branch of Bhakti.

For instance, just as the 'Prayaaja' ceremony is a component part or a subsidiary ritual of a fire sacrifice (such as the horse-sacrifice and other such sacrifices) as well as of the ceremony of the Dikshaa (wherein the patron who would perform the sacrifice initiates himself into it and undertaking the vows needed to complete it), so too Yoga and Gyan are subsidiaries of Bhakti. To wit, both Yoga and Gyan help in the successful completion of Bhakti, and leads the spiritual aspirant to his desired spiritual objective. (19)

[How is Bhakti an aim or objective of Gyan as well as of Yoga? The main purpose of acquiring Gyan, say by deep study of the scriptures, is to make a spiritual aspirant become aware of the true nature and form of the Supreme Being as well as about the true purpose of life and the nature of this gross perishable world. Gyan motivates him to see that there is actually no peace in and nothing worthwhile to gain by pursuing the sense objects of this world, and that true happiness and bliss is obtained by realisation of the 'self' which is pure consciousness. Gyan further enlightens him that his 'self' is a microcosmic form of the supreme 'Self' represented by the cosmic Consciousness. If one were to pursue this 'consciousness' and successfully come face-to-face with it then one would be able to access the fount of spiritual bliss and beatitude that is of an eternal and infinite nature. To wit, Gyan teaches the spiritual aspirant to seek God-realisation. It also teaches him the different ways this can be done.

The word 'Yoga' means to bring about a union between any two entities and make them compatible with each other. Yoga prescribes many practical ways by which a practitioner can control the different faculties of his mind and body so that their combined energy can be harnessed to achieve success in attaining one's spiritual goal in life. In the realm of metaphysics and spiritualism, this goal is to bring about a union between the individual soul of the creature (the "Jiva") and the Supreme Soul (the "Parmatma"; the supreme Brahm).

This is also the aim of Gyan (gnosis; metaphysical and theological knowledge; the knowledge of the scriptures) and Bhakti (devotion and love for the Lord God). They too help the aspirant to have self-realisation and attain God-realisation. Hence, all the three—Yoga, Gyan and Bhakti—can be said to be the three corners of an equilateral triangle. All of them are equally important, but Bhakti is like the apex of this triangle of which Gyan and Yoga are the base.

Just as Gyan alone cannot bestow bliss and beatitude as well as emancipation and salvation to the soul of the creature if it is not accompanied by Bhakti for the Lord so also Yoga that is devoid of Bhakti too fails to provide this blessing to the creature.

The objective of 'Yoga' is to bring about a union between two entities that have been separated due to some reason. Here, this union refers to the coming together of the individual's soul and the supreme Soul of this creation—i.e. to bring the spiritual aspirant closer to his Lord God and make them embrace each other.

The aim of Bhakti is also the same. Bhakti too aims to bring the devotee closer to his beloved Lord. When Bhakti is mature and successful, the devotee experiences the spiritual ecstasy and bliss that comes with attainment of his beloved Lord God that is equivalent to the ecstasy and bliss of self-realisation as experienced by the ascetic who practices Yoga, or that obtained by Brahm-realisation by the person who follows the path of Gyan. The ultimate reward of eternal spiritual peace, bliss, beatitude and felicity, of liberation, deliverance, emancipation and salvation of the soul, are the same whichever path the spiritual aspirant chooses to follow.

But Bhakti is preferred over all other paths because it is hassle free and easy.

It is said in Srimad Bhagvat Mahapuran, 11/14/20 that: "For attaining me (the Supreme Lord) and thereby finding emancipation and beatitude, neither Yoga (meditation), nor Sankhya (a branch of scriptural knowledge), nor Dharma (righteousness), nor the study of Vedas (knowledge), nor Tapa (austerities; penances), nor Vairagya (renunciation) etc. would help if there is no Bhakti or deep and intense sense of love and devotion for me (in the heart of the creature)."

Lord Ram has praised Bhakti over Yoga and Tapa etc. in Ram Charit Manas, Uttar Kand, Chaupai line nos. 3-5 that precede Doha no. 85 when he told the crow-saint Kaagbhusund: "I am very pleased with you and your wisdom of choosing Bhakti over all other things. Indeed you are very lucky and blessed as you have asked for Bhakti which is so soothing and pleasant, but which even the exalted ascetics and sages do not easily want as they rather prefer to follow other difficult paths to me, such as Japa (repetition of the God's name), Yoga (meditation), Tapa (severe penances) etc. which are all like scorching the body in fire."

It is said in Srimad Bhagvat Mahapuran, 4/20/16 that: "I am not known through Yaya, Tapa or Yoga, but I am reveal my brilliant form in the untainted heart of my devotee."

Similarly, in Srimad Bhagvat Mahapuran, 3/32/33 it is said that: "As the same milk with its various qualities or attributes is differently observed through different senses of the body, say through the eye one can see only its colour, through the touch of the skin one can feels its coolness or heat or feel its liquidity, through the tongue one can taste it, but the goodness that the milk contains is of any use only when it is actually drunk. Likewise, Karma (doing righteous deeds), Gyan (gnosis), Yoga (meditation) one may have partial view of the Lord, but it is only through pure Bhakti (love and devotion) that the full spiritual benefits of God-realisation can be had."

Just like Gyan (refer note appended to verse no. 15), 'Yoga' is also a subsidiary of Bhakti as it aids in the fulfilment of Bhakti. Gyan and Yoga are useful for those devotees who are intellectually mature and would like to have full knowledge of Bhakti, what it means, what is its aim, who is the Lord God who is to be worshipped and attained, what are the pitfalls and what precautions one should take, and all other such relevant questions before they embark on this spiritual journey. Being thus fully prepared, they easily attain success in Bhakti.]

१ /२ /१० गौण्या तु समाधिसिद्धिः ॥ २० ॥

1 /2 /10 gauṇyā tu samādhisiddhiḥ || 20||

(1/2/10) Attainment of the eclectic state of 'Samadhi' (a trance-like state of transcendental existence) is a silent and subtle aspect of Bhakti, as it a natural accompaniment of success in Bhakti and plays a subsidiary role in its manifestation. Hence, Samadhi is a secondary form of Bhakti. Or it is a secondary symptom of Bhakti. (20)

[Samadhi is called a secondary form of Bhakti because it is merely a symptom of success in Bhakti. The bliss and ecstasy obtained by Bhakti may or may not lead to the trance-like state usually called Samadhi. A devotee may not attain Samadhi but still be deeply rooted in his love and devotion for the Lord God. The bliss and ecstasy of Samadhi obtained in Bhakti is experienced personally by the devotee just like it is experienced by an ascetic in the higher stages of Yoga (meditation).

'Samadhi' is a state that is reached in higher stages of Yoga. It refers to a state of transcendental existence when the ascetic rises above the sense perception of the gross material world and is unaware of his surroundings because he perpetually remains submerged or engrossed in contemplation and meditating on his 'self' which is pure consciousness, a stage that gives him an extreme sense of bliss and ecstasy. In the realm of Yoga, Samadhi is reached in the Turiya or the Turiyateet states of consciousness when only the pure consciousness prevails and the gross aspect of the body as well as the world cease to exist.

This also happens in the higher stages of Bhakti when the devotee becomes so lost in the thoughts of his beloved Lord God that he lives virtually aloof from the physical world in which his gross body lives. His 'self', i.e. his pure consciousness known as the Atma, is with the Lord God he loves, and so the presence of the body becomes irrelevant for him for all practical purposes. To give an example, this was the condition of the Gopis of Vrindavan as clearly referred to in verse no. 14 and explained in the note appended to this verse.

Samadhi gives perpetual sense of spiritual bliss and ecstasy; it is a state when self-realisation is achieved; it is also a stage of God-realisation as nothing matters after that. Therefore it is said that when the stage of Samadhi is reached, Yoga is supposed to have reached its climax. Similarly, Bhakti is said to be mature when the devotee attains a state of Samadhi.

As we read on, we shall see that there are many other secondary forms of Bhakti—such as doing Kirtan (verse no. 63), auspicious deeds and offering them to the Lord God (verse nos. 64, 71), Japa (verse no. 61), Dhyan (verse no. 65), Padodak (i.e. offering water to wash the feet of the deity being worshipped—verse no. 67), Offerings of different kinds (verse no. 68, 70), and so on.]

१ /२ /११ हेया रागत्वादिति चेन्नोत्तमास्पदत्वात् सङ्गवत् ॥ २१ ॥

1 /2 /11 hēyā rāgatvāditi cēnnōttamāspadatvāt saṅgavat || 21||

(1/2/11) If it is said that since Bhakti is manifested in the form of 'attachment to God' (refer verse no. 2), and 'attachment' itself is not a good virtue as it leads to entanglement with the object of adoration, then this is a fallacious argument.

This is because here 'attachment' ("rāga"; in the case of Bhakti) is not with any gross thing like the material things of the world or objects of the senses, but this 'attachment' is to bring closeness between the individual soul, which is untainted and pristine pure consciousness, and the Supreme Soul represented by the Lord God who is an embodiment of cosmic Consciousness, of Truth, of bliss and beatitude.

When any two pristine pure and untainted entities unite to become one (as in the case of Bhakti which brings the devotee's soul to the cosmic Soul so as to become one with it), it cannot be said to be equivalent to getting attracted to something that is gross and mundane as in the case of attachment to worldly things.#

[#This verse can also be read as follows: "Some say that since Bhakti has 'attachment' (to God) as its component, it is to be avoided as attachment is not an excellent spiritual virtue." They put forth the argument given in Yoga Sutras of Patanjali, verse no. 2/3 that says that attachment and infatuation are negative virtues; it's like an affliction that is to be avoided. But there is a difference here—for this 'attachment' relates to the pure cosmic Consciousness that is untainted by application of any yardstick or criterion. This attachment in Bhakti is to have love and devotion for Lord God, and is therefore different from attachment as understood in the field of Gyan or Yoga where it refers to infatuation with the world and the sense organs. Hence, the difference is obvious and clear. The attachment in Bhakti is of a pure kind, while in Gyan and Yoga it surely has a negative connotation. The two cannot be equalled."] (21)

[This verse clarifies the confusion surrounding the word 'attachment'. Usually it has a negative connotation as it relates to being attracted to the gross world and its objects that appeal to the senses. This attachment leads to entanglements.

On the other hand, attachment with the Lord God creates an affinity and nearness between the devotee and the Lord. It forges a bond of love and affection between the two. It ought to be noted that this is also the goal of Yoga and Gyan—to bring about a union of the individual's soul with the Supreme Soul. So therefore, 'attachment with God' is different from 'attachment with the world'.]

१ /२ /१२ तदेव कर्मिज्ञानियोगिभ्य आधिक्यशब्दात् ॥ २२॥

1 /2 /12 tadēva karmijñāniyōgibhya ādhikyaśabdāt || 22||

(1/2/12) Hence, it is established that a Bhakta (i.e. a person who follows the path of Bhakti, the devotion and love for the Lord God) is superior to a Karmi (a person who follows the path of doing meritorious deeds), or a Gyani (a person who acquires knowledge of the scriptures to become self and God realised) or a Yogi (an ascetic who follows the path of Yoga, the path of meditation and contemplation to attain God-realisation). (22)

[To wit, Bhakti is the best spiritual path to God-realisation. Even the Lord himself has endorsed the primacy and the supremacy of Bhakti over other paths such as Karma (doing righteous and meritorious deeds), Gyan (gnosis; acquisition of metaphysical and theological knowledge; study of the scriptures) and Yoga (meditation and contemplation). In the context of this verse, refer also to verse nos. 8 and 10.

This fact is reiterated in Srimad Bhagvad Geeta, 6/46-47 where Lord Krishna says: "A Yogi (a person who meditates and contemplates upon the Lord's pure cosmic form as personified Consciousness, and remains ever so blissful and ecstatic in this remembrance of the Lord) is superior to a Karmi who does sacred activities without any self-realisation, even to a Gyani who has mere knowledge which he can't put to use in self or God realisation, to a Tapaswi who suffers by doing severe penances only to ask for boons. And of all the Yogis, he who is completely 'devoted to me alone' is surely the best and absolutely the greatest amongst them all because he becomes united with me (which is the ultimate goal of all endeavours)."

Srimad Bhagvat Mahapuran, 6/14/15 says: "Among the innumerable souls who have found Mukti (freedom from the world) or have attained Siddhi (mystical powers), rarely is found a true devotee of the Supreme Lord who loves him whole-heartedly (as a result of which he not only derives immense bliss and beatitude, but also gets emancipation and salvation)."]

१ /२ /१३ प्रश्ननिरूपणाभ्यामाधिक्यसिद्धेः ॥ २३॥

1 /2 /13 praśnanirūpaṇābhyāmādhikyasiddhēḥ || 23||

(1/2/13) The supremacy and primacy of Bhakti is also established by the questions asked by Arjun and the answers given by Lord Krishna (in the 12th Chapter of Srimad Bhagvad Geeta). (23)

[This is known as 'Bhakti Yoga'. An English version of this entire chapter of Geea with detailed explanation has been included in a book titled 'Bhakti' penned by this author and published on-line in an e-book as well as a printed version.

Arjun asks Lord Krishna: "Out of those who constantly, faithfully and most devotedly worship your form that has attributes, and those who meditate upon your cosmic all-pervading form that has no attributes—of these two classes of worshippers, who is excellent and superior?"

Briefly, Lord Krishna's answer is this: "My devotee who worships me with faith and his mind unwaveringly fixed on me, the Supreme Being, is the one who is best and well versed in the essence of Yoga (the primary aim of which is to focus the mind on the Absolute Truth, and to bring about a union between the individual creature's soul and the Supreme Soul of the creation).

On the other hand, those who seek me by controlling their mind and their senses, by seeing me everywhere in my all-pervading form as pure consciousness, who seek me by meditating upon my form known as the supreme Brahm, a form of cosmic dimensions, a form that is too abstract to be understood, a form that is nameless, un-manifested, unthinkable, immutable and all-pervading, also attain me, but they encounter a lot of problems and troubles to reach me for this path is beset with dangers. Contemplation on an undefined and invisible form of Brahm is too difficult to practice for a creature who is accustomed to relating to entities he can see and experience in this world as is the case with my form that is visible and has attributes. For an embodied soul that the creature is, it is very difficult to comprehend the disembodied soul that my cosmic form is. Hence, meditation on my Nirguna form is very difficult, whereas meditation on my Saguna form is extremely easy.

Verily I say that those who single-mindedly worship me, are devoted and dedicated to me, are focused exclusively on me, who meditate and contemplate upon me, and who have placed their mind and themselves in my custody—I take special care of them and look after their welfare; I become their saviour and take them across the vast and fathomless ocean of birth and death."]

१ /२ /१४ नैव श्रद्धा तु साधारण्यात् ॥ २४॥

1 /2 /14 naiva śraddhā tu sādhāraṇyāt || 24||

(1/2/14) 'Shraddha' (meaning the virtues of faith, reverence, belief, conviction) is an excellent virtue and it should not be thought of in an ordinary sense or common way with respect to Bhakti. (24)

['Shraddha' is indeed an excellent virtue, and it is an important component of Bhakti or devotion for Lord God. So it should not be applied to any ordinary or common purpose. It needs an equally excellent objective for its proper and correct application. This 'excellent objective' for a living being is attainment of liberation from the cycle of birth and death, attainment of emancipation and salvation for his soul, attainment of eternity, bliss and beatitude. And these eclectic spiritual objectives cannot be achieved if one applies the glorious virtue of 'Shraddha' to ordinary or common things of this world.

In the context of this verse, refer to verse no. 18 where it is said that offering worship to any sundry god or goddess or any ordinary deity is not the true form or purpose of Bhakti. Merely having faith or belief in a deity or worshipping that deity with reverence is not true Bhakti though these virtues do constitute an important part of Bhakti like love, affection and devotion do. In the same manner one may serve one's worldly master or lord with due 'Shraddha', but this obviously is not Bhakti!

Only the Supreme Being can grant final liberation and deliverance to the soul of the creature from the cycle of birth and death. Other ordinary deities, no matter who they are, can fulfil other wishes of the worshipper, but they cannot deliver him from this cycle. Though the worshipper is devoted to these ordinary deities and may have full faith in them, though he may even love to worship these deities but he does not know or understand the true meaning and benefit of Bhakti. He is deluded and ignorant.

So therefore, though having 'Shraddha' is a common aspect of Bhakti and an important and crucial component of it for it to succeed and bear fruits, but it should applied with due care and diligence; it is not to be applied to ordinary form of devotion but to its best form that is offered directly to the Supreme Being.

Merely having 'Shraddha' will not give the desired spiritual rewards in Bhakti, for one may have Shraddha for ordinary gods and goddesses, one may worship any common deity with due reverence and faith, but that is not true Bhakti, and therefore the reward is also not up to the mark. True Shraddha is when this glorious virtue is applied with respect to the Supreme Being.

We will note here that 'Shraddha' relates to the heart because faith, conviction, belief and reverence have their basic root in the heart as compared to the mind which is the seat of intelligence, logic, analysis and rational thinking. It is also in the heart where the Atma or the soul of the creature dwells. So therefore, Shraddha is also directly related to the welfare of the Atma, and since the Atma is the true 'self' of the creature, Shraddha is directly related to the creature's welfare.

To wit, 'Shraddha' is the first step towards Bhakti for the Lord God; hence it should not be treated as something ordinary or common. Its meaning and application should be properly understood to benefit from this excellent virtue as expounded herein above.

The next verse no. 25 further clarifies this concept of 'Shraddha' vis-à-vis 'Bhakti'.]

१ /२ /१५ तस्यां तत्त्वे चानवस्थानात् ॥ २५॥

1 /2 /15 tasyāṁ tattvē cānavasthānāt || 25||

(1/2/15) Ordinary or common form of 'Shraddha' (as it is understood in its literal meaning) is different from its glorious form that leads to self-realisation and God-realisation, that makes a person realised and enlightened and firmly established in the Truth (i.e. in the pure Consciousness that is his true self as well as embodied in the form of the Supreme Being). (25)

[Refer to verse no. 24 with its note herein above that has clearly explained this point. The dictionary meaning of the word 'Shraddha' is faith, belief, conviction and reverence. One may have Shraddha towards one Guru (teacher), or any ordinary god or goddess, or his worldly master or lord. But that is not equivalent to having Bhakti for them.

One serves one's teacher, or sundry deities or worldly masters and lords such as a king or a boss, but all this service would at best fulfil his worldly needs and desires. None of them would liberate the soul from the miseries it has been suffering through the cycle of transmigration over countless generations. None would provide the person eternal peace, bliss and beatitude. None would grant him emancipation and salvation.

So therefore, 'Shraddha' bears true fruit and is deemed to properly used only when it is applied in its correct sense and employed as a crucial component of 'Bhakti' as has been defined throughout these Sutras. Otherwise it goes in vain and is a futile exercise.

To wit, using Shraddha other than in the context of Bhakti is squarely undermining its spiritual value and importance. It would be a sacrilegious use of Shraddha if it is not employed with Bhakti for the Supreme Being.

The true value of the virtues of faith, conviction, belief and reverence, i.e. the virtue of 'Shraddha' that a person has is when these virtues are applied to the Supreme Being. True Bhakti (devotion and love) is one where Shraddha is directed to the Lord God in a selfless manner. Such a faithful and real devotee of the Lord is the most perfect among the accomplished Yogis, i.e. the ascetics who have successfully established oneness of their own self with the Supreme Self known as Brahm.

To know God, to have firm faith in him, to be whole-heartedly devoted to him—are indeed the steps that lead to spiritual perfection and God-realisation. This exalted state of existence makes a person realise that all his endeavours are directed to the Lord God and not to anyone else, that to realise the Lord and find oneness with him is his only goal of his life, and that the Lord God is the object worthy of his reverence and love. When this firmness of faith and conviction of purpose actually comes alive in a person then one can say that 'Shraddha' has truly revealed its pristine pure form in the heart of this person. Shraddha is a vital step for God-realisation, and therefore applying it for any other purpose is to demote Shraddha and give it ignominy.

To wit, Shraddha helps to create Bhakti; Shraddha cements the bond of love between the devotee and the Lords God.

It ought to be noted here that firm faith, conviction and belief are needed to succeed in any endeavour, whether it is related to the temporal world or to the spiritual world. If one is not fully convinced of the path he has chosen to reach his goal, if he is not firm in his resolve, if he is not convinced that the objective that he has chosen for himself is the best thing for him and it is actually attainable, if he has no faith in his own self and his ability to reach that goal, then he is more likely to fail than succeed in his endeavours. Uncertainty of mind and heart that indicates lack of faith, belief and conviction—or lack of Shraddha—leads to nowhere even in the temporal world where often it is observed that a person fails merely because he was not sure of what he was doing or what his goal is. If this situation is true for the world it surely is true in the spiritual realm as well. Hence the importance of Shraddha in Bhakti is to be properly understood.

The spiritual importance of Shraddha with relation to Bhakti has been succinctly highlighted in the Srimad Bhagvad Geeta, 6/47, where Lord Krishna says: "Of all the Yogis, those who worship me with deep Shraddha for me in their Mana (mind and heart), are regarded as the best of all the Yogis by me."]

१ /२ /१६ ब्रह्मकाण्डं तु भक्तौ तस्यानुज्ञानाय सामान्यात् ॥ २६ ॥

1 /2 /16 brahmakāṇḍaṁ tu bhaktau tasyānujñānāya sāmānyāt || 26||

(1/2/16) The part of the scriptures that is known as 'Brahm-Kand' (brahmakāṇḍaṁ), the chapters or sections that expound and elucidate upon the truth, the nature and the form of Brahm, the Supreme Being who is an embodiment of pure Consciousness, are actually meant to foster the virtue of Bhakti (devotion and affection) for him. Any knowledge of whatsoever kind it may be, if it does not teach this fundamental thing, i.e. if this spiritual knowledge is not gained by the study of the scriptures, than the whole purpose and intent of the scriptures goes to waste. (26)

[It is clear now that Bhakti for the Supreme Being known as Brahm is the sacrosanct and the ultimate purpose of the teaching of all the scriptures. Even though the same scriptures prescribe so many forms of worship and rituals, but their main purpose is to foster devotion for the Lord God and bring the creature closer to him so that ultimately the soul of the creature attains oneness with the Supreme Soul known as Brahm. If this goal is not achieved then all Gyan or acquisition of knowledge goes to waste.

It is commonly believed that imparting the knowledge of Brahm is the main purpose of the scriptures such as the Vedas and the Upanishads. But this is a fallacious interpretation, as their main intent is to bring about liberation and deliverance for the creature by enlightening him about Brahm and the true goal of life, to tell him how emancipation and salvation can be achieved, to show him the path to eternal bliss, felicity and beatitude. If this eclectic spiritual gaol cannot be achieved by reading and studying about Brahm in the chapters of the scriptures that are commonly known as 'Brahm-Kand', then nothing is achieved. And this goal can only be achieved by having Bhakti for the Lord God. However, for Bhakti to mature and reach its natural destiny, Shraddha must be cultivated.

The Vedas are divided primarily into 'Karma Kand' or 'Purva Mimaansa' which deal with rituals, and 'Gyan Kand' or 'Brahm-Kand' or 'Uttar Mimaansa' which is about the knowledge of Brahm. The latter is usually called 'Vedanta' or the 'Upanishad'. Though the Upanishads are intensively knowledge based, but it must be remembered that any knowledge is in vain if it cannot be applied in practice. So the knowledge of Brahm in the Brahm-Kand of the Vedas will be meaningful only if Brahm can be actually realised by the spiritual seeker, not in the theoretical form but in the practical form. And towards this end, Bhakti and Shraddha are necessary.

Now, who attains this perfect knowledge of Brahm? The answer is found in Srimad Bhagvad Geeta, 4/39, which says: "He who is full of faith for me (Shraddha), he who is fully devoted to me and loves me (Bhakti), he who has learnt to control his senses (Jitendra), and he who diligently pursues true knowledge in this way (Gyan Tatparam), is surely able to attain the knowledge of the supreme Truth (represented by Brahm, the cosmic Consciousness and the Supreme Being), and thereby immediately attain supreme bliss and beatitude that naturally comes with it (with Brahm-realisation)."

So therefore, the ultimate purpose of all religious activities as prescribed in the Karma Kand of the Vedas is to attain Brahm. The Brahm-Kand tells the spiritual aspirant who Brahm is, but to actually reach this Brahm, the Supreme Being, the path prescribed is Bhakti along with Shraddha—i.e. to love the Supreme Being, to have devotion for him, to be fully committed to him, and to do it with full faith, belief and reverence for him.]

समाप्तश्च प्रथमोऽध्यायः ॥ १ ॥

samāptaśca prathamō 'dhyāyaḥ || 1||

Thus ends Chapter no. 1

----------*******---------

(4) SHANDILYA BHAKTI SUTRA

Aphorisms for Devotion to God and

The Principles of the Philosophy of Love for Him

[Roman Transliteration of Text, English Exposition, Elaborate Notes]

Chapter 2, Part 1:

Verse nos. 27-55

द्वितीयोऽध्यायः

प्रथममाह्निकम्

dvitīyō 'dhyāyaḥ

prathamamāhnikam

२ /१ /१ बुद्धिहेतुप्रवृत्तिराविशुद्धेरवघातवत् ॥ २७॥

2 /1 /1 buddhihētupravr̥ttirāviśuddhēravaghātavat || 27||

(2/1/1) In order to gain full and correct knowledge it is necessary to keep the mind and the intellect ("Buddhi") focused on it till the time the desired result is obtained just like it is necessary to keep threshing the harvested paddy till the grain is completely separated from the chaff*. (27)

[This is the practical way to learn something. Any student would experience the truth of this statement in his day-to-day life. To master any subject and become skilled in any craft, diligent practice is important. A subject may appear to be difficult in the beginning, but if one studies it with a focused mind and perseverance, if one applies his mind and intelligence to it, then success will be ultimately attained.

So therefore in one's spiritual pursuit as well, concentration of the mind, steadfastness of faith and conviction, and commitment to one's goal are of paramount importance.

Here, the 'knowledge' pertains to Brahm, the Supreme Being, and how the creature can attain Brahm-realisation and self-realisation so that he can obtain eternal peace, bliss and beatitude for himself, as well as attain liberation and deliverance from the cycle of birth and death in this world that leads to the final emancipation and salvation of the soul. This knowledge is of two types—one that is shallow and of a worldly kind, and the other that is deep and far-reaching from the spiritual perspective. The former knowledge is concerned with the performance of many rites and rituals aimed at fulfilment of worldly desires, while the latter knowledge pertains to the soul and its liberation from the world.

The true value of the knowledge of the scriptures lies in what real gain it gives to the person from the long-term perspective of his spiritual destiny, and not one that gives short-term worldly gains. But in both the cases however, intelligent application of the mind is imperative. If the scriptures are studied intelligently and analytically, a person is easily able to gain insight into them and realise that their main aim and purpose is not worldly gain but to provide the creature spiritual blessedness.

This spiritual knowledge contained in the scriptures can be gained by thoroughly studying them, discussing them in detail with others who are well-versed in this knowledge, observing saints and sages to see how this knowledge is being put to practice by them and the gain they derive from it, then personally contemplating upon this knowledge deeply, with the application of a focused mind and intellect, to arrive at the essence and the truth. Once this knowledge is gained in a proper way by a wise aspirant, he would practice it himself with full faith, devotion and commitment.

All the rituals and the knowledge of the scriptures should be pursued only till the time one does not know the true spiritual goal of his life and how to reach it. Once this knowledge dawns upon him, these rituals and knowledge become redundant for him. At this time only pure and untainted love and devotion for the Lord God remains in his heart. After all, this is the ultimate aim of performing all the rituals and having the knowledge of Brahm as contained in the scriptures.

It is said in the Srimad Bhagvat Mahapuran, 11/20/67 and 11/20/9: "I have prescribed three types of Yogas in the Vedas, viz. Gyan Yoga, Karma Yoga and Bhakti Yoga. There is no fourth type of Yoga. So long as one does not develop devotion for me with due faith and reverence, all the rituals and ceremonies and deeds and knowledge go in vain."

The reference to the threshing of the paddy vis-à-vis the study of the scriptures means that one should strive to understand their essence by adopting different means, such as self-study, discussion with wise ones, application of mind on the teaching of the scriptures and deeply contemplating on their purport.

*This instance of the husking of the harvested crop so that the grain can be separated from the chaff by threshing the paddy is also given in the Srimad Bhagvat Mahapuran, 10/14/4 which says: "Those who abandon the path of undiluted devotion for the holy feet of the Lord God who is the source of all well-being and true welfare, and instead labour to have abstract knowledge of Brahm (i.e. pursue the path of Gyan) for the sake of acquisition of the knowledge alone, they are toiling in vain like those foolish people who pound empty husk in an attempt to extract grain from it because in their ignorance they do not know that the grain has already been removed from it."]

२/१/२ तदङ्गानां च ॥ २८॥

2 /1 /2 tadaṅgānāṁ ca || 28||

(2/1/2) The different branches of scriptural (spiritual) knowledge and the various paths or means prescribed to have this knowledge should be diligently pursued till the time one has acquired perfection, and Truth that is free from all doubts and delusions has been understood. That should be the aim of knowledge and the various paths prescribed to gain it. [Otherwise, it is a futile exercise.] (28)

[This verse is an extension of the idea expressed in the previous verse no. 27. All the effort made and the energy and time spent in the studying of the scriptures is deemed to be well-spent if the person gains something worthwhile by it. And the only worthy gain that an aspirant has by this endeavour is to be enlightened about the true nature of his 'self' as well as its relationship with the 'Supreme Self'.

To wit, the real gain of scriptural study and pursuing different paths as prescribed by them is to attain self-realisation and God-realisation, which means that the aspirant understands that the ultimate goal of his study is to learn how to attain oneness with the Supreme Being so that eternal bliss and beatitude can be achieved. He further realises that basically there is no difference between his 'self' known as the Atma which is pure consciousness, and the 'Supreme Self' known as the Parmatma who embodies the cosmic Consciousness. Since there is a natural affinity between the two, only a little effort on the part of the aspirant would fulfil his wishes. He realises that there is actually no need for elaborate rituals or pursuing so many tedious paths as this ultimate goal—i.e. to bring about oneness of the individual soul with the supreme Soul can easily be done by the path of Bhakti. This understanding removes all sense of misery and grief from the inner-self of the spiritual aspirant, fills him with confidence and delight, and he steadfastly moves ahead to attain eternal blessedness. After all, this is the true and real message of the voluminous scriptures. If this is not understood and implemented, nothing is gained by pursuing these scriptures, or doing countless rituals, or keeping endless vows, or observing sacraments, or performing ceremonies, or keeping religious observances.

This verse basically means that all such things are merely branches and offshoots of the main Tree of Knowledge. One must strive to understand the spiritual Truth that is borne in the form of a divine fruit by this tree, instead of wasting the energy of his mind and the effort of his body in trying to understand about the many branches and offshoots of this huge tree.

And this divine fruit of self-and-God-realisation is easily had by following the path of Bhakti. So a wise man would focus his mind to know what Bhakti is, and how it should be practiced. All the other paths are subservient to Bhakti; they are subsidiaries of Bhakti. If there is no Bhakti then none of these many paths to attain blessedness and God-realisation would bear a ripe fruit.]

२ /१ /३ तामैश्वर्यपरां काश्यपः परत्वात् ॥ २९ ॥

2 /1 /3 tāmaiśvaryaparāṁ kāśyapaḥ paratvāt || 29||

(2/1/3) The great sage Kashyap (kāśyapaḥ) was of the eclectic view that only when the mind and the intellect are directed towards understanding of the Transcendental Supreme Truth (paratvāt), it is only then that the seeker is able to attain the supreme form of blessedness and eternity of peace, bliss and beatitude. This knowledge gives emancipation and salvation, known as 'Moksha', to the creature. (29)

[To wit, only when the creature focuses his mind and the intellect on the cosmic Consciousness will he be able to understand about it just like any other subject of study that needs full and devoted application of the mind and the intellect.

There are countless branches of knowledge even in our physical world, and one has to diligently pursue a particular subject or branch of knowledge that he has chosen to study to make a career of it for himself. Once he makes this selection, he has to remain focused on his chosen path and goal. If the limited time that he has at his disposal is not properly used, or if he fails to make a wise decision, then his life and time and energy are wasted away.

The same thing applies in the spiritual realm. The wisest person is one who sets his mind on the main objective of his life—which is to gain true knowledge that would set his soul free from the cycle of transmigration and give him eternal peace, bliss and beatitude. So he concertedly applies his mind and intellect to learn and know about the 'supreme Truth' that will help him attain this objective.

This is what sage Kashyap advised. He said that a wise spiritual aspirant is he who applies the faculty of the mind and the intellect to have the knowledge of the supreme transcendental Truth, and the cause of his miseries and torments. What is this 'Truth' and 'what is the cause of misery'?

The 'Truth' is that the 'self' of the individual creature is not his gross body but it is the Atma that is pure consciousness, that this Atma is the same as the Supreme Atma known as the Parmatma, the Supreme Being, and that true peace, bliss and beatitude is obtained only when the Atma understands its likeness and natural bond and affinity with the Parmatma, its parent, and ultimately becomes one with it. Since the Atma and the Parmatma are the same and both are inherently blissful, enlightened and eternal, the cause of all miseries and torments of the creature is that he does not understand this eternal Truth but remains mired in delusions and ignorance. Sage Kashyap advises the creature to learn this Absolute Truth, and become eternally blissful and blessed. He says that this is the real objective of the knowledge of the scriptures.

It will be noted here that sage Kashyap was of the view that there are two entities, i.e. the individual creature and his Atma, and the Parmatma or the Supreme Atma. Lack of truthful knowledge about the uniformity between the two, and that this knowledge is transcendental in nature, is the cause of worldly torments.]

२ /१ /४ आत्मैकपरां बादरायणः ॥ ३० ॥

2 /1 /4 ātmaikaparāṁ bādarāyaṇaḥ || 30||

(2/1/4) [Sage Veda Vyas, also known as Baadaraayan, has a slightly different view on this subject, though primarily the two views of Veda Vyas and Kashyap are the same.]

The learned sage Veda Vyas (known as "bādarāyaṇ") says that the mind and the intellect that is focused on the Atma (which is the true 'self' of the living being and pure consciousness personified) is the one that leads to final attainment of bliss and beatitude. (30)

[Sage Veda Vyas had penned the Upanishads which are said to be repositories of knowledge of the essence of the Vedas. They are also called 'Vedanta' because they teach the ultimate knowledge that is to be gained by the study of the Vedas, knowledge without which the study of the Vedas is useless.

And what does Veda Vyas teach? He teaches that the individual creature's 'true self' is not his gross perishable body, but it is the Atma. This Atma is pure consciousness personified; it is an eternal entity that is enlightened, wise and blissful. This Atma is the same as the cosmic Atma or the cosmic Consciousness known as Brahm. The creature suffers because he does not know this spiritual Truth. If he becomes aware of this Truth, i.e. if he becomes self-realised, then Brahm-realisation is automatically attained, and with it comes eternal bliss, beatitude and blessedness. This realisation also leads to liberation and deliverance from the delusions and ignorance that bind the creature to this world, and this translates into ultimate emancipation and salvation of the soul that is known as Moksha.

The difference between the views of Veda Vyas and Kashyap is evident, but it is only very slight in its essence. While Veda Vyas treats self-realisation as the main goal of spiritual knowledge that provides eternity and bliss, Kashyap advises Brahm-realisation for this purpose. Examined carefully though, we will see that basically there is no difference between the two views as they both stress that spiritual beatitude and bliss are attained when the creature realises the truth of his 'self' as pure transcendental consciousness that is separate from his gross body, and the fact that it is the same as the cosmic Consciousness known as Brahm. Hence, bringing unification between the two leads to final liberation and deliverance of the creature from the miseries and torments associated with this mortal world of transmigration where out of ignorance and delusions the Jiva, the living being, thinks he is separate from Brahm, the Supreme Being.

So therefore, while sage Kashyap is of the view that the mind and the intellect should be applied to understanding the spiritual truth of the 'self' as well as the 'Supreme Self' as they are two entities, Veda Vyas is of the view that understanding of the true nature of the 'self' is sufficient in itself as there is no difference between this 'self' and the 'Supreme Self' as they are both the same transcendental cosmic Consciousness.

When applied to the spiritual concept of Bhakti, Veda Vyas' view is more relevant because it applies directly to the heart where the soul lives. Bhakti is also directly related to the heart as it primarily consists of love and devotion for the Lord God.

Secondly, Bhakti recognises that there is only one supreme spiritual goal in life, which is to have single-minded devotion for the Lord God, like the view of Veda Vyas who says that there is only one goal of knowledge and it is to know about the truth of the Atma.

From this perspective, the view of sage Kashyap is slightly at variance with the concept of Bhakti because Kashyap applies the mind and the intellect to study two entities, viz. the Atma and the Parmatma, while Bhakti advises concentration on only one entity known as the

Parmatma.

Refer: Brahm-Sutra, 4/1/3 which says: "A wise one endeavours to realise the Atma which is supreme pure consciousness."]

२ /१ /५ उभयपरां शाण्डिल्यः शब्दोपपत्तिभ्याम् ॥ ३१ ॥

2 /1 /5 ubhayaparāṁ śāṇḍilyaḥ śabdōpapattibhyām || 31||

(2/1/5) Sage Shandilya reconciles the two views (of Kashyap and Veda Vyas) and is of the opinion that the mind and the intellect that relies on the Truth envisioned in the words of the Vedas and properly interprets them to understand about Brahm (the Supreme Being representing the transcendental cosmic Consciousness) and the Jiva (the individual creature and his true self which is also pure consciousness)—it is such mind and intellect that leads the creature to emancipation and salvation, and provides him with eternal bliss, beatitude and blessedness.

[This verse can also be read as follows: Sage Shandilya says that emancipation and salvation can be attained by both the paths, i.e. by focusing on the 'self' as well as on the 'Brahm'. This is because both represent the same eternal Truth that is cosmic transcendental Consciousness. So therefore, true knowledge is one that leads to self-realisation or Brahm-realisation, whether it is obtained by the study of the scriptures or got from other sources because both have the same effect, and both provide eternal bliss and beatitude to the spiritual aspirant.] (31)

[Sage Shandilya says that the scriptures should not be neglected, but they should be properly and correctly interpreted and understood. Since the Truth is that the Consciousness is an immutable, all-pervading and eternal entity, it follows that whether it is studied at its microcosmic level as the individual creature and his Atma or at the macrocosmic level as Brahm known as the Parmatma, the same thing is being studied and understood. So where is the cause of difference and dichotomy in it? To say that the living being's Atma is separate or different from the Supreme Atma in the form of Brahm is absolutely wrong and fallacious.

So proper application of the mind and the intellect removes all doubts and confusions regarding whom to have Bhakti for, whom to worship and be devoted to. Because a wise man would understand that by having Bhakti for his beloved Lord God he is actually worshipping Brahm as prescribed in the scriptures such as the Vedas or the Upanishads.

To wit, Bhakti leads a wise and enlightened devotee to Brahm-realisation and self-realisation that gives liberation and deliverance to the soul as envisioned in the Vedas and the Upanishads. The chief aim of the study of these scriptures is achieved if one understands the true nature of Bhakti, as well as that of the Atma and the Parmatma. This is what Shandilya says. In this way, he has reconciled the views of Veda Vyas and Kashyap.

In effect sage Shandilya says that since Bhakti brings about a union between the Atma and the Parmatma, it bridges the views of sage Kashyap and sage Veda Vyas.

Refer: The Chandogya Upanishad, 3/14/1-4 that endorses this view. It says: "Brahm is one and one alone. There is no parallel to Brahm. So a man with intuitive wisdom should worship him (Brahm) alone. The reward that one gets is in accordance with the effort one makes for it. If the spiritual endeavour is directed to Brahm then the spiritual reward is also Brahm-realisation that leads to emancipation and salvation of the soul. For one must remember the truth that 'he'

(Brahm) is the cause of everything, is the one who fulfils all wishes, is the divine Supreme Being who is transcendental, blissful, glorious and all-pervading. It is this Brahm that I worship and devote myself to attain eternal bliss and beatitude."]

२ /१ /६ वैषम्यादसिद्धमिति चेन्नाभिज्ञानवदवैशिष्टयात् ॥ ३२॥

2 /1 /6 vaiṣamyādasiddhamiti cēnnābhijñānavadavaiśiṣṭayāt || 32||

(1/2/6) Though it appears that the Jiva (the living being; the creature) is different from Brahm (the Supreme Being) but this is a wrong understanding of the two. It is because they represent the same pure consciousness that exists at two levels of creation, the Jiva being a revelation of it at the microcosmic level of creation, and Brahm being its revelation at the macrocosmic level.

Since all that is 'true' is nothing but pure transcendental Consciousness that has revealed itself in all these forms, it follows that the Jiva is also a manifested form of Brahm. This is the Absolute Truth. [And, this is also the unequivocal Truth expounded and enunciated by the Upanishads.] (32)

[The truthful nature of the Jiva is his Atma which is pure consciousness. This Atma is his true 'self', the soul of all living beings. It is also the same as the transcendental Consciousness that pervades in this creation as the eternal entity known as the supreme Brahm who is omnipresent, omnipotent, blissful and glorious. Brahm is the Soul of this creation, and therefore it is also revealed as the soul or the Atma of all living beings. This being the case, there is no difference either between any two Jivas or between the Jiva and Brahm. This is the considered view of sage Shandilya as well as of the Upanishads. It is established by the spiritual truth that the Atma is one and without a second.

The Upanishads unequivocally and unanimously endorse this philosophy. For instance, in the Sam Veda's Chandogya Upanishad, 3/14/1 it is said: "Brahm is one and one alone. There is no parallel or second to Brahm".

Similarly, Chandogya Upanishad, 4/8/7 says: "Tattwamasi"—i.e. Thou (the spiritual seeker's true self) art That (the supreme Brahm symbolising cosmic Consciousness)". This is one of the Great Sayings of the Upanishads, known as the 'Mahavakyas'.

Again, Chandogya Upanishad, 6/2/1 says: "There is only One who is without a second or a parallel."

In Shukla Yajur Veda's Brihad Aranyaka Upanishad, 4/4/19 it is said: "There is no duality anywhere in the creation as it is all pure consciousness".

"Aham Brahmasmi"—'I am Brahm': so says the Brihad Aranyaka Upanishad, 1/4/10. This also is one of the Mahavakyas.

"Brahm is the nectar of bliss and beatitude for all the living beings in the form of their Atma"—Brihad Aranyaka Upanishad, 2/5/14.

It is said in Rig Veda's Aiteriya Upanishad, 3/1/1: "Truthful knowledge, true wisdom and true enlightenment are all personified forms of Brahm".

Krishna Yajur Veda's Taitteriya Upanishad, 2/1 says: "The knowledge of Brahm or Brahm-realisation is the supreme knowledge. Brahm is the Truth, he is knowledge and enlightenment personified, and he is eternal and infinite."

The Krishna Yajur Veda's Katha Upanishad, 2/2/13 says: "Those persons who are really wise behold the supreme Brahm with full devotion as the supreme Reality and Truth of existence."

So therefore, from the perspective of the scriptures and the enlightened view of sage Shandilya, Bhakti is to focus the mind for Brahm-realisation, and to serve and have devotion for none but the supreme Brahm.

We observe that in this verse sage Shandilya has addressed the primary question: "To whom should one offer his worship; who is the God to whom Bhakti is to be offered?" His answer is based on the intelligent interpretation of the Vedas and the Upanishads, and it is that: "Bhakti should be offered to Brahm, the Supreme Being; it is Brahm alone who is to be worshipped; it is realisation of this Brahm that is the real aim of all spiritual practices, including that of Bhakti."]

२ /१ /७ न च क्लिष्टः परः स्यादनन्तरं विशेषात् ॥ ३३॥

2 /1 /7 na ca kliṣṭaḥ paraḥ syādanantaraṁ viśēṣāt || 33||

(2/1/7) The Jiva (i.e. the living being, the creature) is subjected to great worldly pain, grief, miseries and torments because it has not understood the real nature of its own 'self'. This 'self' is pure consciousness that is also the nature of the Supreme Self known as Brahm, the Supreme Being, who is an embodiment of eternal bliss and beatitude. So therefore, as long as this realisation does not dawn upon the creature because he is deluded and ignorant, he remains engulfed in all sorts of miseries and torments, which however vanish on their own upon realisation of the 'self'. (33)

[The previous verses have already expounded upon this spiritual principle. The creature's 'self' is his Atma which is pure consciousness and eternally blissful. Therefore the cause of all his miseries and torments is obviously his ignorance of this fact. So as soon as one develops understanding of the Supreme Being, the Lord God, and realises that his Atma is directly related to the Supreme Lord, then all miseries vanish automatically. This is the aim and purpose of Bhakti. It brings about oneness between the individual Atma of the creature and the Supreme Atma known as the Lord God; it helps to merge the microcosmic consciousness represented by the individual's Atma with its cosmic form known as the Parmatma, the Supreme Atma that is eternal and blissful.

Now the question arises, "if the Atma and the Parmatma are one, then why does the creature suffer so much unease and problems; why does he not find peace and bliss?" The answer is that the creature is deluded and is so ignorant that he does not know this fact. This delusion and ignorance can be removed by an intelligent study of the scriptures as indicated in verse no. 27.

In the Katha Upanishad, 2/2/13 it is said: "The person of wisdom who understands that the supreme Brahm is the only Truth and paramount eternal Reality in this creation, that Brahm is the fountain-head of bliss and the primary Consciousness that has revealed itself as the Atma residing inside all living beings as their 'self', and that this Brahm not only controls the creature from within his own self by the virtue of being the prime deity who resides as inside him as his Atma but also rewards him in accordance with his deeds—verily indeed, such a person attains eternal peace and bliss; no one who is ignorant of this fact about Brahm and his own 'self' ever attains peace and bliss."

So therefore, a wise and intelligent person develops steady devotion for Brahm, and he never turns back from this path that provides him eternal bliss and peace—refer: Taitteriya Upanishad, 2/8.]

२ /१ /८ ऐश्वर्यं तथेति चेन्न स्वाभाव्यात् ॥ ३४ ॥

2 /1 /8 aiśvaryaṁ tathēti cēnna svābhāvyāt || 34||

(2/1/8) Supernatural and majestic powers, infinite glories, holiness and divinity (aiśvaryaṁ) are an integral quality or virtue of the cosmic Consciousness, and these virtues cannot be separated from it as they are natural to it. [Refer also to verse no. 35.]

The creature does not exhibit these virtues or divine powers, even though it is said that his true self is pure consciousness, as he is ignorant of the nature of his 'true self' because of which he regards himself as different or separate from the Supreme Self which is represented by the cosmic Consciousness. (34)

[This verse explains why the creature is so diminutive and why he suffers in this world inspite of the fact that his 'self' is a personified form of cosmic consciousness that is all-powerful and possesses infinite glories and divinity. The answer is that the creature has not known who is 'true self' actually is. Had he known this, he would be like the supreme Brahm himself.

To wit, this is the purpose of Bhakti—to enable the individual creature realise Brahm and acquire the glories so characteristic of Brahm, i.e. to become eternally blissful, and to be liberated from ignorance and delusions. Just like Brahm, an enlightened and God-realised devotee becomes powerful enough to easily overcome all miseries and torments associated with this mortal gross world of transmigration even as he attains eternity and beatitude.

Till the time the person becomes God-realised, the grand characteristics of the divinity, holiness and glories of the Atma, the natural tendency of the Atma to be blissful, enlightened and happy, remain dormant and hidden within him.

It can be argued that if the whole creation is a manifested form of Brahm, then the pain, miseries and torments that make the Atma suffer also affect Brahm. This is a fallacious argument because though these negative elements exist in Brahm along with all the positive elements, they do not affect him just like the case of heat being inherently present in the fire element but the fire never feels tormented by its own heat.

Just like the natural brilliance of the sun is not affected by its dull image reflected from a dirty mirror, the glories of Brahm are not affected by the dullness that the Atma is subjected to because of the delusions and ignorance that dominate a creature.

The next verse no. 35 further elaborates on this principle.]

२ /१ /९ अप्रतिषिद्धं परैश्वर्यं तद्भावाच्च नैवमितरेषाम् ॥ ३५॥

2 /1 /9 apratiṣiddhaṁ paraiśvaryaṁ tadbhāvācca naivamitarēṣām || 35||

(2/1/9) Nowhere in the scriptures has it been said that the Supreme Being lacks in any kind of divinity, holiness, majestic powers and other glorious virtues, as these are his natural and inherent qualities.

Since the primary form of the Jiva (i.e. the true self of the living being in the form of his Atma) is the same as the Supreme Being (because they both represent pure consciousness), it follows that the former (i.e. the Jiva) also does not lack in any of the divine virtues. They are also integral to him. (35)

[Though the many divine virtues are an integral part of all Jivas, the living beings, yet they are subjected to modifications due the degree of ignorance and delusions that dominate the Jiva because of which he finds himself separated from the Supreme Being. By having Bhakti, which establishes oneness between the Jiva and the Supreme Being, this disparity or difference is removed. Then Jiva comes to experience the spark of divinity and holiness that are naturally present inside him. This would fill him with eternal joy and bliss.

Hence, the Jiva is able to overcome miseries and pain, and instead attain bliss and beatitude by following the path of Bhakti.

The Chandogya Upanishad, 8/3/4 says: "When the Jiva rises above his gross body, it is then he realises his true transcendental self."]

२ /१ /१० सर्वानृते किमिति चेन्नैवम्बुद्ध्यानन्त्यात् ॥ ३६ ॥

2 /1 /10 sarvānṛtē kimiti cēnnaivambuddhyānantyāt || 36||

(2/1/10) If it is said that one can find complete freedom (liberation, emancipation of the soul) by getting rid of (spiritual) delusions, then this is not practically feasible because the Buddhi (mind and intellect) is infinite, and so if one is able to overcome the delusions under one given situation, others take hold of him in another situation. This is because the Buddhi would look and interpret the second situation differently from the first situation. (36)

[That is why even the wisest of men fall prey to delusions and go astray from their spiritual path. This is also why one needs to constantly study the scriptures and practice Bhakti diligently so that he is able to counter the confusions and doubts that the Buddhi continues to create for him.

For instance, the person may be convinced about the falsehood of the charms of the material world and is assured that true happiness comes by renouncing it. Then his mind and intellect pesters him that the knowledge about the Atma etc. are too abstract to be of any practical value, so he must rather enjoy the practical world instead of pursuing an abstract idea. The person begins to falter in his spiritual beliefs, and it would be ruinous for him if he does not recover in time. So herein comes the necessity of constant study of the scriptures and practice of Bhakti which together help him overcome the constant pestering of the Buddhi which tries to make him look rationale and secular and modern in his outlook by neglecting his spiritual pursuit and instead follow the path of the material world.

This is the meaning of this verse. The mind is not constant; it keeps on changing and interpreting things differently. That is why control of the mind has been prescribed in the Upanishads as a necessary step towards self-realisation and final liberation.

To wit, those who are atheists in heart though pretending to be ethical in word and deed, those who read the Vedas well but disparage the Lord God by not accepting him and his existence, those who are arrogant, insolent and demoniac by nature inspite of studying the scriptures as they have not cultivated the glorious virtues of humility and piety taught by them—it is sure that these people can never find emancipation and salvation for themselves as their mind and intellect have been hijacked by delusions.]

२ /१ /११ प्रकृत्यन्तरालादवैकार्यं चित्सत्त्वेनानुवर्तमानात्
|| ३७ ||

2 /1 /11 prakṛtyantarālādavaikāryaṁ citsattvēnānuvartamānāt
|| 37||

(2/1/11) The Supreme Being employs his delusion-creating powers (known as 'Maya', and which is one of his many powers) to create Prakriti (physical world; Nature). So to imagine that the Supreme Being has lost his characteristics of being invisible, infinite, immutable, indivisible and constant just because he has created this world that is visible, finite, ever-changing and perishable, is a wrong proposition. (37)

[The Supreme Being known as Brahm used his delusion-creating powers to create a physical world that is so different from the unique characteristic qualities of its creator even though the scriptures say that the world (Prakriti) is a revelation of Brahm, that everything in existence is nothing but Brahm, that Brahm created this world and the Jiva, the living being who came to live in this world, in his own likeness.

Nothing appears to be 'in likeness' between Brahm and either the Jiva or the world—for while Brahm is sublime, subtle, invisible, immutable, infinite and eternal, both the Jiva and the world are gross, visible, changeable, perishable and finite. The reason is that Brahm created this world by employing his Maya, his delusion-creating powers which are one of his countless majestic powers.

Therefore, inspite of this Prakriti (world and Jiva) being corrupted by so many negative qualities it does not mean that Brahm is also corrupted.

Since Brahm had initiated the process of creation, it is said that he is the 'creator' or the 'doer of deed' that resulted in the production of this creation. But Brahm is free from his creation and its taints, so inspite of being the 'doer of a deed' (that resulted in this creation), he is free from its negative effects.

Now a question arises: If everything is created by Maya or delusions, and not by Brahm, then why is it said in the scriptures that all that exists is Brahm, and it is Brahm that is established in creation? The next verse no. 38 answers this question.]

२ /१ /१२ तत्प्रतिष्ठा गृहपीठवत् ॥ ३८॥

2 /1 /12 tatpratiṣṭhā gṛhapīṭhavat || 38||

(2/1/12) [Since Prakriti, Nature, owes its origin directly to Maya as said in the previous verse no. 37, then why is it said that everything that exists has its origin in Brahm, the Supreme Being who is a personified form of the cosmic Consciousness? This question is addressed now.]

Since the origin of Maya as well as Prakriti can be traced back to Brahm, there is no wrong in concluding that owe their origin ultimately to Brahm; that they are ultimately established in 'that' (i.e. Brahm) which lends them their validity, authority and authenticity (tatpratiṣṭhā).

It is like the case of a man seated on a stool in his home (gṛhapīṭhavat)—here it is always said that the man is sitting in his home, and not on a stool. (38)

[This example is self-explanatory. When we want to know where a person is, we are told 'he is in his home'. If we enquire further and wish to be specific as to where inside the home he exactly is then we are told 'he is sitting on a chair or a stool inside his home'. Now this stool or chair on which the person is sitting are also a part of his home, and they can be shifted anywhere inside the building, but we still say that the person is 'sitting on a stool or a chair in his home'.

Likewise, this creation or Prakriti can have its origin in anything related to Brahm, it may be Maya or any other virtue of Brahm, but still the primary source of its coming into existence is Brahm and Brahm alone, and nothing else. It is Brahm's prerogative to decide what he will use to create Prakriti. Hence it is said that this creation that is revealed as Prakriti or Nature has its ultimate seat in Brahm.

Just as we do not separate the stool or the chair from the home while being told where the person is, so likewise we do not treat Maya and Brahm separately while learning where Prakriti (Nature) and its Jivas (the living beings who inhabit this creation) have their root or origin. We identify their seat as Brahm.

Again, just as a spider creates and withdraws its web without any effort, so also this world proceeds forth from Brahm and falls back in Brahm. Another example is this: Just as hairs grow unconsciously from the body of a conscious man without his even being aware of the creation of hairs, and these hairs fall off from his body again without his being aware of this happening, and in due course of time new hairs grow afresh again without the man being aware of it, similar is the case with Brahm vis-à-vis the Prakriti (Nature) and its inhabitants known as the Jivas (living beings) who are created and destructed continuously in a rhythmic cycle of creation and destruction without Brahm being involved in it. And just as we say that it is the spider's web or a particular man's hair, so we say that the Prakriti and the Jiva have their origin in Brahm.

Further, the spider's web and the hairs of a man will have their respective genes or DNA in them, so likewise the Prakriti and the Jiva have the 'genes' of Brahm in them. So it is said that Brahm dwells in all the units of creation, animate or inanimate. Refer: Chapter 6 of the Chandogya Upanishad of Sam Veda.

Lord Krishna says in Srimad Bhagvad Geeta, 9/10 that: "Prakriti or Nature, propelled by me—i.e. under my instructions and supervision, gives birth to this universe which consists of both animate as well as inanimate beings. It is in this way that the wheel of creation goes on and on."

It is said in the Srimad Bhagvat Mahapuran, 4/11/17 that: "It is due to the Supreme Being that the universe, made up of a system consisting of a cause and its effect, ever remains in a state of flux just as iron pieces are set in motion by the presence of a magnet."

Aiteriya Upanishad of the Rig Veda tradition describes the process of creation. It goes on to say that Brahm, after having initiated the process of creation, wondered as to how he would control the monster he has self-created. So he decided to enter his creation and control it from within. Refer: Aiteriya Upanishad, 1/1/1—1/3/14.

The entire Shvetashvatara Upanishad of the Krishna Yajur Veda tradition is dedicated to the theme of how this creation is established in Brahm. An elaborate English version of this great Upanishad has been published by this author along with other Upanishads of the Krishna Yajur Veda in his series on all the 108 Upanishads classified according to their respective Vedas.]

२ /१ /१३ मिथोऽपेक्षणादुभयम् ॥ ३९॥

2 /1 /13 mithō 'pēkṣaṇādubhayam || 39||

(2/1/13) Therefore we conclude that both Brahm and Maya play a role in creation. Hence, both can be said to be the cause of Prakriti (Nature; creation), and this statement will not contradict anything said.

There is another way of interpreting this verse as follows: Neither Maya nor Prakriti, or Prakriti and Jiva, are able to independently do anything without the overall command and supervision of Brahm—because they have their source of authority in Brahm. It is from Brahm that these two units of creation derive their powers and authority, both at the macro level as well as the micro level of existence. (39)

[Brahm represents pure 'consciousness', and it is this 'consciousness' that does anything at all at any given level of creation. It is very obvious—because a 'dead and lifeless' entity—i.e. that which does not have 'consciousness' or 'the fundamental element or the spark of life' in it, won't do anything even if it tries to do it.

Taitteriya Upanishad, 2/7/1 says: "For who indeed would be able to breathe and remain alive if Brahm, who is eternal and blissful consciousness, does not remain present as the supervisor having its seat in the soul or the Atma of the creature?"

Lord Krishna says in Srimad Bhagvad Geeta, 9/10 that: "Prakriti or Nature, propelled by me—i.e. under my instructions and supervision, gives birth to this universe which consists of both animate as well as inanimate beings. It is in this way that the wheel of creation goes on and on."

This verse no. 39 brings to the conclusion the arguments put forward in verse nos. 37-38.

The next verse no. 40 elaborates on this theme by saying that besides Brahm and Prakriti, or Brahm (Parmatma) and Jiva, there is no other third element. There is the 'cause' in the form of Brahm, and there is the 'effect' in the form of Prakriti, there is the Parmatma from whom the Jiva was born, and there is nothing besides it. So they depend upon each other. Still, Prakriti depends upon Brahm, and Jiva upon Parmatma as the latter is the progenitor of the former.]

२/१ १४ चेत्याचितोर्न तृतीयम् ॥ ४०॥

2 /1 14 cētyācitōrna tr̥tīyam || 40||

(2/1/14) Other than the pure consciousness (which is the cause of everything in this universe) and the revelation of this consciousness (which is the effect of it in the form of creation of this universe, the material world), there is no third element.

To wit, there is no third element (na tr̥tīyam) other than Brahm ("cita"—i.e. pure cosmic Consciousness) and Prakriti or Nature ("cētya"—i.e. the material world). (40)

[Put simply, there is the primary aspect of creation that is its 'cause', and it is known as 'pure cosmic Consciousness'; it is also known as Brahm. The second aspect of this creation is the 'effect' of the 'presence of this consciousness', and it is known as the Prakriti or Nature; it is the revealed aspect of the cosmic consciousness in the form of the material world as we know it.

So therefore, there are two entities to be researched and known: one is 'consciousness' that is at the root of everything, and the other is the effect of this consciousness that is revealed in the form of the 'material world' (cētyācitta). There is no other third thing to be researched and known (ōr-na tṛtīyam). The next verse no. 41 herein below further reiterates this fundamental principle.

Shukla Yajur Veda's 1st Upanishad is called 'Ishavashya Upanishad', meaning 'where does Isha, the Supreme Lord, lives'. Its verse no.1 says: "Verily, all this universe is Brahm—i.e. a man who is wise and enlightened realises that the world has come from Brahm, is sustained by Brahm, and it finally dissolves in Brahm." So therefore, we see that there is no 'third element' present.]

२ /१ /१५ युक्तौ च सम्परायात् ॥ ४१ ॥

2 /1 /15 yuktau ca samparāyāt || 41||

(2/1/15) Prakriti and Brahm (i.e. the gross aspect of creation represented by the material world, and the subtle and sublime aspect represented by pure consciousness respectively) have coexisted ever since the time creation came into being. (41)

[To wit, this creation has always had two components—viz. one is its subtle aspect represented by pure consciousness, and the other is its gross aspect that is represented by the material world. There is no 'third' component.

This verse clearly implies that the material world or the Prakriti came into being because of consciousness known as Brahm—because of the simple reason that only an entity that has 'consciousness' in it can think and do something. But at the same time it is also important to note that the very existence of Prakriti proved the existence of Brahm. To wit, how would anyone know that Brahm is consciousness if it does not do something actively to produce a tangible result to show that it is a living entity and not a lifeless one? And in the same vein, what is the use and relevance of Prakriti if it is like a dead tissue if there was no presence of life or consciousness represented by Brahm in it? Hence, Brahm and Prakriti help each other to make this creation relevant.

So therefore, both Brahm and Prakriti coexist and compliment each other. Hence, to have a comprehensive knowledge of existence and the truth behind it, it is equally important to learn about the material world known as Prakriti or Nature as well as the subtle world represented by the pure consciousness that is known as Brahm at the macro level and as the Atma at the micro level of creation.]

२ /१ /१६ शक्तित्वान्नानृतं वेद्यम् ॥ ४२॥

2 /1 /16 śaktitvānnānṛtaṁ vēdyam || 42||

(2/1/16) The revelation of this creation is a vivid manifestation of the supernatural and cosmic powers of Consciousness.

Therefore one must understand that both the Prakriti (Nature) and the Maya (the delusory powers that are behind it) are a vivid manifestation of Brahm (cosmic Consciousness); they represent the cosmic powers of Brahm to create and regulate.

Hence, the object of knowledge and spiritual research is the cosmic energy and dynamism of Consciousness (that would actually provide the desired reward in the form of liberation, deliverance, emancipation and salvation to the spiritual aspirant; it is this positive energy that helps the aspirant to neutralise his negative energy so that he can overcome his worldly miseries and torments to attain eternal peace, bliss and blessedness). (42)

[The very fact that this fantastically magnificent creation which seems to have no end in its dimensions as well as in the variations of its form and nature proves the stupendous powers and the majesty that is possessed by the cosmic Consciousness that has created this wonder.

The cosmic Consciousness represented by Brahm is the cause of Prakriti and Maya as we have already read in previous verse nos. 37-41. They represent the stupendous dynamism of Brahm; they symbolise the profound creative energy of Brahm.

So this verse gives the reason why one should strive to have Brahm-realisation. It is because then he would be able to harness the positive energy and dynamism of the pure cosmic Consciousness, and then put it to good use by employing it to neutralise the negative energy that is present inside him due to his continued association with this gross mundane world. When the dirt of negativity is scrubbed clean from his inner-self, the divine light of his own conscious Atma would shine through. This would remove all darkness symbolised by ignorance and delusions that had dominated him earlier, and instead fill him with spiritual enlightenment and a sense of blessedness.

So therefore, Brahm-realisation naturally leads to attainment of eternal peace, happiness, bliss and beatitude for the spiritual aspirant.

After having established why it is so important to have Brahm-realisation or God-realisation, sage Shandilya now turns his discourse back to the main theme of this book—i.e. Bhakti. This follows from the next verse no. 43.]

२ /१ /१७ तत्परिशुद्धिश्च गम्या लोकवल्लिङ्गेभ्यः ॥ ४३॥

2 /1 /17 tatpariśuddhiśca gamyā lōkavalliṅgēbhyaḥ || 43||

(2/1/17) The attainment of perfection in Bhakti, i.e. attaining its purest form, and being firmly established in the true form of Bhakti, is revealed in the form of signs that are visibly observed in this world. (43)

[When a spiritual aspirant has reached the transcendental state of Brahm-realisation, it becomes evident by his behaviour. He would be perpetually ecstatic, live in a blissful state, be meditative and contemplative, and indifferent to the mundane world and its affairs.

Similarly, when Bhakti has matured in the heart of the spiritual aspirant, he would be lost in the thoughts of his beloved Lord God, be oblivious of the surrounding world, be perpetually ecstatic and blissful, and virtually exhibit all the signs of one who has become Brahm-realised. Here a parallel is drawn between maturity of Bhakti and Brahm-realisation.

Just as Brahm representing pure consciousness is invisible, but the Prakriti or the material world created by Brahm is visible, so is the case with Bhakti. In Bhakti, when it matures, the devotee experiences the subtle presence of the Divinity, the Lord God, inside his own heart. This is an esoteric experience that manifests itself in the form of some signs exhibited by the devotee's physical body—such as it would be thrilled, have goose-bumps, tears would roll down his eyes, he would not be aware of his surroundings, would behave like a mad man, laughing, weeping, singing and dancing or even sitting in a trance, and so on and so forth.

Though attainment of maturity in Bhakti is not something to be expressly said or divulged to others, it is still revealed on its own accord by the many signs exhibited by the devotee.

So therefore, just as the glorious presence of Brahm can be understood by observing the world, so likewise one can understand the maturity of Bhakti by observing certain signs that are apparent in a devotee. This is basically what this verse says.

The next verse no. 44 tells us some of the characteristics of true devotees of the Lord.]

२ /१ /१८

सम्मानबहुमानप्रीतिविरहेतरविचिकित्सामहिमख्यातितदर्थ-प्राणस्थानतदीयतासर्वतद्भावाप्रातिकूल्यादीनि च स्मरणेभ्यो वाहुल्यात् ॥ ४४॥

2 /1 /18

sammānabahumānaprītivirahētaravicikitsāmahimakhyātitadartha-

prāṇasthānatadīyatāsarvatadbhāvāprātikūlyādīni ca smaraṇēbhyō vāhulyāt || 44||

(2/1/18) [This verse outlines some of the characteristics of the devotees of the Lord God.]

The scriptures have outlined certain signs that denote the maturity of Bhakti. To wit, these examples are the practical ways Bhakti can be practiced by a devotee. Some of these are enumerated here:

(i) To have great respect and reverence for the Lord God (like was the case of Arjun who had great reverence and respect for Lord

Krishna) [sammāna] {refer: Mahabharat, Drona Parva, 2822};

(ii) to have great respect and reverence for anything that has any likeness with the Lord such as any name or form that is closely like that of the Lord (because this likeness reminds the devotee of his beloved Lord God and ignites love and devotion in his heart as was the case with king Ikshwaku of Ayodhya) [bahumāna] {refer: Nrisingh Puran, 25/22};

(iii) to feel exceptionally happy by seeing or meeting a devotee of the Lord as much as meeting the Lord himself (as was the case of Bidur) [prīti] {refer: Mahabharat, Udyog Parva, 88/3124};

(iv) to feel intense pain of separation from the Lord (as was the case with the Gopis of Vrindavan who were separated from Lord Krishna) [viraha] {refer: Mahabharat, Shanti Parva, 12883};

(v) not to be interested in anything that is not directly related to the Lord (as was the case with Umpanyu and the residents of Shwet-dwipa) [ētaravicikitsā] {refer: Mahabharat, Anushaashan Parva, 14/7077};

(vi) to always remain engaged in glorifying the Lord and talking and discussing about his divinity and grand virtues that are famed in the world and so much praised in the scriptures; to constantly sing the glorious virtues of the Lord God and chant his holy name; to invoke the grace of the Lord and always remember him and his glories [mahima-khyāti] {refer: Vishnu Puran, 2/6/39-45);

(vii) to live for the sake of the Lord and serve him alone (as was the case with Hanuman whose life was entirely dedicated in the service of Lord Ram, and with the residents of Vrindavan whose life revolved around Lord Krishna) [tadartha-prāṇasthāna] {refer: Valmiki's Ramayan, Uttar Kand, Canto 107, verse no. 31; Srimad Bhagwat Mahapuran};

(viii) to be of a firm conviction that whatever things are

presently possessed or whatever is due actually belongs to the Lord God (as was the case with king Bali who had gladly offered his entire empire as well as his own body to Lord Vaaman, the dwarf incarnation of Lord Vishnu; and Uparichara Vasu) [tadīyatā] {refer: (a) the story of king Bali and Lord Vaaman appears in Srimat Bhagwat Mahapuran, 8/15-23; and (b) Mahabharat, Shanti Parva, 337/12718 respectively; the story of Bali and Lord Vaaman is described in Vaaman Puran's chapter nos. 73-75, 77, 89, 91-95 in great detail};

(ix) to see the Lord God in every creature, in every thing and everywhere in this world (as was the case with Prahalad who had told his angry father, the demon Hiranyakashipu, that he sees his beloved Lord everywhere and in every living being) [sarvatadbhāva] {refer: Vishnu Puran, 1/17; 1/19/36-38; Srimad Bhagwat Mahapuran, 7/4-8};

(x) not to act in any way that is against the wishes of the Lord or do not conform to the noble ideals of righteous and auspicious conduct that is favoured by the Lord (as was the case with Bhisma, Yudhisthir etc. in the epic story of the Mahabharat) [aprātikūlyādīni] {refer: Mahabharat, Bhishma Parva, 58/2604}.

These are but some of the examples can remembered as to how Bhakti can be practiced and what its signs are [smaraṇēbhyō vāhulyāt]. [There are of course many other forms.] (44)

२ /१ /१९ द्वेषादयस्तु नैवम् ॥ ४५॥

2 /1 /19 dvēṣādayastu naivam || 45||

(2/1/19) Any trace of any kind of jealousy, hatred, malice, ill-will and animosity (and all other such negative traits) are not present in a true devotee of the Lord God. (45)

[A true devotee's heart is pure and holy as it becomes a dwelling place of the Lord God himself. So therefore there is no scope of any negativity being present inside it. Such emotions as hatred, jealousy, malice etc. are totally unbecoming of a pious and holy person that a devotee of the Lord is expected to be.

In the epic Mahabharat, Anushasan Parva, Chapter 149, verse no. 133, it is said: "Neither anger nor envy, nor greed, nor jealousy, nor impure thought of any kind can dwell in the heart of those who are devoted to the Supreme Being."

In Ram Charit Manas, Uttar Kand, Doha no. 112, Lord Shiva tells goddess Uma: "Listen Uma. Those who love to worship and are always devoted to the holy feet of Lord Ram are free from desires and passions (Kaam), hypocrisy, ego and arrogance (Mada), as well as anger, malice and hatred (Krodha). They see their beloved Lord everywhere and in each individual in this creation, so where is the cause of their hating or opposing anyone in this world; why should they hate or oppose anyone at all?"

A true devotee of the Lord God sees his beloved Lord everywhere, in each individual living being. So where is the cause of his harbouring any trace of malice or jealousy or any other negative sentiments against anyone? Hence, even if he is shown lack of respect or courtesy by others he still treats them with full respect because he knows that the other person is an image of his Lord, and probably it is the Lord who is testing his sincerity of faith in him, his depth of devotion for him, and the presence of good virtues such as equanimity, tolerance, fortitude, renunciation and calmness of mind that are expected in a devotee of the Lord by employing this ruse to observe how he reacts in the face of disrespect shown by others for him.]

२/१/२० तद्वाक्यशेषात् प्रादुर्भावेष्वपि सा ॥ ४६ ॥

2 /1 /20 tadvākyaśēṣāt prādurbhāvēṣvapi sā || 46||

(2/1/20) The devotion (Bhakti) that is directed towards the various manifestations of the Supreme Being is also deemed to be a genuine kind of Bhakti. (46)

[We have read in the earlier verses that sage Shandilya has emphasised that true Bhakti is one that is directed to Brahm, the Supreme Being who represents the cosmic Consciousness as advised in the Upanishads. Refer to verse nos. 28-42 in this context.

So here he wishes to remove any doubt that may emerge in a person's mind as to whether the various incarnations of Brahm, such as Lord Ram, Lord Krishna and others, are worthy of reverence and having devotion for or not. Yes surely they are, and the spiritual rewards are equal too, for these different forms are visible manifestations of the same the Supreme Being whose cosmic form is invisible and incomprehensible for a common man. Since the main aim of Bhakti is to bring the individual closer to the Supreme Being, and since everyone does not have the intellectual ability to realise Brahm as expounded in the Upanishads, so therefore an easy alternate path should always be provided so that all living beings can access the spiritual nectar in the form of Bhakti for the Lord God, for all living beings have the right to find liberation and deliverance for themselves, and enable their souls to attain emancipation and salvation even if they are not too intellectually sharp, wise and enlightened enough.

In Srimad Bhagvad Geeta, 7/23, Lord Krishna says: "Those who worship me in any form finally attain me irrespective of the form they choose to worship (because it is me who is being ultimately worshipped in this way)."

The Brahmasamhita, verse no. 46, says: "As from one original lighted candle other candles are lit and all of them show the same light as the original, so in the same way from the same divine form of the Supreme Being other divine forms such as Lord Ram, Lord Nrisingh etc. are manifested. So they all are the same in their essence and virtues."

The next verse no. 47 reiterates the views expressed in this present verse.]

२ /१ /२१ जन्मकर्मविदश्चाजन्मशब्दात् ॥ ४७॥

2 /1 /21 janmakarmavidaścājanmaśabdāt || 47||

(2/1/21) The words of the scriptures also endorse the view that those devotees of the Lord God who have properly understood the mystery of the birth and the numerous deeds of the Lord during his many incarnations find liberation from the cycle of birth and death. (47)

[Why should one study the scriptures? It is because they enlighten him about the form that the Supreme Being has taken while he revealed himself in this world, to distinguish the divine form of the Lord from all other forms of the Jivas (living beings) so that the devotee knows correctly whom to adore, whom to have devotion for, and whom to offer his worship. Since the external form of the Lord is like that of other living beings, the devotee would be at a lost to recognise his Lord God if the scriptures were not there to guide him in this respect.

For instance, Lord Ram and Lord Krishna were like other human beings in their external appearances; they took a birth and had a gross physical body like other human beings, they grew up like others, did many worldly deeds, exhibited so many emotions and generally had other characters that are so common to all human beings, and they even had to suffer pain and pass through difficulties like ordinary men—but they were different from other men, for they were divine incarnations or a living manifestations of the Supreme Being unlike other ordinary human beings. The scriptures tell us this fact, and without their help no one would be able to distinguish between Lord Ram or Lord Krishna and other exalted men who lived on this earth. In the absence of this knowledge, how would a person know whom to offer his worship and devotion, whom to adore, and before whom to surrender? He will not know whose worship and devotion would grant him spiritual blessing, who will be able to deliver him from the trap of the cycle of transmigration, who will provide his soul with salvation and emancipation, who will give him beatitude and felicity?

So once a person understands that the various incarnations of the Supreme Being in this world, such as his manifestation in the human forms of Lord Ram and Lord Krishna, are simply a visible form of the Lord who is invisible and without any attributes in his primary cosmic form as the Supreme Lord of the universe, and that there is no difference between worshipping the Lord's macrocosmic, all-pervading, infinite and invisible form and his microcosmic form that is visible and easily comprehensible—then such persons would realise that the Lord he is worshipping is not an ordinary man but the Supreme Being himself. So by worshipping and having devotion for the various manifestations of the Supreme Being, the devotee gets the same spiritual reward as got by ascetics and enlightened sages who worship Brahm directly in order to become Brahm-realised.

To wit, even ordinary devotees who may not have the wherewithal to do Yoga and acquire Gyan can also find liberation from the cycle of birth and death in this mortal world by having Bhakti for the various incarnations of the Supreme Being. The humble devotee's soul is delivered and he easily finds emancipation and salvation by finally merging his own soul with the supreme Soul represented by the form of the Supreme Being he worships in the same way that highly enlightened and self-realised ascetics and sages do by meditating upon the 'self' which is pure consciousness known as the Atma, as well as upon Brahm who represents the cosmic Consciousness known as the Parmatma.

Now, a question arises: Why has the eternal and divine Brahm, the Supreme Being who has no forms, taints and attributes, assumed a gross form with the attributes and characteristics that are so characteristic of this mortal, gross and mundane world? The answer is this: The Supreme Being has done it for the benefit of his devotees. He has been gracious enough to assume a visible gross form in a world that is characterised by the cycle of birth and death so that his ordinary devotees can enjoy his presence amongst themselves. Since the laws that regulate this world have been ordained by the Lord himself, he feels it obligatory to follow them—and that is why the Lord takes a birth and assumes a gross body, and also goes through the entire process of life in this world like any other living being who has a physical gross body so that there is no transgression of the laws of Nature.

It is said in Ram Charit Manas, Baal Kand, Chaupai line no. 3 that precedes Doha no. 185 that the Supreme Lord reveals himself at any place if the devotee has sufficient devotion and love for him, and wishes to see the Lord personally.

Further it is said in Ram Charit Manas, Baal Kand, Chaupai line nos. 6-8 that precede Doha no. 121 that: "Whenever sins and evil qualities become dominant, and righteousness and good virtues are on the verge of extinction, the Lord God manifests himself at such times to restore the balance in favour of the goodness and put things in order in a general way."

Similarly, in Ram Charit Manas, Baal Kand, Doha no. 33 along with Chauapi line nos. 6-8 it is said: "Lord Ram is eternal and infinite, and so are his glories. Though his invisible all-pervading cosmic form has no origin or birth, but he does reveal himself and assumes a visible form from time to time in different eras of the celestial cycles of birth and death. So a wise person should not doubt the divinity of the Lord in any of these births and forms."

So a wise and intelligent devotee understands that the visible form of the Lord God he is offering his worship to is the same supreme Divinity, the same Supreme Being to whom the scriptures advise a creature to be devoted to and offer worship.

This devotee also realises that the Lord has simply followed the Laws of Nature and Creation by taking birth like other ordinary living beings and have a gross perishable body as this is the natural process of creation and destruction in this mortal world, for the Lord cannot set a bad example by violating the sacrosanct laws of creation that he has set and ordained himself.

In Srimad Bhagvad Geeta, 10/9, Lord Krishna says: "My form and activities are divine. A person who knows and understands this reality does not have to take a birth again after leaving his body, but he comes to me (i.e. he finds liberation and deliverance from the cycle of birth and death)."

In Srimad Bhagvad Geeta, 4/7-8, Lord Krishna says: "Oh Arjun! Whenever righteousness is on the decline and unrighteousness is on the increase, I assume a physical body (i.e. I reveal myself) for the protection of goodness and elimination of evil, and to establish Dharma on a strong footing. In this way I am born in different eras of the celestial cycle of birth and death."

Srimad Bhagvat Mahapuran, 10/29/14 and 10/36 say: "The Lord descends for bestowing the boon of final beatitude on human beings; out of his infinite merciful nature he does so to show grace upon his devotees; so that his devotees can remember his divine life and its glories in order to find freedom from the humdrum affairs of life in this gross mundane world."

This spiritual reward is obtained because the devotee would have cleared his mind of all delusions that cause so many doubts and confusions regarding the divinity of the soul and its relationship with the supreme Soul. This state of awareness or spiritual enlightenment leads to 'Mukti'—freedom from all fetters that tie a soul to the cycle of transmigration.]

२ /१ /२२ तच्च दिव्यं स्वशक्तिमात्रोद्भवात् ॥ ४८॥

2 /1 /22 tacca divyaṁ svaśaktimātrōdbhavāt || 48||

(2/1/22) The deeds done and activities undertaken by the Lord in his various manifestations are all divine by nature, and they are beyond the usual grossness associated with this mundane world.

The Lord has revealed himself by his own wish, and it is his own cosmic power known as Maya (the power that causes delusions) that creates an illusion of his being an ordinary person doing ordinary deeds like any other ordinary living being. (48)

[The Lord wishes to keep his identity secret. He wishes that only a selected few get to know who he actually is. So he uses the powers of Maya, the cosmic power of the Lord that creates delusions, to hide his divinity and cosmic form.

A wise and enlightened devotee understands this. That is why he does not doubt the Lord's divinity, and hence he does not get confused by the Lord's ordinary behaviour in this world. He relies on the words of the scriptures that tell him to be careful not to be deluded by the Lord's seemingly ordinary-looking life in this world—because the Lord is simply following the Rules of Nature ordained by himself when he behaves in an ordinary way. The Lord does not want to break his own laws by acting superhumanly if he had chosen to assume the form of a human being. But every now and then some incidents do occur that clearly reflect that the human form of the Lord is just a veil hiding the cosmic powers of the Supreme Being. It is only the rare wise person who sees through this mystery.

A simple example of this is that during the entire bloody war of Mahabharata, Arjun remained unharmed because Lord Krishna was driving his war chariot. Further, it is indeed remarkable that Krishna was not wounded during the war while all other participants suffered grave wounds. Arjun had not fully realised the gravity of the situation, and thought that it was he who had won the war. So at the end of the war, Lord Krishna told him to get off the chariot first. As soon as the Lord stepped down, the chariot was reduced to a heap of crumpled iron and burnt wood.

In the story of the Ramayana we read that Lord Ram gave a signet ring to Hanuman to be used as an identity proof to be shown to Sita when the monkey army was sent to search for her. There were hundreds and thousands of monkeys and bears who were dispatched for this purpose, but Lord Ram knew that only Hanuman would make it. That is obviously why the Lord gave the ring to him—because he was certain that Sita would be found, and that it was Hanuman who would find her.

This are small examples to show that every now and then some small event took place that proved the divinity and super-natural powers of a particular form of the Lord.

In Srimad Bhagvad Geeta, 4/6, Lord Krishna says: "Though I am without a birth and death as I am eternal, and am present as the Atma or the soul of all living beings in this creation, yet often I reveal myself independently by employing my own cosmic powers (known as Maya that create delusions). But even then, I keep my nature under strict control and conform to my divine origin."]

२ /१ /२३ मुख्यं तस्य हि कारुण्यम् ॥ ४९॥

2 /1 /23 mukhyaṁ tasya hi kāruṇyam || 49||

(2/1/23) The chief reason why the Supreme Lord takes birth in this world to live amongst ordinary creatures is his extreme gracious, benevolent and compassionate nature which obliges him to bless the world and its inhabitants whenever they require his presence. So the Lord comes down to personally live with them and to provide them with an opportunity to be close to him during his manifestation. For other generations that follow, the Lord provides a mean by which they can have an easy access to him by remembering his glorious life and deeds. (49)

[It is said in Ram Charit Manas, Baal Kand, Chaupai line no. 3 that precedes Doha no. 185 that the Supreme Lord reveals himself at any place if the devotee has sufficient devotion and love for him, and wishes to see the Lord personally.

Further it is said in Ram Charit Manas, Baal Kand, Chaupai line nos. 6-8 that precede Doha no. 121 that: "Whenever sins and evil qualities become dominant, and righteousness and good virtues are on the verge of extinction, the Lord God manifests himself at such times to restore the balance in favour of the goodness and put things in order in a general way."

Similarly, in Ram Charit Manas, Baal Kand, Doha no. 33 along with Chauapi line nos. 6-8 it is said: "Lord Ram is eternal and infinite, and so are his glories. Though his invisible all-pervading cosmic form has no origin or birth, but he does reveal himself and assumes a visible form from time to time in different eras of the celestial cycles of birth and death. So a wise person should not doubt the divinity of the Lord in any of these births and forms."

In Srimad Bhagvad Geeta, 4/7-8, Lord Krishna says: "Oh Arjun! Whenever righteousness is on the decline and unrighteousness is on the increase, I assume a physical body (i.e. I reveal myself) for the protection of goodness and elimination of evil, and to establish Dharma on a strong footing. In this way I am born in different eras of the celestial cycle of birth and death."

Srimad Bhagvat Mahapuran, 10/29/14 and 10/36 say: "The Lord descends for bestowing the boon of final beatitude on human beings; out of his infinite merciful nature he does so to show grace upon his devotees; so that his devotees can remember his divine life and its glories in order to find freedom from the humdrum affairs of life in this gross mundane world."

In Srimad Bhagvad Geeta, 10/9, Lord Krishna says: "My form and activities are divine. A person who knows and understands this reality does not have to take a birth again after leaving his body, but he comes to me (i.e. he finds liberation and deliverance from the cycle of birth and death)."

These verses answer the question: Why should the Lord take birth and engage himself in activities though he has no need for them? He does this to bless his devotees and give them a chance to attain liberation and deliverance from this world of grossness and mundanity by the simple method of remembering the Lord's divine life and the glories associated with it.]

२ /१ /२४ प्राणित्वान्न विभूतिषु ॥ ५० ॥

2 /1 /24 prāṇitvānna vibhūtiṣu || 50||

(2/1/24) It ought to be remembered here that worship, devotion and affection for other living beings or rendering service to them, no matter how exalted they may be or what excellent virtues and mystical powers they may possess, is not equivalent to worshipping, rendering service to, and having devotion and affection for the Supreme Being himself (in his manifestation as a living being as mentioned in the previous verses). (50)

[This verse is meant to caution the devotee that he should be very careful while selecting the object of his adoration, worship and devotion. To wit, adoration, worship and devotion for a manifested form of the Supreme Being is quite different from adoring and showing respect to other exalted souls no matter who they may be.

One should note that though it is true that the Atma or the soul of all living beings is the same, and that it is also true that the individual's Atma is the microcosmic form of the supreme Atma that has a cosmic presence and is known as the Supreme Being, yet there does exist some subtle difference at the spiritual level between ordinary human beings and the Supreme Being. It is because no matter how wise, enlightened and learned a person may be, he will invariably have some traces of grossness that is so characteristic of all the Jivas, the living beings, by the virtue of their having a gross physical body made of the five elements of earth, fire, water, air and sky, as opposed to the form that the Supreme Being assumes during his incarnation in this world because the Lord's form is free from any traces of grossness that are associated with this mundane world. To wit, the Lord's form is divine and holy as opposed to the form of other living beings, whether he is a great king, a sage, a saint, or for that matter any other exalted person or creature.

So therefore, a wise devotee ensures that his Bhakti is directed to the Supreme Being himself even when he worships the Lord in his various manifestations as advised in the scriptures, and not to someone else no matter how high he may be, or what mystical powers he may possess. The latter form of Bhakti is deemed to be improper and of an inferior kind. In this context, refer to verse no. 18 where it is said that worship offered to gods and deities other than the Supreme Being is of an inferior and degraded kind.

In Srimad Bhagvad Geeta, 9/23, it is said that: "Those who are devoted to other gods and worship them with unwavering faith, such worship is not recognised as the right method of worship even though all these forms are my own images. Such forms of worship deprive the worshipper of direct access to me, and hence they are also deprived from the eclectic spiritual reward of immortality and beatitude. Whereas my devotees come to me and are freed from the cycle of transmigration, those who worship others go to them and remain trapped in this cycle."]

२ /१ /२५ द्यूतराजसेवयोः प्रतिषेधाच्च ॥ ५१ ॥

2 /1 /25 dyūtarājasēvayōḥ pratiṣēdhācca || 51||

(2/1/25) Service to Kings is prohibited in the scriptures (for a true devotee of the Lord God) because such service needs cunning, deceit and conceit to be successfully done.

[*This verse can be read as follows: "One need not serve a king or engage in gambling or any other deceitful activities as they are prohibited (in the scriptures)."] (51)

[This verse is an extension of the idea expressed in the previous verse no. 50.

It is impossible for a simple-hearted, pious, honest and straightforward person to be successful in serving any king. All royal courts are plagued by intrigue and are rife with complex political plays. So it becomes well neigh impossible for a holy man to be in the good looks of a king. On the other hand, there is a grave danger of falling prey to the scheming of selfish courtiers who would certainly not like such a man in their midst. The king himself likes flattery and sycophancy, he would like that his subjects treat him as a living god. So the king would treat a devotee with utter contempt and disdain when he finds out that the latter is worshipping some one else instead of the king himself.

Hence, this verse gives a prudent advice to a devotee to shun any service to any worldly king or emperor—or for that matter any lord or master in this world. For the devotee, his real 'King' and the real 'Master and Lord' is his beloved God to whom he is devoted and whom he loves from the core of his heart. So why should and why would he like to serve other human beings, no matter who they may be or how powerful they might be?

In Ram Charit Manas, Uttar Kand, Chaupai line no. 3 that precedes Doha no. 46, Lord Ram has declared: "If one says that he is my devotee but expects something from others, say what faith does he have in me; how can he claim to be my true devotee if he can't rely on me alone for his well-being and has to seek favours from others?"]

*If we take into account the second version this verse can be read, it would mean that a devotee should shun all activities that are deceitful and unrighteous such as gambling or playing the game of dice besides shunning any service to worldly kings and lords. He should rather focus on his Lord God and serve him along with practicing the glorious virtues of honesty and up-righteousness.]

२ /१ /२६ वासुदेवेऽपीति चेन्नाकारमात्रत्वात् ॥ ५२॥

2 /1 /26 vāsudēvē 'pīti cēnnākāramātratvāt || 52||

(2/1/26) If it is argued that the manifested form of the Supreme Being in the form of Lord Vasudeo (one of the names of Lord Krishna) too had a gross body like other living beings, or that the Lord also ruled the earth like other great Kings (when he became established his capital at Dwarka), so it would be wrong to worship him and have devotion for him (as advised especially in verse nos. 50 and 51), then this would be a fallacious argument.

It is because the Lord's true identity and subtle form is sublime, pure, divine and holy as opposed to the forms of other living beings including great Kings. (52)

[Lord Vasudeo, literally meaning the Lord of Vasus, is another name of Lord Krishna. He had established his kingdom in Dwarka. Further, it is well documented and known that Krishna had played a pivotal role in the epic war of Mahabharata. So is it advisable to worship such a Lord in the context of what has been said in verse nos. 50 and 51 herein above?

This present verse addresses this question and removes any doubt that may arise in the mind of the devotee. The answer is 'Yes, Lord Vasudeo or Lord Krishna is to be worshipped as a manifestation of the

Supreme Being known as Lord Vishnu'.

How can we be certain of it? The answer is 'By studying the scriptures that never tell a lie or mislead.' The scriptures speak in an unequivocal language about the divinity of Lord Krishna and his primary form as being the Supreme Being. So worship and devotion offered to Lord Krishna or Lord Vasudeo is deemed to be offered to the Supreme Being. He was no ordinary man or king. Refer verse no. 53 herein below that reiterates this principle.

Here it will be pertinent to have a look at the term 'Vasudeo'. The word has two parts: viz. 'Vasu' and 'Deo'. The second part 'Deo' means a Lord, while 'Vasu' refers to the many mystical powers and divine qualities that are uniquely possessed by the Supreme Being.

There are said to be eight 'Vasus' and they have been described in the following Upanishads: (i) Atharva Veda's Atharva Shikha Upanishad, Kandika 1; Brihajjabal Upanishad, Brahman 4, verse no. 16, Brahman 6, verse no. 12; Nrisingh Tapni Upanishad, Canto 1, verse no. 3.

The 'Vasus' are the various patron Gods who preside over the essential elements of life. They are eight in number as follows—Vishnu who is the sustainer, Shiva who is the annihilator, Kuber who is the treasurer of the wealth of the Gods, the Sun, Water, Fire, Wealth represented by gems and gold, and 'Ray' representing glory and fame. The element 'Fire' is the most potent, prominent and essential force in creation, because without fire the world would freeze to death. Hence, the Fire-God is said to be the chief amongst the Vasus. The 'fire' element is the active force in creation and is primarily responsible for kindling the cosmic cauldron that set in motion the process, and once having set it in motion it then sustained it and would finally annihilate it by burning it to cinders. On the other hand, Lord Vishnu is the passive force of creation represented by his other form of Viraat Purush which is the primary male aspect of creation. Lord Vishnu, who is the sustainer of the creation, is the Lord of Laxmi who is the Goddess of wealth, and is the supreme creator because Brahma, the old patriarch of creation who created the visible world and its creatures, was himself born atop the divine lotus that emerged from the navel of Lord Vishnu. Lord Vishnu utilizes the services of Laxmi who is the personification of the active forces of creation to create, sustain and annihilate the world. The Vasus are symbolic Gods who represent those essentials aspects of creation without which life would be difficult to conceive and sustain and finally conclude.

The eight Vasus are the patron Gods who provide succour and a dwelling place for the whole creation. They symbolise those primary necessities of life without which existence is not possible. They are— (i) Kuber (the God of wealth and prosperity), (ii) the Sun God (who provides energy and food) and his rays and radiance (i.e. sunlight and the energy that it provides), (iii) Shiva (the concluder or annihilator of the creation), (iv) Vishnu (the sustainer), (v) the Water God (called Varun), (vi) the Fire God (called Agni), (vii) any body of water such as a pond, a river etc., and (viii) holy and pious people (who give advice and guidance to the creatures of the creation). According to Brihad Aranyak Upanishad 3/9/3, the Vasus are the following—Fire, Earth, Air, Antariksha (the space of the solar system), Aditya (Sun), Duloka (heavens), the Moon, and the Nakshatras (the stars and the planets).

According to Purans, the eight Vasus are the following—Dhruv, Dhar, Som/Soma (the sap of an elixir-providing plant called Som/Soma which is used during religious ceremonies as sanctified liquid offered to the Gods; it is white in colour and is said to be stored in the moon), Aapha (water), Anil (wind), Anal (fire), Pratush, and Prabhaas.

These eight Vasus are the semi-Gods who symbolise the various types of assets needed to sustain this world. They therefore represent such assets as jewels, precious stones and gems, gold and other forms of wealth and property. Vasus also refers to the fire and water elements as well as their grosser forms as the terrestrial fire and water bodies such as ponds and lakes; to the virtue of radiance, splendour and glory; to the ray of light; to Kuber (the treasurer of Gods), Shiva, Sun, Vishnu, and a simple and pious gentleman.

The Ekakchar Upanishad of Krishna Yajur Veda, in its verse no. 7, says that these Vasus are manifestations of Brahm in order to provide the creation with the necessities of life.

The Atharva-shikha Upanishad of the Atharva Veda, in its Kandika (Canto) 1 says that the Vasus were created in the beginning of creation from the first Matra 'A' of OM representing the first leg of the supreme Brahm along with Brahma the creator, the Rig Veda, the Gayatri Chand and the Grahapatya Agni.

The Brihajjabal Upanishad of the Atharva Veda, Brahman 4, verse no. 16 lists the eight Vasus as follows—Ghar, Dhruv, Soma, Kripa, Anil, Anal, Pratyush and Prabhash. [The Vasus are the personified forms of the essential things that the supreme Creator created in this world so that the forthcoming creation would be well provided for and its essential needs taken care of. Some of these essentials were Fire ('Anal') that gave light, heat and energy, Air ('Anil') that breathed life into the creature's body and prevented suffocation, Water that acted as the soothing balm, the lubricating liquid and the nectar of life ('Soma'), a dwelling (a 'Ghar'), whether it was a cave, a crevice, a tree branch or a mud hut that the creature needed for its residence and protection against the vagaries of Nature, the virtue of compassion and kindness ('Kripa') to let one's neighbour too live and enjoy life to the full, and so on and so forth. These were the 'assets' that were personified as various Gods named here.]

The Nrisingh Purvatapini Upanishad of the Atharva Veda, in its Brahman 1, verse no. 3 says that the Vasus, along with the Rudras and Adityas etc., were born out of the third step of the divine Anushtup Chanda in which the Mantra of Lord Nrisingh was revealed to the creator Brahma when he did severe Tapa in order to initiate the process of creation.

The Devi Upanishad of the Atharva Veda tradition, verse no. 4 says that the Vasus are manifestations of the Mother Goddess, who actually represents the dynamism of the supreme transcendental Brahm, the

Supreme Being. The Goddess is the energy, authority and powers of Brahm that are employed by the latter to create and control this creation, both at the macrocosmic level as well as the microcosmic level.

The Vasu is this dynamism of Brahm revealed at the macrocosmic level.

The Ram Uttar Tapini Upanishad of the Atharva Veda, Canto 5, verse no. 4/32 says that the Vasus are none but manifestations of Lord Ram who himself is the supreme transcendental Brahm himself.

The Vasus are the Nature's gift to creature. They were the natural assets formed by the supreme Brahm so as to make life feasible and convenient in creation. In other words, the supreme Brahm who is also known as Lord Ram not only created this world but ensured that it is well provided for and its basic needs are taken care of by manifesting himself in the form of these eight primary requirements of life. This is the reason why one of the names of Vishnu is 'Vasudeo'—the Lord of Vasus. It ought to be noted here that Lord Ram is an incarnation of Vishnu or Vasudeo.

The Tripura Tapini Upanishad of the Atharva Veda tradition, Canto 4, paragraph no. 9 describes the great characteristics of Lord Vishnu as follows—

"Those who are wise, learned and erudite see the divine abode of Lord Vishnu as stretching in the clean space of the sky as far as the eyes can see. It stretches across the sky from one end to the other. Therefore, the abode of Lord Vishnu is the 'sky' itself. On the one hand it is as vast, fathomless, indescribable, remote and inaccessible as the bottomless reaches of the infinite sky element, and on the other hand it is easily reached, viewed, touched and accessed as the sky that is seen with the naked eyes, that surrounds everything at close quarters, and that touches each and every creature directly.

Lord Vishnu is many-faced (i.e. he has uncountable forms and shapes; all the creatures and all the aspects of creation are some or the other form of Vishnu). He uniformly pervades everywhere in this creation; whatever that exists is completely soaked in and surrounded by Vishnu. There is nowhere where the Lord is not present. His divine abode is the sky with a high summit. The Gods headed by Brahma the creator and the Sun God always look up to this divine abode of the Lord in the heaven to have his divine glimpse. They bear the Lord in their hearts.

Lord Vishnu lives in a subtle form in all the creatures of this creation. That is why is known as 'Vasudeo'—one who lives in all.

There is another connotation of the term 'Vasudeo'. It means the Lord of the eight Vasus. These Vasus are the primary assets created by the supreme Creator, the Brahm, to provide for the welfare of the creation that he created. Thus, the Vasus include such elementary needs of creation as water and fire etc.

Lord Vishnu is also known as the Viraat Purush, the infinite, invisible macrocosmic gross body of Brahm, the supreme transcendental Consciousness from which the entire creation evolved or emerged. The Viraat Purush was the first gross form of Brahm. It was 'gross' only in a relative term vis-à-vis the Brahm himself, but when compared to all the other units of the forthcoming creation, this Viraat Purush was almost as subtle as Brahm himself. The difference between Brahm and the Viraat Purush was only of a measurement of a millionth of a million degree in subtlety. Now, it was from this Viraat Purush that the rest of creation evolved. Even the creator of the visible world, Brahma, emerged atop a divine lotus that rose from the navel of the Viraat Purush. Once the creation took shape, the Viraat Purush assumed for himself the role of its keeper and sustainer. Hence, Brahm assumed the role of the Viraat Purush to create the primary forces of creation, including the Gods of the Trinity, i.e. Brahm, Vishnu and Shiva, and once it was done, he assumed the role of the overall commander and controller of creation in the form of Lord Vishnu. This is why Vishnu is primarily regarded as being synonymous with Brahm, and treated as the

Supreme Being.

Besides this, the virtues of Vishnu that he is all-pervading and all-encompassing are also applicable to Brahm only, making him synonymous with the latter."

Lord Vishnu is called 'Vasudeo' because he is the sustainer and protector of creation, signifying his undisputed lordship over all the essential elements in Nature, called the Vasus of which there are eight in number, which were created at the beginning of creation to help sustain the upcoming creation. It ought to be noted here that Vishnu is also called Viraat Purush, the macrocosmic gross body of Brahm, and it is from this form of Brahm that the creator of the visible creation, i.e. Brahma the old patriarch of creation, had emerged atop a divine lotus that sprouted from the navel of Vishnu. In other words, everything has its origin in the supreme Brahm.

The Krishna Yajur Veda's Suk Rahasya Upanishad, verse no. 25 lists the names of Vishnu as Vasudeo, Sankarshan, Pradumna and Aniruddha.

The Atharva Veda's Devi Upanishad, verse no. 5 says that Vishnu is actually a manifestation of the Shakti, which is the cosmic dynamic powers and energy of Brahm, the Supreme Being, employed by the Lord to take care of this creation which the same Lord has created in his manifestation as Brahma the creator. It also goes on to say that the terrestrial world is the foot of Vishnu.

The glories of the Vishnu as the Viraat Purush have been enumerated in the Tripadvibhut Maha Narayan Upanishad of the Atharva Veda tradition, Canto 2, paragraph no. 11, and Canto 6, paragraph no. 11.

The same Upanishad enumerates the glorious virtues of Vishnu independently in its Canto 1, paragraph no. 1, 6; Canto 2, paragraph no. 11; and Canto 8, paragraph no. 17. These together collectively present a combined picture of the grand form of the Viraat Purush.

It is said in the Vishnu Puran, 4/11/4, 5/1/2, 5/3/3 that: "The Lord who has revealed in the Yadav clan as Krishna is the one who eliminates all sins; he is the supreme Brahm who is all-pervading and omnipresent in this universe; he is Lord Vishnu himself who has manifested in the form of Lord Krishna who gives delight to the whole world."

So we see that Lord Vasudeo is not an ordinary King or Emperor, but he is the Supreme Lord himself in a human form. And therefore, he is worthy of worship and devotion like the Supreme Being himself is.

The following verses reiterate and endorse this principle again.]

२ /१ /२७ प्रत्यभिज्ञानाच्च ॥ ५३ ॥

2 /1 /27 pratyabhijñānācca || 53||

(2/1/27) [And how do we know it—that Lord Vasudeo is the same Lord as the Supreme Being, and therefore he is worthy of adoration, worship and devotion?] This fact has been endorsed by the scriptures. (53)

[As has already been emphasised earlier, we look up to authentic scriptures whenever there is a doubt in our minds. So when it comes to the question whether Lord Vasudeo should be treated like other human kings or is he a manifestation of the Supreme Being, we consult the scriptures to arrive at a conclusive answer. These scriptures tell us that indeed, Lord Vasudeo is a manifestation of the Supreme Being known as Lord Vishnu. A detailed note has been appended to verse no. 52 herein above in this regard.

Srimad Bhagvat Mahapuran, 1/2/28 says: "The Vedas ultimately treat Lord Vasudeo as being the Supreme Lord, the different religious sacrifices themselves are aimed at the attainment of Vasudeo, the various Yogas eventually lead to Vasudeo, and all sorts of rituals too have their end in Vasudeo. Therefore final attainment is Lord Vasudeo."

In Srimad Bhagvat Mahapuran, 1/3/28 we read that sage Markandeya tells Ydhishthir: "The Supreme Being whom I witnessed at the time of dissolution of this creation is the same Lord who has now revealed himself as Lord Krishna."

In Srimad Bhagvat Mahapuran, 4/24/28, Lord Rudra (one of the many forms of Lord Shiva) tells Prachetas: "A devotee who has surrendered himself to Lord Vasudeo is very dear to me. Indeed, Lord Vasudeo is beyond the triple Gunas of Prakriti, and also he is superior to all the Jivas including the celestial beings."

Srimad Bhagvat Mahapuran, 1/2/7, says: "Steadfast devotion to Lord Vasudeo forthwith endows one with full philosophical knowledge of the Supreme Being and his Divinity, as well as it helps such a person to develop aversion to worldly enjoyments."

Sage Markandey told Ydishthir in Mahabharat, Vanaparva, Chapter 189, verse no. 13002 says: "The Lord with beautiful lotus-like eyes that I saw previously, the same Lord has now revealed himself as Lord Vasudeo to become your friend and guide."

In Vishnu Puran, 4/4/2, sage Parashara says: "Men listening to the history of the race of the Yadus will get rid of impurity of their hearts for in the said race was born the Supreme Lord known as Vasudeo."

The divinity and glories of Lord Vasudeo have been described in Gopal Tapini Upanishad of the Atharva Veda tradition.]

२ /१ /२८ वृष्णिषु श्रैष्ठ्येन तत् ॥ ५४॥

2 /1 /28 vṛṣṇiṣu śraiṣṭhyēna tat || 54||

(2/1/28) Indeed, Lord Vasudeo is a manifested form of Lord Vishnu, the Supreme Being, himself. There is 'that' Supreme Being himself (who is so much praised and honoured in the scriptures). (54)

[This verse clears the air about the divinity of Lord Vasudeo. It is an extension of the previous verse nos. 52-53.]

२ /१ /२९ एवं प्रसिद्धेषु च ॥ ५५॥

2 /1 /29 ēvaṁ prasiddhēṣu ca || 55||

(2/1/29) In this way it is well established that worship, devotion and service rendered to the different manifestations of the Supreme Being (such as Lord Krishna, Lord Ram, Lord Vaaman etc.) are all equivalent to rendering such worship, devotion and service directly to the Lord himself. All such forms of service are deemed to be proper forms of devotion and worship of the Lord God. Hence, all of them are equal, and all of them would grant the spiritual reward of liberation, deliverance, emancipation and salvation to the devotee. (55)

[This verse concludes the discussion revolving around the proper way of offering worship to the Lord God. We have observed that primarily there are two levels at which one can worship the Supreme Being—viz. (i) the higher intellectual level that involves Gyan and Yoga where the spiritual aspirant aspires to have God-realisation by focusing on the cosmic form of the Lord known as Brahm that symbolises pure Consciousness; and (ii) an ordinary level suitable for ordinary living beings where he is advised to have Bhakti or devotion for the many manifestations of the Lord. The second method is easy, hassle-free and within the reach of the common devotee as opposed to the first method that is possible only for a rare devotee of high intellectual abilities, and who has already attained some level of spiritual enlightenment, to implement successfully.]

---------********---------

(5) SHANDILYA BHAKTI SUTRA

Aphorisms for Devotion to God and

The Principles of the Philosophy of Love for Him

[Roman Transliteration of Text, English Exposition, Elaborate Notes]

Chapter 2, Part 2:

Verse nos. 56-84

॥ शाण्डिल्य भक्ति सूत्रम् ॥

द्वितीयोऽध्यायः

द्वितीयमाह्निकम्

|| śāṇḍilya bhakti sūtram ||

dvitīyō 'dhyāyaḥ

dvitīyamāhnikam

२ /२ /१ भक्त्या भजनोपसंहाराद्गौण्या परायै

तद्धेतुत्वात् ॥ ५६ ॥

2 /2 /1 bhaktyā bhajanōpasaṁhārādgauṇyā parāyai
taddhētutvāt || 56||

(2/2/1) 'Bhajan' (worshipping the Lord God by remembering him, his glories and his divinity, by reciting his holy stories and repeating his holy name, by keeping the mind focused exclusively on the Lord and to exclude everything else from its ambit, and to derive ecstasy and bliss by doing so) is one of the primary ways by which Bhakti can reach its maturity. (56)

[Srimad Bhagvad Geeta, 9/14-15, clearly delineates the paths to God-realisation. Lord Krishna says: "My devotees engage themselves in constantly chanting my divine Name with firmness and steadfastness of mind, with all humility and sincerity, and bowing repeatedly before my form (i.e. my manifested form or its representation in the form of a picture or an image)—verily indeed, this way they attain me. Others (who follow the path of Gyan or knowledge and Yoga or meditation) too attain me when they offer their self to me and worship my absolute form that is without attributes, a form that is eternal, infinite and pure consciousness. While still there are others who worship me in the form of my celestial revelations (in the form of Nature and its components) by the path of different rituals and religious sacrifices—they too attain me (because it is me who exists in all these forms)."

These two verses of the Geeta clearly indicate that there are three levels of worshipping the Supreme Being—viz. (i) worshipping a manifested form of the Lord by the path of Bhakti of which Bhajan is an important tool; (ii) worshipping the cosmic form of the Lord as Brahm or pure Consciousness for which knowledge and meditation are important tools; and (iii) worshipping the different dynamic forces of Nature or aspects of creation which represent the dynamic form of Brahm, as there is nothing in creation that is not one or the other form of Brahm, by doing rituals and sacrifices.

In Srimad Bhagvad Geeta, 9/29, Lord Krishna explicitly declares the importance of being devoted to the manifested form of the Supreme Being: "I (in my all-pervading and subtle form as the Atma, the soul, the cosmic Consciousness) am equally present in all beings, animate or inanimate. There is no one who is hateful or dear to me (as I am equally present in all). However, those who worship me and are devoted to me, I do surely reveal myself in them (i.e. they feel my presence up close inside their own heart), and they abide in me—i.e. I and my ardent devotee become one and inseparable."

In the earlier verses we have read that 'Gyan' or knowledge and enlightenment, and Yoga or meditation and contemplation, are other important tools for attaining success in Bhakti or having devotion for the Lord God.

Gyan and Yoga are more relevant to obtain success in realisation of that form of the Supreme Being which has a cosmic dimension, the form that is known as Brahm representing pure cosmic Consciousness that is infinite, eternal, invisible, all-pervading, without any attributes, subtle and sublime.

On the other hand, Bhajan is more apt as a tool for worshipping the Lord's form that is more easily accessible to a common human being because he can better relate to it. So Bhajan is a form of devotion that is offered to that divine aspect of the Supreme Being which his manifested in a visible form in this world. It is a form that is easily identifiable and known because it has taken a birth right here in this world to live amongst his devotees as if the Lord was one of them. This manifested form of the Lord God is easily understood by even an ordinary man as he can comfortably relate to it because this visible form of the Lord is like the other known forms he is well acquainted with in this mundane world. This manifested form of the Lord God is not like the Lord's cosmic form known as Brahm that represents pure Consciousness that is too far and too abstract for a person to comprehend. This latter form is attainable by only a rare few highly enlightened and spiritually evolved sages and ascetics, but it eludes the common man.

So the scriptures devised this easy device of 'Bhajan'—which means worshipping the Lord God by remembering him, his glories and his divinity, by reciting his holy stories and repeating his holy name, by keeping the mind focused exclusively on the Lord and to exclude everything else from its ambit, and to derive ecstasy and bliss by doing so—to enable even a common man to have access to the nectar of spirituality, to attain eternity, peace, bliss and beatitude that are usually achieved by following the higher path of Gyan and Yoga that culminates in Brahm-realisation.

The general idea conveyed in verse nos. 46-49 and 55 herein above is that offering worship and service to a manifested form of the Supreme Being, such as to his human incarnations known as Lord Ram or Lord Krishna, is equivalent to doing so directly to the Lord in his cosmic form known as Brahm. To wit, having Bhakti for Lord Ram or Lord Krishna would yield the same spiritual reward that is obtained by following the path of Gyan and Yoga to attain Brahm-realisation.

The present verse no. 56 now tells us how to do Bhakti for the manifested form of the Supreme Being. The way to do this is 'Bhajan'—i.e. to remember the divine story related to the life and time of the Lord on this earth, to sing or recite this story with great faith, devotion, love and affection in one's heart, to feel joy and rupture and experience the Lord's presence while singing his glories and deeds, to repeat the Lord's holy name and derive immense spiritual bliss while doing so, and to be so delighted in getting involved in these activities that the person does not want to do anything else related to this mundane world. The feeling of spiritual fulfilment and blessedness, of ecstasy and bliss should so overwhelm the devotee that he would gradually move away from the gross world and towards the spiritual world where he finds a sense of eternal closeness with his beloved Lord God. This state marks the culmination of Bhakti; it is a state of mature Bhakti.

Hence, like Gyan and Yoga that bring about Brahm-realisation for an ascetic and sage, 'Bhajan' too helps the devotee to become God-realised, albeit it is in the Lord's manifested form.

Bhajan is an easy spiritual tool recommended for a common man who may not have the mental calibre and the intellectual ability to comprehend the Lord's cosmic invisible form that seems to be too abstract for him to grasp. The devotee has the opportunity to worship and love his favourite Lord God by reciting the divine story of the Lord's exemplary life on earth, by remembering the great deeds the Lord had done, the magnificent virtues he had, and by recalling the legend of devotees who were liberated and delivered by their association with the Lord. This opportunity is surely not available if one worships the Lord's cosmic, invisible and infinite form known as Brahm who represents pure Consciousness.

The story of the Lord's life here in this world is definitely more appealing and attractive and easy to comprehend and relate to as compared to the abstract philosophy of the Upanishads and the Vedas that deal directly with the invisible, infinite, subtle, sublime, attributeless and cosmic form of the Supreme Being that is pure Consciousness.

The next verse no. 57 tells us that 'Kirtan' is another important component of worshipping the Lord God, and it is complimentary to doing 'Bhajan'.]

२ /२ /२ रागार्थप्रकीर्तिसाहचर्याच्चेतरेषाम् ॥ ५७॥

2 /2 /2 rāgārthaprakīrtisāhacaryāccētarēṣām || 57||

(2/2/2) Doing 'Kirtan' with full devotion and affection for the Lord God (i.e. worshipping the Lord by singing his divine glories, reciting his holy stories, repeating his holy name and chanting his Mantras, either singly or in a group, with a rapturous mind that leads to ecstasy and bliss) is another important tool by which Bhakti can be practiced successfully and reach maturity. Kirtan brings the devotee close to his Lord*. (57)

[Refer also to verse no. 63. It ought to be noted here that like other forms of symbolic service done to the Lord God, Kirtan is also secondary form of Bhakti. It is one of the many ways a devotee can offer his worship to the Lord God.

The question arised: If Kirtan and other such means of Bhakti are 'secondary or subsidiary' in nature, then what is the 'primary' form of Bhakti? The answer is: The primary form of Bhakti is having undiluted and pure love and devotion for Lord God as envisaged in verse nos. 2 and 83. All others are aids in Bhakti, and so are secondary to this main objective.

The glory and importance of 'Kirtan' is highlighted in Srimad Bhagvad Geeta, 11/36, when Arjun told Lord Krishna: "Oh Lord! The world exults and is filled with love and ecstasy by singing your glories and virtues, and by chanting your holy name. Evil and demonic forces run away when they hear such auspicious words, while mystics and pious souls bow their heads in reverence."

Similarly, in Ram Charit Manas, Ayodhya Kand, Chaupai line nos. 4-

5 that precede Doha no. 128, sage Valmiki tells Lord Ram: "Oh Lord, you should live in the heart of those whose ears do not tire of listening your holy stories and divine glories just like the ocean that never gets filled by the rivers that continuously flow into it."

Once again, in Ram Charit Manas, Ayodhya Kand, Chaupai line no. 6 that precedes Doha no. 129, sage Valmiki tells Lord Ram: "Oh Lord, you should live in the heart of those who regularly repeat your holy Mantra which is deemed to be like a king amongst all the spiritual formulas."

In the previous verse no. 57 we have read that 'Bhajan' is an important way by which a devotee can practice Bhakti and bring it to maturity. Now this present verse tells us that 'Kirtan' is also another important tool for doing Bhakti successfully.

Like Bhajan, 'Kirtan' too is an easy tool for spiritual fulfilment and bring Bhakti to its maturity as it does not need any special efforts, any specialisation or any sort of expertise in the scriptures to be practiced successfully.

Moreover, since the method used in this practice is 'singing, chanting and reciting the divine glories of the Lord', it directly touches the heart. It is also an attractive and simple method to keep the mind occupied with the thoughts of the Lord God by excluding all other thoughts from it—because one needs to be attentive and focused in his mind to correctly remember the events associated with the life of the Lord and his countless glories and holy names if one were to keep the rhythm and maintain the symphony of singing and dancing. Any sort of mental distraction will obviously disrupt the process.

Another positive aspect of doing 'Kirtan' is that it motivates others to join the process of Bhakti because singing and reciting the Lord's glories and repeating his divine names etc. as done in Kirtan usually involves a group of devotees rather than the single devotee as compared to 'Bhajan' that is usually done as a private affair.

Besides this, Kirtan involves an active participation of many organs of the body than is the case with Bhajan. For instance, for doing Kirtan the mouth is used for singing and reciting, the ears are used to listen, the hand is used to clap and make joyful gestures, the legs are used to dance, the mind is used to recollect and remember the Lord's glories and the events associated with his life in a coherent manner, the heart is involved to lend the emotive support that is needed for singing rapturously, and the whole body lends its own support by becoming thrilled and thoroughly enjoying the process. To wit, the devotee's whole 'self' gets involved in remembering and worshipping the Lord in the process of Kirtan.

Kirtan also helps to spread the auspicious aura of spirituality as it is done aloud by way of singing, recitation and chanting, rather than remembering and worshipping the Lord God silently by the devotee.

*So it is said that 'Kirtan brings the devotee closer to his Lord God' because the Lord loves him exceedingly; this devotee becomes a favourite of the Lord as he not only attains spiritual bliss himself but he also helps others to have it by making them participate in the singing and chanting of the Lord's glories and names.]

२ /२ /३ अन्तराले तु शेषाः स्युरुपास्यादौ च काण्डत्वात् ॥ ५८ ॥

2 /2 /3 antarālē tu śēṣāḥ syurupāsyādau ca kāṇḍatvāt || 58||

(2/2/3) All other forms of worship and service offered to the Lord God are of equal importance, and they all contribute towards the spiritual objective of attaining maturity of devotion (Bhakti) that leads to eternal bliss, beatitude and ecstasy that comes with God-realisation. All forms of devotion lead to the same spiritual goal, they are all parts of the composite body known as 'Bhakti'; this is also the conclusion drawn by the different units of the scriptures (ca kāṇḍatvāt). (58)

[Besides the two tools mentioned in previous verse nos. 56-57, i.e. 'Bhajan' and 'Kirtan', there are other equally important spiritual tools that are available to a devotee. These have been enumerated in Srimad Bhagvad Geeta, Canto 9, from verse no. 13—to verse no. 29.

Briefly they are the following: Vrat (keeping religious vows and observing sacraments), Namaskar (to bow before the Lord God or his image), Dhyan (contemplation and remembering the Lord God and his various forms, their virtues and glories), Yaag (offering formal forms of worship as done in rites and rituals), Daan (making charity and giving alms and donation in the name of the Lord God and as a service rendered unto him), Arpan (offering all deeds and their rewards to the Lord God, and not personally expecting anything by way of reward for doing auspicious deeds), and so on. It ought to be noted here that all these tools of Bhakti are dedicated to worshipping the 'manifested form of the Supreme Being'. Refer: verse nos. 46-55 in this context.

Not only this, even Gyan (knowledge, enlightenment and self-realisation) and Yoga (meditation) are equally important tools for the maturity of Bhakti as they guide the devotee to the primary form of the Supreme Being, the cosmic form of the Lord that is known as Brahm and which represents pure cosmic Consciousness, whom he worships through the Lord's manifested or revealed form by adopting the various other tools mentioned herein above.

To wit, the chief aim of all methods of worship and service rendered to the Supreme Being is the same—and it is to provide eternity to the soul of the individual creature, grant him bliss and beatitude, and free it from the cycle of birth and death which leads to emancipation and salvation of the creature. The Upanishads that mark the culmination of the wisdom contained in the Vedas too speak of the same thing.]

२ /२ /४ ताभ्यः पावित्र्यमुपक्रमात् ॥ ५९ ॥

2 /2 /4 tābhyaḥ pāvitryamupakramāt || 59||

(2/2/4) All these different ways of worshipping and having devotion for the Lord God (as outlined in the previous verses) are equally effective and purifying for the soul of the devotee. (59)

[This fact has been endorsed in Srimad Bhagvad Geeta, 9/2, where it is said: "This knowledge of the two forms of the Supreme Being, i.e. the cosmic form known as 'Nirguna' as it has no attributes, and the manifested form known as 'Saguna' as it has known attributes, provides true blessedness to the Jiva (living being) as it removes all chances of doubts, contradictions and confusions. Hence, this knowledge is supreme. It is sovereign knowledge; it is supremely holy and liberating as it eliminates all delusions; it is blissful because whatever forms the aspirant chooses to worship the Lord God in accordance with his individual temperament and mental liking, he knows that the same Supreme Being is being worshipped and served by him. All in all, such wisdom grants joy to the devotee and he feels happy and contented."

The devotee feels reassured that the method he has personally chosen to worship his beloved Lord God is not inferior to any other method, that he will get the same spiritual reward that is got by pursuing other so-called superior paths—because all the paths lead to the same goal!

In Srimad Bhagvad Geeta, 2/46, Lord Krishna says: "Different purposes are served by different small reservoirs of water, but a large lake serves all purposes at once. Similarly, different paths such as Yoga and Gyan may be employed for attaining different goals in life, but a man of wisdom alone knows that the true purpose and the best use of all these paths is to attain God-realisation and final beatitude. To wit, the enlightened person has the same use of the knowledge of the scriptures as the person who is surrounded by water on all sides, as he need not go anywhere to quench his thirst. So therefore, the enlightened person realises that the ultimate goal of the teaching of all the scriptures is self and Brahm realisation that grants eternity, bliss and beatitude as well as liberation and deliverance to the soul, and so he may pick up any method that suits him with the assurance that the result would be the same."]

२ /२ /५ तासु प्रधानयोगात् फलाधिक्यमेके ॥ ६०॥

2 /2 /5 tāsu pradhānayōgāt phalādhikyamēkē || 60||

(2/2/5) Since attaining maturity in God-realisation with its attendent bliss and beatitude is the ultimate and the chief aim of all spiritual practices of which Bhakti (devotion) is the dominant one, and other methods enumerated herein above (e.g. Bhajan, Kirtan, Yoga, Gyan, etc.) being its important components or tools that aid it, so therefore it follows that if they are all employed judiciously and in the right manner, Bhakti would give a better result and quicker reward to the devotee.

But it ought to be clearly kept in mind that Paraa Bhakti (i.e. the supreme form of Bhakti that refers to complete devotion and love for Lord God) is the chief objective of all spiritual efforts, and these Gauna Bhaktis (secondary forms of Bhakti) will give desired result only if the

Paraa Bhakti is robust. (60)

[The meaning is crystal clear. A wise person would not treat any of the spiritual practices as being inferior to any other method as they are all equally important and equally effective for God-realisation in their own way. They are like the many spokes of the wheel which together give shape to the latter, and all the spokes have their own place in the broader scheme of things.

It is also like the many organs of the body of a person. Each organ has its own place and function, and they together make life comfortable and enjoyable for a person. It is not that the person can't do without any single organ, for example it is not that a man would die if he loses his eyes or hands, but surely life would be so much the harder and less comfortable to live in their absence. Similarly, when a wise devotee uses all the components of spiritual practices, such as Gyan, Yoga, Dhyan, Bhajan and Kirtan etc. to realise his spiritual objective, success comes to him easily and more conveniently as opposed to him employing some selected method alone.

But at the same time he must remember that these secondary kinds of Bhaktis would yield result only if the spiritual aspirant has single-minded devotion for Lord God, if he is fully committed and dedicated to the Lord, and employs these different forms of secondary Bhaktis only as aids towards the fulfilment of the main objective. To wit, the secondary forms of Bhakti, known as Gauna Bhakti, are subsidiaries to Paraa Bhakti, or the main form of Bhakti; they are tools for realisation of Bhakti in its best form. In this context refer to verse no. 84.]

२ /२ /६ नाम्नेति जैमिनिः सम्भवात् ॥ ६१ ॥

2 /2 /6 nāmnēti jaiminiḥ sambhavāt || 61||

(2/2/6) According to the illustrious sage Jaimini, repeating and chanting the Lord's holy name or listening to it being done regularly, with due devotion and faith (nāmnēti), is the way by which success in Bhakti (and God-realisation) can be easily and conveniently achieved. (61)

[The same idea is expressed by sage Valmiki in Ram Charit Manas, Ayodhya Kand, Chaupai line no. 6 that precedes Doha no. 129 when he tells Lord Ram: "Oh Lord! You should dwell in the heart of such persons who regularly repeat or chant your holy name and divine Mantras (spiritual formulas)."

Refer also to Srimad Bhagvad Geeta, 9/14 where Lord Krishna says: "My devotees engage themselves in constantly chanting my divine Name with firmness and steadfastness of mind, with all humility and sincerity, and bowing repeatedly before my form (i.e. my manifested form or its representation in the form of a picture or an image)—verily indeed, this way they attain me."]

२ /२ /७ अत्राङ्गप्रयोगानां यथाकालसम्भवो गृहादिवत् ॥ ६२॥

2 /2 /7 atrāṅgaprayōgānāṁ yathākālasambhavō gr̥hādivat || 62||

(2/2/7) The different components of Bhakti and the tools that aid it (such as Bhajan and Kirtan etc. mentioned earlier) should be employed wisely and in the correct way as and when they are needed because they all help the devotee prepare himself to attain maturity in Bhakti (and attain God-realisation with its spiritual reward of eternity, bliss and beatitude). It is just like the case of a wise person planning and collecting all things needed to construct his home. (62)

[When one starts to build his home, he begins to plan and collect all items needed for completing his project. He may need some of the things immediately and some at a later stage, but nevertheless he either actually collects them and keeps them in his stock or else at least gathers information about their availability and price etc. so that they can be acquired at short notice. A wise person never leaves things to chance.

Likewise, a wise devotee would use all tools of Bhakti, such as Bhajan, Kirtan, Gyan, Yoga, Dhyan, Japa etc., in order to reach his spiritual destination. He will not exclude any of them as he knows that all play their own part in the composite structure of spirituality. He may use one or two of the different tools of Bhakti at a given point of time, but he will collect as much knowledge about all of them as possible, such as what they mean, how they are practiced, what are their requirements, and all other relevant details so that when he needs their help he would be ready with it.

For instance, he may fix some moments for doing personal form of worship of the Lord God at his home by silently doing Bhajan in the form of repeating the Lord's holy Mantras, offering prayers, bowing before the Lord's image or portrait, reading from the scriptures that describe the life and times of the Lord's incarnations, etc. Then at some other time he may join a group of people in a congregation to do Kirtan and community worship. At other times he can make charities, or attend religious ceremonies and festivals or participate in formal rituals and rites dedicated to the Lord God. Or else he can preach others about the Lord's glories and divinity if he is qualified enough to do so. The opportunities are endless, and a wise devotee would not shun any one of them. Rather, he would judiciously employ all of them with the singular aim of God-realisation and attainment of liberation and deliverance for his soul.

But it should be clearly understood that everything depends upon the concerned devotee. If he decides against multiple paths to God-realisation and aids to maturity of Bhakti, and rather determines that he would select and follow only one or two paths, then that would also be alright. This fact is clearly endorsed in the following verse no. 63.]

२ /२ /८ ईश्वरतुष्टेरेकोऽपि बली ॥ ६३॥

2 /2 /8 īśvaratuṣṭērēkō 'pi balī || 63||

(2/2/8) If even one of the different tools or methods listed herein above is employed faithfully and with sincerity to pursue devotion for the Lord God, then that particular method is enough to please the Lord (īśvaratuṣṭa). (63)

[In the previous verse nos. 56-62 we have read that there are many methods by which a devotee can worship the Lord God, and that all can be judiciously employed for success.

Now in this verse we learn that though it is true that all the different methods can be successfully employed to attain God-realisation and lead to maturity in Bhakti, but this does not mean that it is compulsory to use all of them, or that it is a binding doctrine that ought to be followed by all the devotees. For it has also been said that all of them are equally effective and powerful. So it follows that if the devotee decides to follow only one of these paths over others, then he is welcomed to do so because if he follows his chosen path diligently and with due faith, then the Lord would be fully pleased with him in the same way as he would have been pleased with the devotee if he would have used more then one path.

In Ram Charit Manas, Aranya Kand, from Chaupai line no. 7 that precedes Doha no. 35—to Chaupai line no. 7 that precedes Doha no. 36, Lord Ram has listed nine forms of Bhakti. The Lord says that if a person has 'even one' of these nine forms of Bhakti in him then he is loved by the Lord.

Similarly we read in Srimad Bhagvat Mahapuran, 7/5/23 that Prahalad has taught about the nine forms of Bhakti. If a devotee practices any of these forms of Bhakti he attains the Lord God and is loved by him.]

२ /२ /९ अबन्धोऽर्पणस्य मुखम् ॥ ६४॥

2 /2 /9 abandhō 'rpaṇasya mukham || 64||

(2/2/9) The deeds that are selflessly offered to the Lord God do not create any kind of entanglements or fetters for the doer (i.e. the devotee) because no result, either good or bad, of such deeds accrues to the doer. He is freed from the chain of 'cause and effect'; so he attains liberation and deliverance from the cycle of birth and death.

Since such deeds do not create any sort of fetter or bondage for the devotee, it is a tool of Bhakti. (64)

[In this context, refer verse no. 71 also. If one does selfless service to the Lord God and offers all his deeds and their results or fruits to the Lord unconditionally, the devotee is deemed to be practicing Bhakti. It is because he has neutralised all his desires and expectations as he does not want anything in return for his deeds and actions, he has overcome all worldly temptations and attachments which usually impel a person to get involved in doing deeds and taking some action for the realisation of his desires and dreams in the first place. Instead, he has focused his mind and heart on the Lord. This is indeed the aim of Bhakti.

The way to emancipation and salvation is complete self-surrender to the Lord God. A person who has surrendered himself to his master cannot own anything for himself, including the results that are got by carrying out the master's orders. Similarly, the devotee who has surrendered himself and his deeds to the Lord is not held responsible for the effects of his actions and deeds. His soul remains free from all consequences.

This verse deals with the theory of 'Karma' which states that every deed done by an individual produces some result for him. If he does anything with the hope of getting something in return, he gets emotionally attached to that deed, to his actions. The result may be to his liking and expectation, or it may be not. In both the cases, however, the person remains deeply involved in the chain symbolised by the doing of deeds and their consequences.

It is not easy not to expect anything from the deeds done and to be neutral towards their consequences, for otherwise one would not be inclined to do anything at all. In this world that is kept alive and active by the 'doing of deeds and taking of actions', it is not possible in practical terms to remain indifferent to deeds and their results. More often than not, such deeds become mechanical and robot-like, and this is not the way true service is done; it is not the correct way of doing anything wisely. So how does one break free from this endless chain of doing deeds and either enjoying or suffering from its consequences? How would one find liberation and deliverance from this trap to get eternal peace and happiness for his soul?

This verse seeks to address this problem. Its advice is simple and straightforward: One should offer all the deeds done by him to the Lord God, and treat his deeds as his service to the Lord. He must think that he is simply obeying the Lord's orders because it is the Lord who wants him to do certain things. Like a servant carrying out his master's commands and not expecting the result of what he has done to accrue to him personally, except that his master will be pleased with him if he does things properly and diligently, the devotee too does what comes his way for the sake of his Lord God, for the sake of pleasing his beloved Lord who is also his Master. Then he is not worried about the outcome of such deeds. That translates into his being free from the many worries and anxieties associated with doing any deed, either worrying about his failure or being anxious of achieving success in his efforts. Instead of the common forms of problems faced by a person who gets mentally and emotionally involved in doing of deeds, the devotee, on the other hand, gets a bonus and a pat on his back in the form of the Lord's grace and benediction upon him for a job well done, and done selflessly!

Srimad Bhagvad Geeta, 18/66 says: "Take refuge in me, the almighty Lord of the world, and surrender all your deeds and duties to me. If you do so, then don't worry for I shall absolve you of all your sins."

A similar idea is expressed in Ram Charit Manas, Ayodhya Kand, Doha nos. 129 and 131 where sage Valmiki tells Lord Ram: "Oh Lord! A person who does everything and then offers them to you, wanting nothing but affection for your holy feet, verily indeed the heart of such a person is your dwelling place." "Oh Lord! A person who does not want anything at all for himself, and has unwavering faith and affection for you, his heart is your residence."]

२/२/१० ध्यानियमस्तु दृष्टसौकर्यात् ॥ ६५॥

2 /2 /10 dhyānaniyamastu dṛṣṭasaukaryāt || 65||

(2/2/10) The importance of 'Dhyan' (contemplation; deep thought; concentration and focusing of the mind attentively on an object; constant and attentive remembrance of the Lord God) in the realm of Bhakti is that it helps one to focus his mind on the Lord God, to remember the Lord constantly and persistently at all times of his life, and to turn his mind away from the world and its temptations and instead concentrate its efforts towards God-realisation.

It is for this obvious reason that one should diligently practice Dhyan properly in order to succeed in Bhakti. (65)

[One should try all available methods in order to attain purity of mind and fixing it on the objective—which here is God-realisation through the path of Bhakti. Refer verse no. 27 in this context. Earlier we have read about Bhajan and Kirtan in verse nos. 56-57, about Gyan and Yoga in verse nos. 16-17 and 19, and about other means in verse no. 58 which all aid Bhakti. And now in the present verse no. 65 we see that 'Dhyan' is another important tool of Bhakti.

In conventional terms, 'Dhyan' is a vital component in the system of doing Yoga (meditation). It generally refers to contemplation and deep thought that are needed for success in meditation. Since Dhyan helps the ascetic to attain success in Yoga, so now this verse uses its benefits for the purpose of getting success in Bhakti.

To wit, if a devotee is able to keep his mind focused on the memory of his beloved Lord God, if he contemplates upon the Lord and meditates upon him, if he manages to deeply think of the Lord and make him an important component of his sub-conscious mind, then it becomes easy for the devotee to focus his conscious mind on the Lord at all times of his life. His life then becomes fully dedicated to the Lord

God, and he remembers the Lord while he is awake as well as while he is asleep. This means he has become inseparable and indistinguishable from his Lord, his whole being has been possessed by the Lord and his thoughts, and he thinks of nothing but the Lord—which is indeed the intent of Bhakti, for Bhakti aims to remove the distance and distinction between the devotee and the Lord God.]

२ /२ /११ तद्यजिः पूजायामितरेषां नैवम् ॥ ६६ ॥

2 /2 /11 tadyajiḥ pūjāyāmitarēṣāṁ naivam || 66||

(2/2/11) The root word 'Yaja' (tadyajiḥ) is usually interpreted to mean 'sacrifices' when it is used by the scriptures (such as the Vedas) which deal elaborately with the fire sacrifices. But actually it is not so (naivam). [Its correct meaning and interpretation is different.] It actually refers to the 'worship that is offered to the Supreme Being' (selflessly, and as a means of self-surrender rather than to fulfil any of desire by the performer of the sacrifice or worship). (66)

[The root word 'Yaja' is used to denote different rituals during fire sacrifices where offerings are made to different patron gods. These fire sacrifices are usually done for fulfilment of some desire. This desire may be worldly or spiritual, but nevertheless it is a 'desire', a wish that needs to be fulfilled by propitiating certain gods by offering oblations and libations to them through the means of the fire sacrifice. But the actual 'offering' and the actual 'sacrifice' is one where the individual offers his own self to the Lord God and expects nothing in return. Then the Supreme Lord, being most compassionate, gracious, benevolent, beneficent, merciful and kind, feels obliged to grant as much largesse as he can upon the person who has unconditionally surrendered everything to him, even if it for the sake of upholding his own reputation as being the greatest of all the Lords and Gods in creation. So the Lord showers his benediction upon the devotee and grants him eternal bliss, beatitude and felicity. Not limited to this alone, the Lord ensures that the devotee finds liberation and deliverance from the cycle of birth and death, and his soul attains final emancipation and salvation.

Verily indeed, this is the eclectic reward that the Supreme Lord gives to the devotee who understands the true meaning of making offerings and doing sacrifices. On the other hand, those who are of a low intellect and lack in proper wisdom remain trapped in the cycle of doing this and that sacrifices, making this and that offerings to this and that god, yet achieve nothing worthwhile.

The greatest and the biggest proof of not fully understanding the meaning and intent of the 'Yajas', or offerings and sacrifices, as prescribed by the scriptures is that the individual needs to do them again and again because he does not find full contentment and fulfilment of desires by doing such fire sacrifices for any number of times. On the other hand, if he understands the true meaning and purpose of the 'Yaja', then he would surrender himself before the Lord God and ask for nothing in return. The result would be that he will find eternity of peace and bliss that will leave no room for any more wants; he will attain a sense of extreme spiritual blessedness that liberates him from all wants forever.

This idea is also expressed in Srimad Bhagvad Geeta, 9/23-25, where Lord Krishna tells Arjun: "Those who have Bhakti inside them (i.e. in their heart) but use this virtue to worship gods other than the Supreme Being (in the hope of fulfilment of certain desires), then though it is true that they are worshipping me in these forms yet this kind of worship is not the proper way to worship me. Since such worshippers are deluded under the influence of Maya because they do not recognise who I am (as they worship other Gods instead of directly worshipping me), they fall back into the cycle of transmigration instead of breaking free from it and attaining deliverance. This is because those who worship other Gods go to them (and all these Gods are said to preside over different aspects of creation that are assigned to them, but surely not the supreme state of beatitude and blessedness that is the sole realm of Brahm). Only those who worship me (the Supreme Being) come to me to get final deliverance."

In the context of Bhakti, or having devotion for the Lord God, this kind of 'Yaja'—i.e. offering of the self, or surrendering of the self to the Lord God—is spiritually far superior to and more rewarding than the different types of material offerings that are made during mechanical rituals in formal worships and fire sacrifices.]

२ /२ /१२ पादोदकं तु पाद्यमव्याप्तेः ॥ ६७॥

2 /2 /12 pādōdakaṁ tu pādyamavyāptēḥ || 67||

(2/2/12) The word 'Padodak' (pādōdakaṁ) refers to the water that is used to wash the feet of the Lord God. But it is not practically possible to 'actually' wash the Lord's physical feet as the Lord is not present before the worshipper. So therefore, even a mental offering of any kind, even of one's own self, at the holy feet of the Lord God is deemed to be equivalent to actual worshipping of the Lord as done during formal worshipping rituals. (67)

[During the process of formal worhipping rituals, water is used to wash the feet of the deity being worshipped. Then this water is distributed by the priest amongst the worshippers as a holy and sanctified liquid which is said to have some sacred powers. Sage Shandilya invokes this tradition to stress that it is merely a mechanical ritual as no one has actually seen the Lord nor was the Lord actually present at the time when his feet was being ritually washed.

To wit, just like the case of 'Yaja' as explained in previous verse no. 66, the real meaning of 'Padodak', or the offering of water to wash the Lord God's feet, is to mentally honour the Lord and welcome him reverentially to take a seat right inside one's own heart. This 'water' or 'Padodak' should be in the form of 'tears' that fall spontaneously from one's eyes as he remembers the Lord and feels ecstatic by this thought. If this happens, i.e. if one can reverentially wash the Lord's feet by the natural water of love and affection that is produced by his eyes in the form of 'tears', then it is deemed that such a devotee has actually offered real-time 'Padodak' to the Lord.

In the context of Bhakti, or having devotion for the Lord God, this kind of 'Padodak'—i.e. the tears of love and affection for the Lord—is spiritually far superior to and more rewarding than the plain water that is used in mechanical rituals during formal worship.]

२/२/१३ स्वयमर्पितं ग्राह्यमविशेषात् ॥ ६८॥

2 /2 /13 svayamarpitaṁ grāhyamaviśēṣāt || 68||

(2/2/13) #When one surrenders one's own 'self' to the Lord God, then it is the best and the supreme form of offering indeed. [Nothing is better or superior to that.] Just like the case that anything which has been offered to a deity no more belongs the worshipper, once the devotee offers himself to his Lord God, he has no right whatsoever on his 'own self'. [To wit, now onwards, the devotee's 'self' belongs to the 'supreme Self' represented by the Lord God. Indeed, this eclectic state is equivalent to the 'devotee being one with the Lord himself'.]

{*This verse can be interpreted and read also as follows: "The offerings that are made to a deity become holy and purified, and hence become worthy of acceptance by the devotees of the Lord God. Hence, when a devotee offers himself to the Lord, he indeed becomes worthy of respect and acceptance by one and all."} (68)

[#When something is offered during formal worship rituals, the person who has made this offering has no more claim over it. The thing offered is now shared amongst the worshippers without distinction.

This principle is invoked here in the context of Bhakti to mean that once the devotee truly offers or surrenders himself to the Lord God he loves, he has no right to claim any independent identity, for now onwards he belongs to the Lord; he is Lord's. This means that when a devotee has truly understood the meaning of Bhakti, he would no longer treat himself as an independent individual who is separate from his beloved Lord, but he will think that he is "Lord's". To wit, at the culmination of Bhakti, the distinction between the devotee and the Lord God he worships is removed.

*If we carefully examine this eclectic state of spiritual existence we will see that offering of deeds to the Lord God as mentioned in verse no. 64, and other symbolic offerings as mentioned in verse nos. 66-67, all culminate in total surrender before the Lord: their aim is complete surrender of the devotee before the Lord he worships so much so that the devotee ceases to be an independent person. He ceases to have an independent identity or existence of his own, for now he belongs to his Lord God, and his identity is directly linked to the Lord himself. It is just like the case of a servant who is known and recognised by the name and majesty of the master he serves. The servant no longer has an independent stature of any kind of his own. This servant gets his respect and recognition in the society by the virtue of his being a servant of a certain great master who is highly respected and deeply revered by one and all in the society. Likewise, a true the devotee derives his strength and powers by the virtue of Bhakti that he has for the Supreme Lord.]

२ /२ /१४ निमित्तगुणाव्यपेक्षणादपराधेषु व्यवस्था ॥ ६९ ॥

2 /2 /14 nimittaguṇāvyapēkṣaṇādaparādhēṣu vyavasthā || 69||

(2/2/14) There may be occasions when some offense or error or sin that occurs while offering of worship. This offense or error or sin may be intentional, inadvertent or accidental. There are methods for expiation to neutralise their negative effects, and these methods depend upon the type of offense or error or sin committed. (69)

[One may commit some offense out of free will during worship in order to insult the deity, or to test the effectiveness of the worship that is being offered, to see if the errors that he has committed purposely really affect the outcome of the worship, or is such worship merely a ritual with no actual fruit. All such things are deemed to be sinful and offensive in worship.

In other instances, a person may commit some sin or offence or error without any knowledge that he is doing anything wrong. Then there may be cases when something goes wrong accidentially or by providence, over which no one has any control and which no one can even predict so as to take precautions against.

Out of these three situations, the offense that is made or the sin that is committed by accident is the least harmful; that which happens inadvertently is of the medium kind and its harmful consequences are not too grave; but that which is done intentionally are very serious, and they have grave and long-lasting negative impact upon the offender.

Refer also to verse no. 74 which tells us that sins and other spiritual offenses can be remedied or neutralised by doing 'Smaran' (remembering the Lord, his glories and his holy name), 'Kirtan' (singing the Lord's glories and holy name), 'Katha-Srawan' (hearing the divine stories of the Lord), and other such methods.

Varaha Puran, chapter 25, verse no. 36 lists thirty-two such sins or faults in worship. The Vishnu Puran, Part 2, Canto 6 describes the different 'hells' and the numerous types of sins that condemn a person to them.]

२ /२ /१५ पत्रादेर्दानमन्यथा हि वैशिष्टयम् ॥ ७० ॥

2 /2 /15 patrādērdānamanyathā hi vaiśiṣṭayam || 70||

(2/2/15) Even if a simple thing as a leaf or a flower is offered by the devotee to the Lord God with love and devotion then it is cheerfully accepted by the Lord as if it was a special kind of gift or offering made to him.* (70)

[The idea is very simple and straightforward: The Lord is so kind and graceful that he does not need elaborate worship or expensive offerings to be pleased. What he expects is love and devotion in the heart of the devotee. So if a devotee offers a mere leaf, a flower or even plain water, then such offerings are accepted by the Lord delightfully. He treats such offerings as a special kind of gift given to him by his devotee.

A similar idea is expressed in Srimad Bhagvad Geeta, 9/26, where Lord Krishna says: "Whosoever offers anything to me with love, even as simple a thing as a leaf or a flower, I gladly appear before this pure-hearted and dispassionate devotee to cheerfully accept his offerings for me because they have been made with love."

We read in Ram Charit Manas, Ayodhya Kand, Chaupai line nos. 1-2 that precede Doha no. 129 that sage Valmiki advises Lord Ram to live in the heart of those devotees who accept anything, even the food that they eat, the clothes that they wear etc., after it has first been offered to the Lord God as then such things become sanctified and holy, and the devotee exults that what he has got has come to him by the Lord's grace and benediction."

*This verse can be interpreted in a different way also. During religious ceremonies and sacrifices, the patron who presides over them holds some flowers and leaves in his hands while making oblations to the deity being worshipped or making offerings to the sacred fire itself. These flowers and leaves are symbolic of reverence and honour shown to the deity or the sacred fire. Once an offering is made in this way, the things that are offered belong to the deity being worshipped.

Likewise, if one gives charities, alms and donations in a similar manner, then they are also deemed to be equivalent to sacred offerings made during the sacrifice, and the spiritual rewards that accrue to the giver of such charities, alms and donations are also special because they are equivalent to a selfless service done to the Lord God, on behalf of the Lord and for the Lord.

This tradition is being invoked in this verse to say that when a devotee makes selfless charities or gives alms and donations with the thought that he is doing it as a service to his Lord God, that he is making these charities and giving these donations as offerings to his Lord, then they become a form of his selfless worship of the Lord. Hence, the person gets special spiritual rewards for such charities, alms or donations made in the name of the Lord God.

Such auspicious deeds, if done in a proper way, become a form of Bhakti for the devotee. The Lord duly blesses him. Refer also to verse nos. 58, 67-68 in this context.]

२ /२ /१६ सुकृतजत्वात् परहेतुभावाच्च क्रियासु श्रेयस्यः ॥ ७१ ॥

2 /2 /16 sukṛtajatvāt parahētubhāvācca kriyāsu śrēyasyaḥ || 71||

(2/2/16) If one does selfless deeds, with a pure and auspicious mind, for the good of others, then such deeds are regarded as the best deeds done, and consequentially their rewards would be also the best in spiritual terms.

[This verse can also be interpreted and read as follows: "If one gives something to others, and if the thing given has been acquired by auspicious and righteous means, then this method of giving is of an excellent kind, and so are its results in spiritual terms."] (71)

[In this context, refer also to verse no. 64. Two points are to be noted here: one is that only things that have been acquired by rightful means should be offered to the Lord God or given as charity for his sake or as a service rendered unto him; and two, that such deeds should be done selflessly and with a pure mind that is free from any wordly corruptions. Only then does a devotee become entitled for any worthwhile spiritual rewards; only then such deeds or offerings give him auspicious results by way of getting freedom from the cycle of 'cause and effect', the ever-turning cycle of Karma (deed) and its results which trap a creature endlessly.

So, merely doing worship of the Lord God, or offering one's deeds and their results to the Lord would not yield any spiritual reward of any worth if one did not follow the guideline of this verse. If he does follow the instructions as laid down in this present verse then he accumulates spiritual merit that stands him in good stead and leads him to his aim of attaining freedom from the cycle of transmigration that revolves around the Theory of Karma.

What is this 'Theory of Karma?' Briefly it states that a person who does some deed or takes any action with the hope of any result from them, then he gets mentally and emotionally attached to such deeds and actions. Since one desire leads to another in an endless cycle, since all the desires cannot be fully fulfilled in a person's single life, and since some of the results of deeds and actions done during the lifetime still remain due at the time of a person's death, his soul has to take another birth to finish the unfinished task of the previous birth, and either enjoying or suffering from the results of the past deeds and actions. In the new birth fresh deeds are done, which in turn generate new results, and these add up with the previous ones to build up a formidable balance of spiritual merits or demerits for the soul. The trap gets stronger and deeper unless the person is wise enough to start dismantling this structure from its very root—and the way to do is not to get involved in any new deed and accumulate any new result in the present life. How is it made possible? Well, the answer lies in doing deeds selflessly and offering them and their results to the Lord God. Since a devotee acts like a servant who merely does what he is told to do by his master, the devotee who thinks that he is merely doing what the Lord requires him to do would not accumulate any result of the deeds done by him. By-and-by he is freed from the trap of 'deeds'.

Countless fish live in the holy water of the sacred river Ganges, and flocks of pigeons and other birds live in temples and other shrines. Do they get liberation and salvation; do they feel blessed and spiritually rewarded? The answer is 'no'. Merely living in the sacred water does not provide any spiritual reward to the fish, nor does living in a sacred place such as a temple give any benefit to the bird. Likewise, merely offering worship to the Lord God or doing charity in the Lord's name would not give the necessary spiritual reward to a person if it is not done with love and devotion for the Lord God, and further, this love and devotion should be sincere and true, and not as a pretension of being a holy person to get honour and respect in the world!]

२ /२ /१७ गौणं त्रैविध्यमितरेण स्तुत्यर्थत्वात् साहचर्यम् ॥ ७२॥

2 /2 /17 gauṇaṁ traividhyamitarēṇa stutyarthatvāt sāhacaryam || 72||

(2/2/17) These different ways of worshipping or serving the Lord God (as enumerated in the forgoing verses) are called 'Gauna Bhakti' or the secondary forms of Bhakti. This Gauna Bhakti is of three types (gauṇaṁ traividhyamitarēṇa): viz. Aarta Bhakti, Jigyaasa Bhakti, and Arthaathirtha Bhakti (Ārta Bhakti, Jijñāsā Bhakti, and Arthārthitā Bhakti).

Although these three kinds of Bhaktis are said to be secondary in nature but they have their own importance as they are all meant to be aids in Bhakti. However, the best form of Bhakti that is praised by all is the one that is based on the words of the scriptures, and is therefore called Gyan Bhakti (Jñāna Bhakti). It is because true knowledge and wisdom is the basis of enlightenment and it shows the correct way

Bhakti should be practiced. Gyan enlightens the devotee about the true purpose of Bhakti, whom to offer worship, the way Bhakti is to be properly practiced, what are the different ways it can be done, the pitfalls and their precautions, the spiritual rewards that accrue to the devotee, and so on. Hence, Gyan Bhakti is the best companion for the spiritual aspirant. (72)

['Aarta Bhakti' is when one is extremely distressed he takes refuge with the Lord God in order to overcome his sufferings and adverse circumstances, 'Jigyasaa Bhakti' is when one has heard about the Lord and wishes to explore more about him and to know what the spiritual rewards of Bhakti are, and so he follows this path more with an intention to examine it than for the sake of love for Lord God, and 'Arthaarthi Bhakti' is when one expects any worldly reward from doing Bhakti and offering worship to the Lord.

But the true aim of Bhakti is God-realisation. This would mean establishing a communion between the devotee and the Lord God. Out of all the paths available to a devotee, the best one is said to be the path of 'Gyan', known as 'Gyan Bhakti', as it enlightens the devotee about every aspect of Bhakti. A person who walks on any path with full knowledge of the path and where it leads to is able to move ahead with steady steps and confidence. Otherwise, it would be like walking down a blind alley; or travelling on an unknown and uncharted path that creates uncertainties and doubts. Hence the importance of Gyan Bhakti cannot be under estimated.]

२/२/१८ बहिरन्तस्थमुभयमवेष्टिसववत् ॥ ७३॥

2/2/18 bahirantasthamubhayamavēṣṭisavavat || 73||

(2/2/18) The various external forms of Bhakti (such as Kirtan, Bhajan, Japa, Daan, offering of worship etc. as described earlier) have a dual role. They can play a direct and independent role in success of Bhakti by helping the devotee to overcome his sins and their negative consequences by engaging himself in the many exercises that are collectively called 'Gaun Bhakti' so as to sufficiently purify himself and become eligible for God-reslisation that would lead to spiritual blessedness, or they can can play a subsidiary role by helping the devotee to focus his energy and efforts to develop intense internal love and devotion for the Lord God which would directly connect him to the Lord.

Both these roles of Gaun Bhakti, i.e. the direct and the indirect roles, serve the same purpose though—as they both lead to attainment of God-realisation and beatitude. (73)

[The different ways of practicing Gaun Bhakti, or secondary Bhakti, have been enumerated in the previous verses. Some of these ways are Kirtan (verse nos. 57, 63), Bhajan (verse no. 56), Yaja (verse no. 66), Japa (verse no. 61), Karma (verse nos. 64, 71), Dhyan (verse no. 65), Yoga (verse no. 19), making different kinds of offerings (verse nos. 58, 67-68, 70), and so on. All these forms of Bhakti are paths that help the spiritual aspirant to clean his slate of the various sins and evil consequences of his past deeds that hinder his spiritual progress and come in his way of developing true Bhakti or true love and devotion for the Lord God.

The 'Gaun Bhakti' helps as an aid to 'Paraa Bhakti'; it makes Paraa Bhakti steady and more robust; it is a vital tool for attainment of Paraa Bhakti. A devotee would take recourse to Gaun Bhakti when he cannot develop Paraa Bhakti directly in his heart.

So even if a person is not sufficiently spiritually elevated and intellectually wise and enlightened enough to attain God-realisation by understanding that the Supreme Lord lives right inside him as his own Atma or soul, that this Atma is blissful, eternal and pure consciousness, that self-realisation is equivalent to God-realisation that brings bliss, beatitude and felicity in its wake, and therefore one would derive the nectar of spiritual bliss and beatitude not by searching the Lord outside anywhere but by turning inwards for the Lord dwells inside his own 'self'—he can still reach this supreme spiritual goal by a little bit of practice and help from the various forms of Gaun Bhaktis as enumerated in these verses.]

२ /२ /१९ स्मृतिकीर्त्योः कथादेश्चार्तौ प्रायश्चित्तभावात् ॥ ७४ ॥

2 /2 /19 smṛtikīrtyōḥ kathādēścārtau prāyaścittabhāvāt || 74||

(2/2/19) Such practices as remembering and singing the Lord God's divine name and glories (smṛtikīrtyōḥ), hearing auspicious stories that narrates the Lord's life and deeds, and other such means that are adopted in practicing Aarta Bhakti (kathādēśc-ārtau) are symbolic forms of expiation or repentance (prāyaścitta-bhāvāt) that help the devotee overcome the adverse effects of certain circumstances that have caused distress to him. By practicing these methods he becomes entitled to receive the Lord God's grace and benediction. (74)

[Here it ought to be noted that the need to do penance or expiation or repentance in order to atone for some guilt arising from some form of sin or misdeed, or to overcome the adverse circumstances that may have arisen due to any sin done by the devotee during the course of his life in this world, or caused by providence, or due to some error of omission or commission while offering worship to the Lord God and performing some religious duty as referred to in verse no. 69.

The next verse no. 74 further clarifies this point when it says that by invoking the Lord's holy and divine name even the gravest of sins and misdeeds can be neutralised.

In Ram Charit Manas, Aranya Kand, Chaupai line no. 8 that precedes Doha no. 35, Lord Ram has told Sabari, the old tribal woman who was the Lord's devotee, that listening to the divine stories of the Lord is one of the nine ways by which Bhakti can be practiced.]

२ /२ /२० भूयसामननुष्ठितिरिति चेदाप्रयाणमुपसंहारान्महत्स्वपि ॥ ७५॥

2 /2 /20 bhūyasāmananuṣṭhitiriti cēdāprayāṇamupasaṁhārānmahatsvapi

|| 75||

(2/2/20) Even for expiation or doing repentance for the gravest of sins and misdeeds, one need not do some kind of severe penance (such as doing the Chandrayan Vrata etc.), because remembering the Lord God and chanting his holy name constantly with devotion till the time of death ensures that the person gets liberated from the evil consequences of his sins and misdemeanours of whatever kind they are. (75)

[This verse reassures a devotee that even if he has committed any wrong and finds that he will be unable to do some form of severe of penance to repent for his sins or misdeeds, he has an easy way out of the dilemma. He need not worry because even by invoking the divine form of the Lord God and chanting his holy name he will be able to easily atone for his sins and misdeeds.

This fact is endorsed in Vishnu Purana, 2/6/37-44, which says that the best form of expiation for any kind of sin is the remembrance and chanting of the holy and divine name of the Lord God with steadfastness of devotion and faith. The Lord has many names such as Vasudeo (Krishna), Narayan, Vishnu etc., but the beneficial effects of invoking any of them are the same (verse nos. 39-40, 42). Further, a person can invoke the name of the Lord and remember him any time of the day and night, as all time is auspicious for remembering the Lord God (verse no. 41). Again, a person who keeps his mind steadily fixed on Lord Vasudeo even while he is engaged in doing various religious activities such as doing sacrifices, offering worship, making charity, offering oblations and libations to deities, and so on—he attains the highest state of liberation and deliverance (verse no. 43). Verily indeed, he attains a stature that is superior to going to heaven as the latter keeps him trapped in the cycle of birth and death while the stature obtained by a devotee of the Lord gives him final beatitude; he attains salvation and emancipation for his soul (verse no. 44).

In Vishnu Puran, 3/7/18, we read that Yama, the god of death, does not torment a devotee of Lord Vishnu who worships the Lord's holy feet with due devotion and purity of mind.

Again, in Vishnu Puran, 3/7/26, we read that Yama leaves alone a devotee of Lord Vishnu whose heart is devotedly fixed on the Lord, and whose inner self has been purified of all impurities such as pride, arrogance, ego, malice and jealousy.

Further, Vishnu Puran, 3/7/32-34, says that Yama does not torment a devotee of Lord Vishnu in whose heart the Lord dwells permanently, and who has taken the shelter of the Lord by surrendering himself to him and begs for the Lord's protection.

In fact, Vishnu Puran, 3/7/38, says that he in whose heart Lord Vishnu lives is protected by the Lord himself so much so that neither Yama (the god of death), nor any of his messengers, nor Yama's baton, or his shackle or any other weapon would be able to harm such a devotee.

Srimad Bhagvat Mahapuran, 11/5/42, says: "If a beloved devotee who has forsaken all other attachments and sought shelter at the holy feet of the Lord incurs any sin for any reason (although as a rule he is so purified that he does not commit any sin), the Supreme Lord Hari, who is enshrined in his heart, washes off all those sins."

Srimad Bhagvat Mahapuran, 11/20/29, says: "He who constantly worships me through the path of devotion is enabled to enthrone me in his heart with the result that I eradicate all of his evil propensities from his heart."

A similar idea is expressed in Ram Charit Manas, Ayodhya Kand, Doha no. 129 along with Chaupai line nos. 4-6 that precede it, sage Valmiki tells Lord Ram that he should live in the heart of a person who repeats his holy name constantly, who worships the holy feet of the Lord, who has no other support or hope except the Lord, and who wants nothing in return by doing various auspicious deeds except to have affection and devotion for the holy feet of the Lord.

The next verse no. 76 once again reiterates the same basic idea that for a devotee of the Lord God there is no other better option for repentance for sins than to surrender before his Lord, and pray for the Lord's mercy and grace.]

२ /२ /२१ लघ्वपि भक्ताधिकारे महत्क्षेपकमपरसर्वहानात् ॥ ७६ ॥

2 /2 /21 laghvapi bhaktādhikārē mahatkṣēpakamaparasarvahānāt || 76||

(2/2/21) Remembering the Lord God and invoking his grace even once is enough to free the devotee from the gravest of sins and their consequences. It is said that a devotee of the Lord must abandon all other means of expiation, penance or repentance for his sins and misdeeds except to surrender before the Lord and invoke his mercy and grace. (76)

[This verse is an extension of the idea expressed in the previous verse no. 75 that lays stress on having devotion and love for the Lord God, remembering the Lord, chanting his holy name, and invoking the Lord's mercy and grace as a means to repent for sins and misdeeds.

We read in Srimad Bhagvad Geeta, 18/66, that: "Surrendering all your duties and responsibilities to me, the all-powerful and all-supporting Lord, take refuge in me along. If you do so then don't worry, I shall take responsibility to absolve you of all your sins and misdeeds."

Vishnu Puran, 5/8/19-21, says that by remembering and singing or chanting the holy name of Lord Hari (the Supreme Being; Lord Vishnu) even once, a person is freed from the fear of the gravest of sins; all his sins get dissolved like a metal melting away in a fierce fire; and the greatest of torments of hell are eliminated.

The astounding glory, the stupendous authority and the majestic spiritual value of the Lord's holy name have been elaborately described in Ram Charit Manas, (a) Baal Kand, from (i) Chaupai line no. 1 that precedes Doha no. 19—to Chaupai line no. 2 that precedes Doha no. 28; (ii) Chaupai line nos. 2-3 that precede Doha no. 46; and (b) Aranya Kand, Chaupai line no. 1 that precedes Doha no. 36 (where Lord Ram tells Sabari that repeating the holy Mantra of the Lord with due devotion is one of the nine ways by which Bhakti can be practiced successfully.

Similarly, Vishnu Puran, Part 2, Canto 6, verse nos. 39-44 also emphasise the great importance of remembering, invoking, chanting or repeating the holy name of the Lord God as the sole method for freedom from all torments, spiritual as well as temporal. It is because the Lord immediately attends to the call of his devotee and takes care of his well-being. Of course this requires an exemplary level of faith, depth of conviction and steadfastness in devotion on the part of the devotee for the Lord, and for the Lord's divinity, holiness, greatness, cosmic authority and omnipotence.]

२ /२ /२२ तत्स्थानत्वादनन्यधर्मः खलेवालीवत् ॥ ७७॥

2 /2 /22 tatsthānatvādananyadharmaḥ khalēvālīvat || 77||

(2/2/22) Since deep love and devotion (Bhakti) for the Lord God ensures that the almighty Lord dwells inside the heart of the devotee, so therefore no other special exercises are needed to be done by the devotee for expiation of his sins or repentance for his misdeeds because Bhakti serves this purpose fully. It is just like case of the post of the threshing floor of the farmer's yard. (77)

[During a sacrificial ritual, the animal to be sacrificed is tied to a post or a pole. If the 'post of the threshing floor' from a farmer's yard is used for this purpose then one need not worry about the many criterions that are fixed for the proper way a post or a pole is to be selected to tie the sacrificial animal, such as that it should be made octagonal, or made from a particular type of wood, have a certain height etc. It is because the post from the threshing floor is regarded as inherently sanctified, and no further purification of it is needed before it can be used for the purpose of the fire sacrifice. In ancient times, a bull or an ox was tied to a pole around which harvested crop of wheat or rice was piled. When the animal was made to go around this pole, the grain was separated from the stalk by the beating of the hooves of these animals. Another way of separating the grain was to beat bundles of stalk manually against the pole so that the grains fell to the ground.

Likewise, if a person has deep and true devotion for the Lord God then he need not do any special penance for the expiation of his sins, because his devotion and love for the Lord, i.e. his Bhakti, is a great purifier in its own right, and no other purification rite is better or more effective than it. This happens because the Lord God, the supreme purifier of all, lives right inside the devotee's own heart, making him already purified and holy, and eligible to attain spiritual rewards of bliss and beatitude.

To wit, a true devotee of the Lord God who has enshrined the Lord in his own heart by the virtue of the depth and sincerity of his love, affection and devotion for the Lord, need not take recourse to other methods for attaining spiritual blessedness, for attaining bliss, felicity and beatitude, as these come to him automatically by the grace of the Lord. He may, if he so wishes, engage in doing Kirtan or Bhajan or Dhyan or Japa or Yaja or Daan (verse nos. 56-57, 61-66, 70) or other means of spiritual purification (verse nos. 58, 67-68) etc., but they become superfluous for him.

It is said in Vishnu Puran, 2/6/40-41, that: "If a person regrets for his sins and wishes to repent, then though there are many ways he can do it but the remembrance of the holy name of Lord Vishnu is a complete method for expiation of sins no matter how grave they may be." "If a person invokes the holy name of the Lord anytime of the day or night, his sins are neutralised immediately."]

२ /२ /२३ आनिन्द्ययोन्यधिक्रियते पारम्पर्यात् सामान्यवत्

॥ ७८ ॥

2 /2 /23 ānindyayōnyadhikriyatē pāramparyāt sāmānyavat

|| 78||

(2/2/23) Everyone, from the highest born to the lowest, has an equal right to have spiritual peace, happiness, bliss and beatitude that comes with Bhakti. To wit, in the spiritual path of Bhakti it has been an established tradition that everyone has equal right, no matter what his birth or race or caste or belief is, or what custom he follows. It is just like the case of everyone having equal right to life, and to live a life of righteousness and auspiciousness, to follow the meritorious path of truth, abstinence from violence, renunciation, detachment, non-possession, equanimity etc. Verily, this is the considered view of Authorities on this subject such as great sages and saints. (78)

[Every living person has the right to be a good person. It is obvious and an unsaid law. Similarly, it goes without saying that every person has a right to have devotion, love and affection for the Lord God, and to derive spiritual bliss and beatitude by it. It also goes without saying that every living being has the right to attain liberation, deliverance, emancipation and salvation. There is no discrimination in this.

So therefore this verse says that the path of Bhakti that revolves around having devotion, love and affection for the Lord God and complete surrendering before him, and its supporting methods such as Kirtan, Bhajan, Japa, Dhyan, Yoga, Yaja etc., are open to one and all, without any discrimination whatsoever.

It is also like the case of the huge Banyan tree that does not discriminate between anyone while giving its shade. Like this tree that gives refuge to all and provides them shade, the Lord too gives refuge to all and shows his benediction on everyone without discrimination.

Narad Bhakti Sutra, verse no. 72, also says: "Birth, scholarship, external appearance, wealth and occupation etc. make no difference for having devotion for the Lord God."

We read in Srimad Bhagvat Mahapuran, 11/14/20, that: "I, who am the beloved of self-realised souls, am attainable only through exclusive devotion. Single-minded and unswerving devotion to me absolves even the untouchables, e.g. those who may cook and eat the flesh of dogs, from the stigma attached to their births."

Srimad Bhagvad Geeta, 9/32, Lord Krishna says: "Persons who take complete shelter in me alone, whoever they may be, such as those who are born from the sinful wombs of women (as such being born as outcastes or fallen men known as Mlecchas or Yavanas), or may be of any caste such as Vaishyas (members of the trading community) and Sudras (members of the labour class)—all of them attain the supreme state of spiritual blessedness and beatitude by the virtue of their single-minded devotion to me."]

२ /२ /२४ अतो ह्यविपक्वभावानामपि तल्लोके ॥ ७९ ॥

2 /2 /24 atō hyavipakvabhāvānāmapi tallōkē || 79||

(2/2/24) Hence, even those who have not attained the highest state of enlightenment and self-realisation, or whose spiritual efforts have not matured and bear the desired fruits for them, they too can practice

Bhakti for the Lord God in whatever simple way they can in this world. (79)

[Bhakti is a simple and straightforward way that leads to God-realisation and attainment of spiritual blessedness. No special efforts are to be made or vows are to be kept in it, and one need not even abandon his duties in this world in order to follow the path of Bhakti. If one simply surrenders himself unconditionally before the Lord God and offers everything to him, if one simply begins to love the Lord and have complete faith in him, if he is completely devoted to the Lord and has no other succour or solace anywhere except the Lord—then all his spiritual objectives are deemed to be fulfilled. The merciful, graceful and ever-obliging Lord takes care of him.

To wit, even if one has not attained the highest level of purification and self-realisation, even if one has not done severe penances or sacrifices, even if one has not attained success in meditation and contemplation or any other spiritual practice, but if he has Bhakti (devotion and love) for the Lord God in him then he is deemed to have done all these, and thus become eligible for liberation, deliverance, emancipation and salvation.

In Srimad Bhagvad Geeta, 6/37-40, we read: "Arjuna asks Lord Krishna, 'What happens to a person who has faith but is not able to overcome passions, and therefore his mind gets diverted from the path of Yoga (meditation and contemplation) so that he does not reach perfection in it. As he has strayed from the path leading to God-realisation and has nothing to support him, is such a person not like shreds of clouds floating aimlessly in the sky, neither being able to have God-realisation nor being able to enjoy the sensual pleasures of the world? Oh Lord, please remove my doubts.' Lord Krishna replied, 'Oh Arjun, listen! He who is endowed with devotion for the Lord God never falls from the path leading to beatitude and perfection; he never suffers either here or hereafter.' "]

२ /२ /२५ क्रमैकगत्युपपत्तेस्तु ॥ ८० ॥

2 /2 /25 kramaikagatyupapattēstu || 80||

(2/2/25) Thus, those who could not attain maturity in Bhakti but are diligently following it will attain the highest stature of spiritual blessedness in a gradual manner, whether it is obtained in one generation or many generations, but those who have attained maturity in Bhakti attain God-realisation forthwith in this life itself. (80)

[This verse teaches us to remain steady in the path of Bhakti. One should not abandon Bhakti midway because he has not got the fruit of God-realisation immediately. He must remember that everything takes time to mature. A person sows a seed but he has to wait till the seed produces a tree and fruits ripen on it; he can't eat the fruit immediately after sowing the seed!

We read in Mahabharat, Shanti Parva, Canto 394, verse nos. 13383-89 that: "Those whose hearts are untainted and neutral to either virtues or vices, whose minds are perfectly tranquil and self-controlled, such single-minded devotees do attain Lord Vasudeo."

In Mahabharat, Shanti Parva, Canto 350, verse nos. 13548-50, we read: "Those whose sins have been burnt, those who have overcome virtues and vices alike, they follow the spiritual paths as prescribed in the scriptures, and gradually progress in them to finally attain the state of beatitude and God-realisation. However, those who follow the path of unstinted devotion for Lord Narayan (the Supreme Being) straightaway attain this eclectic spiritual stature without having to go through the process."

In Srimad Bhagvad Geeta, 18/55-56, Lord Krishna says: "Through supreme devotion for me my devotee comes to realise me, and thus he becomes one with me immediately. However, for others who are engaged in the affairs of the world but offer everything to me and depend upon me, they too come to me to attain eternity and perfection (but it is a gradual process)."

The next verse no. 81 further elaborates on this principle.]

२ /२ /२६ अत्क्रान्तिस्मृतिवाक्यशेषाच्च ॥ ८१ ॥

2 /2 /26 atkrāntismr̥tivākyaśēṣācca || 81||

(2/2/26) Even the scriptures endorse this view that those who have attained perfection in having undiluted and deep Bhakti for the Lord God attain liberation and deliverance immediately, but for those who have not attained such perfection a gradual and step-by-step path is prescribed. (81)

[In Srimad Bhagvad Geeta, 8/14-15, Lord Krishna tells Arjun: "He who always thinks of me with a focused and undivided mind, who remains absorbed in me, to him I am easily attainable. Exalted souls who have attained highest level of perfection come to me to attain eternity, and for them there is no re-birth, which is the cause of all sorrows and is transient by nature."

Then a little later Lord Krishna shows the destiny of those who do not have perfection in Bhakti. In Srimad Bhagvad Geeta, 8/24-25, he describes the path they take after death: “He follows the path led by the Fire-God who is all-effulgent in nature, or other deities whom he had worshipped in life. He follows these paths to finally reach the abode of the Supreme Being who lives in heaven. Others follow a different path that takes them to the lower heaven presided over by the Moon God. They abide there for some time, enjoying its pleasures, and then come back to the mortal world.”

In Srimad Bhagvad Geeta, 8/16, Lord Krishna says: “All the worlds, right from the abode of the creator Brahma to the mortal world, are liable to come and go as everything in creation is transient. But for those who attain me, there is no re-birth. Hence they attain eternity.”

So we see that final liberation and deliverance from the cycle of transmigration is easy to attain by following the path of Bhakti as compared to other paths prescribed by different scriptures.]

२ /२ /२७ महापातकिनां त्वार्तौ ॥ ८२॥

2 /2 /27 mahāpātakināṁ tvārtau || 82||

(2/2/27) Even the worst and the greatest of sinners have the right to seek the Lord God’s mercy and grace just like those who are in grave distress and seek the Lord’s intervention to save themselves from the horrors and miseries they face. Indeed the Lord grants them their wishes, and blesses them so that they have devotion for the Lord to ensure that they are not subjected to the same ill-fate again. (82)

[When anyone is in great distress and suffering a lot, he fervently prays to the Lord God to help him out of his miserable condition. And the merciful Lord obliges immediately by not only eliminating the cause of distress but also blessing the person with the gift of Bhakti, the magnificent gift of devotion and love for the Lord God that would shield the person from the attack of miseries and troubles in the future. The Lord effectively grants the devotee the umbrella of his protection. We have two well-known examples of this: one is the story of Draupadi and the other is that of Vibhishan. Draupadi invoked Lord Krishna as a last resort when she was being publicly disrobed in full royal court. Then and there Lord Krishna had assumed the form of a seamless piece of cloth that wrapped Draupadi from all sides so that her modesty and self-respect were protected instantly. In the other case of Vibhishan, when he was kicked out by his own elder brother Ravana, the demon king of Lanka, he was in utter distress as his life was in danger and he had no where to go. So he immediately came to Lord Ram and surrendered before him. The merciful Lord immediately accepted him and granted him immunity from all fears.

We may cite one more well-known incident in this regard: it's the story of 'Gajraj'. He was the king of elephants. Once when he was taking a bath in a river, a ferocious crocodile caught hold of his foot and began to pull him in the water. The elephant king first tried all his might to pull himself away, but when he failed in his effort and was about to be drowned he plucked a lotus flower from the river and offered it to Lord Vishnu even as he said his last prayer. The Lord immediately rushed to protect him from death; he cut-off the crocodile's head and saved the elephant.

The above three examples are of devotees who had prayed to the Lord God when they were in grave distress that required an urgent invocation of the Lord. The Lord had however granted them immediate relief even though they had not remembered the Lord out of any kind of devotion or love for him at that particular moment. The point to note here is that though they were not sinners, yet they did not surrender to the Lord out of any Bhakti for him. But still the Lord did not wast time to save them.

This verse teaches us that the same thing would happen to great sinners if they honestly turn to the Lord God, seeking forgiveness and mercy. The gracious Lord would not only absolve them of their misdeeds but also grant them the fruit of his Bhakti so that they don't go back on the evil path they had followed earlier, the path that had caused them so much misery and torments. To wit, once a creature turns to the Lord he is assured of redemption from all his sins and their evil consequences. Henceforth he is deemed to be purified and holy.

We read in Srimad Bhagvad Geeta, 9/32, that Lord Krishna declares: "Persons who take absolute shelter in me, though they may be born from sinful wombs of women such as harlots, or are of the trading community known as Vaishyas, or belong to the labour class known as the Shudras, or are of the lowest of the classes including the outcastes—even they can attain the supreme goal of liberation and deliverance if they have true and sincere devotion for me, the Supreme Being, for there is no bar of caste, creed, colour, sect, sex or community for having Bhakti for the Lord God."

And what kind of surrender to the Lord should it be? Well, it should be 'complete and absolute and honest' to bear any result. We read in Ram Charit Manas, Baal Kand, Chaupai line no. 5-6 that precede Doha no. 131 that "Lord Ram dwells in the heart of those who have abandoned all hopes of help from one's own class, creed, race, religion, wealth, honour, family and household ties, et al, and instead takes shelter with Lord Ram alone."]

२ /२ /२८ सैकान्तभावो गीतार्थप्रत्यभिज्ञानात् ॥ ८३ ॥

2 /2 /28 saikāntabhāvō gītārthapratyabhijñānāt || 83||

(2/2/28) To have single-minded devotion and love for the Lord God, with no other thoughts to disturb or cause distraction in this single-mindedness, is the best form of Bhakti. This principle is clearly evident when one examines the words of Srimad Bhagvad Geeta of Lord Krishna. (83)

[Here the following sampe verses of Lord Krishna's Geeta can be cited: (i) Canto 6, verse no. 30; (ii) Canto 6, verse no.47; (iii) Canto 9, verse no. 22; (iv) Canto 9, verse no. 34; (v) Canto 11, verse no. 55; (vi) Canto 12, verse nos. 6-7.

Now, let us read each of them so see what they say:

(i) Canto 6, verse no. 30:-

"A person who (is wise and enlightened enough to) see me (the Supreme Being symbolising the cosmic Consciousness) in all living beings, and vice versa—verily indeed he never loses sight of me (as he sees me all around himself in the form of those who see in this world), and I too don't lose sight of him (because I reside in his own self as his Atma, his wise and enlightened 'self' that is pure consciousness which sees and knows everything)."

(ii) Canto 6, verse no.47:-"An ascetic (Yogi) who worships me (the Supreme Being) with a single-minded devotion is regarded by me as the best amongst ascetics."

(iii) Canto 9, verse no. 22:-

"The devotee who thinks of no one else but is devoted to me alone and loves me alone, who worships me selflessly, and who are therefore united with me in thought and spirit—verily indeed, I bring full security to him, and I personally attend to his needs (both the temporal and the spiritual)."

(iv) Canto 9, verse no. 34:-

"Fix your mind on me, be devoted to me, worship me, make your offerings and pay your obeisance to me. In this way, link yourself with me, and depend solely upon me. Verily indeed, then you shall come to me."

(v) Canto 11, verse no. 55:-

"Oh Arjun! He who performs all his duties for me and for my sake, who depends solely upon me, who is devoted to me alone, who has no attachment (except with me), and who is free from evil traits such as malice, ill-will, jealousy towards all living beings (because he sees me everywhere in all forms)—verily indeed, he comes to me and me alone."

(vi) Canto 12, verse nos. 6-7:-

"Those who exclusively depend upon me, who surrender all their action to me, who worship me alone, who constantly meditate upon me and contemplate upon me alone with single-minded devotion—verily indeed, I forthwith deliver them whose mind is fixed on me from the ocean of transmigration."

Mahabharat, Narayan Section of Shanti Parva, Canto 35, verse nos. 13151, 52, 54, say: "Those Brahmans who are duly intent on observing all the rules of religion, who read the Vedas along with the Upanishads, as well as exalted ascetics who are strict in all of their spiritual performances—verily indeed, the devotee of the Lord God who has single-minded devotion for the Lord and offers everything to him is far superior to all of them. This is not said only by the gods or wise sages but by the Lord himself (i.e. Lord Krishna) to Arjun in the battlefield of Kurushetra."]

२ /२ /२९ परां कृत्वैव सर्वेषां तथा ह्याह ॥ ८४॥

2 /2 /29 parāṁ kr̥tvaiva sarvēṣāṁ tathā hyāha || 84||

(2/2/29) The chief aim should be to have Paraa Bhakti (the supreme form of devotion and love for Lord God). The other secondary forms of Bhakti (such as Kirtan, Bhajan, Japa, Dhyan, Yaja etc. as mentioned in verse nos. 56-58, 61, 63, 66-68 etc.) are merely tools for its realisation, and they bear fruits or give results only when one has steady and firm devotion and love for the Lord in him. This principle has been endorsed by the Lord God himself*. (84)

[*We read in Srimad Bhagvad Geeta, 18/68, that Lord Krishna says: "He who has deep love and single-minded devotion for me advises other faithful followers about the secret of Bhakti, such a devotee would come to me. There is no doubt about it."

What is this 'secret'? The summary of this entire Chapter is this 'secret'. And what is it? The answer is briefly this: A person who has single-minded devotion for Lord God, who loves the Lord dearly from the deepest recesses of his heart, who has completely and honestly surrendered himself and his deeds to the Lord in a selfless manner, it is only then that he becomes eligible to attain supreme bliss and beatitude as well as liberation and deliverance from the cycle of birth and death with its attendent sufferings. This is called having 'Paraa Bhakti'. However, in his path he can take the help of many tools called 'Gaun Bhakti', such as Kirtan, Bhajan, Yoga, Japa etc. which are tools that are secondary to the main objective of Bhakti but nevertheless play a vital role for its successful accomplishment and maturity. These Gaun Bhaktis are not the aim but means to attain Paraa Bhakti. They bear fruits only when Paraa Bhakti is there. This fact has been reiterated earlier also in verse no. 60.

So it is important for a wise and enlightened devotee to know this principle of Bhakti himself and also to enlighten others who may not be aware of it, because if he does not do it and only enjoys its rewards himself then he is being selfish.]

समाप्तश्च द्वितीयोऽध्यायः ॥ २॥

samāptaśca dvitīyō 'dhyāyaḥ || 2||

Thus ends Chapter 2 of Shandilya Bhakti Sutra

----------*********----------

(6) SHANDILYA BHAKTI SUTRA

Aphorisms for Devotion to God and

The Principles of the Philosophy of Love for Him

[Roman Transliteration of Text, English Exposition, Elaborate Notes]

Chapter 3, Part 1:

Verse nos. 85-92

|| शाण्डिल्य भक्ति सूत्रम् ||

तृतीयोऽध्यायः

प्रथममाह्निकम्

|| śāṇḍilya bhakti sūtram ||

tṛtīyō 'dhyāyaḥ

prathamamāhnikam

३ /१ /१ भजनीयेनाद्वितीयमिदं कृत्स्नस्य तत्स्वरूपत्वात्
॥ ८५॥

3 /1 /1 bhajanīyēnādvitīyamidaṁ kr̥tsnasya tatsvarūpatvāt
|| 85||

(3/1/1) The Lord God who is to be worshipped, honoured, invoked, loved and meditated upon, i.e. the Lord for whom one should have Bhakti (devotion) is none else but the Supreme Being. He is the only one who is worthy of having Bhakti for.

Verily indeed, this whole creation, from its minutest element to the most colossal entity, is a manifestation of the same Supreme Being who has revealed himself in each of the units of this universe. There is nothing in existence that is not an image of the Supreme Being, which does not reflect the presence of the Supreme Being. To wit, each unit of this creation is an inseparable part of the whole that is known as the Supreme Being ('Brahm' in the words of the Upanishads), and there is no other truth except this—because everything in this creation is a manifestation of the Lord in one way or the other.

To be enlightened about this fact and worshipping the Lord God with this clear understanding is the supreme form of Bhakti (known as the Paraa Bhakti), and it is this kind of Bhakti that leads to attainment of final beatitude and felicity for the devotee; it is this Bhakti that provides the spiritual aspirant liberation and deliverance from the cycle of transmigration, and it ensures salvation and emancipation of his soul. (85)

[In this context, refer also to verse no. 87 herein below.

The unequivocal and irrefutable metaphysical truth of creation as affirmed in this present verse no. 85 is also the chief philosophical doctrine expounded by all the Upanishads where the Supreme Being is referred to as Brahm. The Upanishads assert that Brahm is the cause and end of this creation; Brahm pervades this creation uniformly; Brahm is omnipresent, all-pervading and all-encompassing; there is nothing that is not Brahm, and there is nothing beyond Brahm.

And what or who is 'Brahm'? Upanishads say that Brahm is the personified form of the cosmic Consciousness that is the root cause of everything in existence. Brahm does everything via the medium of its cosmic dynamic energy known as Shakti. Maya, or delusions, is one of the many ways this Shakti is revealed. Prakriti, or Nature, is another aspect of Brahm, i.e. Prakriti is a revelation of Brahm at the cosmic level. The Jiva, the living being, is a manifestation of Brahm at the micro level of creation. Lord Vishnu, also known as the Viraat Pursuh, is a manifestation of Brahm at the macro level of creation, so are the many gods and goddesses and other celestial bodies. To wit, the entire animate and inanimate world is a manifestation or revelation of Brahm. Hence, whatever exists in this world or the universe is Brahm in that form, individually and collectively.

The term Brahm (pronounced often times also as Brahmn) has wide connotations—it means any one or all of the following: The Supreme One, the Supreme Being, the Viraat Purush (the cosmic form of the Supreme Being), the Parmatma (the supreme Atma or Soul; the ethereal Spirit), the cosmic Consciousness, the Absolute Truth, the Universal Truth, the Divine Being, the subtle and sublime entity that is all-pervading, all-encompassing, immanent, omnipresent, omnipotent, omniscient and all-knowing, that which is both invisible as well as visible, that which has an existence both at the macrocosmic level of creation as well as the microcosmic level, that which predates creation and lasts beyond creation, that from which the entire known as well as the unknown world has emerged, that which is impossible to prove but incontrovertibly there, that which even the scriptures have failed to define and describe in certain terms, and so on and so forth.

The Atharva Veda's Mahavakya Upanishad, verse no. 10 says that Brahm is the Supreme Being. To quote—"It is the divine, eclectic Brahm whose glories and majesties are being eulogized by ancient Gods and saints; it is Brahm who is held in high esteem by them. It is this Brahm who is pursued and worshipped by them. It is this Brahm who is the ultimate 'Deva' or the exalted Lord God known as the Supreme Being."

In fact, Brahm is the object of all Upanishadic discussions, all metaphysical and theological debates and ponderings. It is the object of all meditation and worship and knowledge. It is the final frontier of knowledge that is achievable with honest endeavour, and it is called the ultimate Truth and the absolute Reality in all that exist. Without Brahm, nothing is true and real.

Brahm in metaphysical context refers to the *pure Consciousness* that has two levels of existence—one is the macro level, and the other is the micro level. At the macro level this refers to the cosmic Consciousness that is universal and uniform throughout this creation, and this fact that the cosmic Consciousness is the Supreme Being himself personified is endorsed in the Atharva Veda's *Annapurna Upanishad*, Canto 5, verse no. 56. At the micro level of creation, the term 'consciousness' refers to the individual's Atma, i.e. the soul of the individual creature. This Atma is his truthful 'self'.

Since everything in creation is a revelation of Brahm, it naturally follows that the term 'Brahm' also applies to the inanimate things of this world as much as it applies to the animate creatures. At a more subtle and more microscopic level of physical existence, the term 'consciousness' implies the dynamic forces and energy of creation that subtly live inside the atom of all elements, and thereby of all things that exist in this physical world because the atom is the basic unit in this creation and all elements are basically made up of atoms. The atom is the fundamental unit that represents the unique identity of any given element. In the field of metaphysics, the basic elements are earth, water, fire, air and sky, and the dynamic force that are inherent in all of them which enables them to harbour and sustain life is known as the 'Brahm' factor—for otherwise they would have not been able to harbour and sustain 'life'.

Therefore we see that whereas the term Brahm refers to the 'consciousness' that is present in all 'living beings' such as plants and animals, it also applies to the apparently 'non living' aspect of creation because all things that exist are made of the basic elements, and all elements have 'atom' as their basic unit. The atom has dynamism and stupendous cosmic energy trapped in its core—as is evident in modern times when we are all well acquainted with the phenomenon of 'atomic energy'.

The Annarpurna Upanishad of the Atharva Veda tradition, Canto 2, verse nos. 17-18 describes the uniqueness of Brahm as follows—

"Verse no. 17 = Whatever is visible in this world consisting of two facets, one that is animate and the other that is inanimate, has something at its core without which this world would just not exist.

The transcendental vision which enables a man to see this hidden entity without which nothing would exist, the entity that is not visible and apparent in its external form but nevertheless constitutes the very core and the very basis of creation, helps him to realise the universal presence of the invisible Brahm that forms the core, known as the 'Atma', of the entire creation.

This eclectic vision of creation enables the wise and enlightened aspirant to see Brahm everywhere in creation, to realise that Brahm is the essence of existence, and that it is the truth that is universal, uniform, all-inclusive and all-pervading (17)."

"Verse no. 18 = A person who has any kind of attraction for or attachment with any of the things that are visible in this world is said to be one who is bonded to this world, who is fettered and bound in shackles. [This is because all things that are visible in this mortal world are gross in nature, are perishable and transient by nature.]

To be freed from such attractions or attachments is deemed to be Mukti or freedom.

It is impossible to describe one's feelings in tangible and comprehensive form about what one has 'seen' behind the external façade of the visible world.

[The reference here is to 'Brahm' and not to the physical sights of the world. In other words, the 'Brahm' that the wise, enlightened and Brahm-realised man 'sees', or of whom he has a divine vision, or whom he perceives as the basis and fundamental essence of creation, cannot be described in words. This is because words have their own limitations, and Brahm is such a divine, esoteric, enigmatic and mysterious entity that it can only be experienced and never defined in words. Brahm is not something gross that can be 'seen' with the gross organ of sight (eye) and therefore it cannot be described, because a man can only correctly describe things that he has 'actually seen with his eyes'. The Brahm that he 'sees' is with the 'eyes of self-realisation, erudition, wisdom and enlightenment'; this Brahm exists in the subtle plane of existence and not in the physical plane like other sense objects. Just like the physical eyes cannot see the 'air' or the 'atom' to be able to define or describe them, it is also not able to do so with Brahm.

Even in the physical world when one sees any object, he would not be able to completely describe it in its entirety because of the fact that words have their limited use, but supposing he is able to narrate any thing seen in physical form completely, the narration might not hold good after some time because the thing would have undergone a change, howsoever miniscule.]

In fact, this sight or vision (of Brahm) can only be witnessed and experienced and endorsed, but never defined or described (18)."

Thus, a wise man who has developed this holistic view of Brahm realises that his 'true self' is the Atma (the 'atom' in the above illustration) which is Brahm or consciousness personified (in a microcosmic level of existence), and that this same Brahm is the one who lives in each unit (atom) of creation (at the macrocosmic level of existence).

The eclectic divine virtues of Brahm have been enumerated in countless Upanishads, for instance in the following—

(a) Rig Veda's Mudgal Upanishad, Canto 3, verse nos. 1-3; Canto 4, verse no. 1; Atma Prabodh Upanishad, Canto 1, verse nos. 2-4, 6.

(b) Sam Veda's Chandogya Upanishad, Keno Upanishad and Avyakta Upanishad.

(c) Shukla Yajur Veda's following Upanishads—Adhyatma Upanishad, verse nos. 61-64; Brihad Aranyaka Upanishad Canto 2, Brahman 3 describes this Brahm's two forms in detail.

(d) Krishna Yajur Veda's Yogshikha Upanishad, Canto 2, verse nos. 15-19, Canto 3, verse nos. 17-22; Kathrudra Upanishad, verse no. 12, 27-28, 30-31, 42; Taittiriya Upanishad Valli 3, Anuvak 10, verse no. 2-5; Skanda Upanishad, verse no. 13; Dhyan Bindu Upanishad, verse no. 4; Varaaha Upanishad, Canto 2, verse nos. 16, 20-21, 26, 29; Canto 3, verse no. 2; and Canto 4, verse nos. 31-32; Yog Kundalini Upanishad, Canto 3, verse no. 35; Saraswati Upanishad, verse no. 50-52; Shwetashwatar Upanishad;Tejobindu Upanishad, Canto 6, verse nos. 35-43, 47-57, 66-67, 103, 106 (virtues of Brahm); Kaivalya Upanishad, verse nos. 8-16, 21-23.

(e) Atharva Veda's = Mundak Upanishad, Mundak 1, section 1, verse no. 6; Mundak 2, section 2, verse no. 7, 9-11; Mundak 3, section 1, verse no. 3-5, 7-9; Atharvashir Upanishad, Kandika 4 (full); Naradparivrajak Upanishad, Canto 8 which is fully dedicated to enumerating the grand virtues of Brahm; Canto 9, verse nos. 3, 19-22; Tripadvibhut Maha-Narayan Upanishad, Canto 1, paragraph 4, Canto 4, paragraph no. 1; Shandilya Upanishad, Canto 2, section 1, verse nos. 2-5, and Canto 3, section 1, verse nos. 1-8, 11-14; Annapurna Upanishad, Canto 2, verse nos. 17-18; Canto 4, verse no. 27-31, 33, 67; Canto 4, verse nos. 35-38, 67; Canto 5, verse nos. 10, 20-21, 66-67, 72, 113; Atma Upanishad, verse nos. 1-D and 1-E, verse nos. 2-4, 9, 30-31; Pashupat Brahm Upanishad, Purva Kanda/Canto 1, verse nos.11, 13-16; Uttar Kanda/Canto 2, verse nos. 13-16, 26, 27-30, 44; Tripura Tapini Upanishad, Canto 1, verse no. 4; Canto 5, verse nos. 6, 8-9, 16-17, 22; Ram Purva Tapini Upanishad, Canto 1, verse no. 7; Par Brahm Upanishad, verse no. 1; Bhasma Jabal Upanishad, Canto 1, paragraph no. 1; Canto 2, paragraph nos. 3, 5-8 (albeit in the guise of enumerating the glorious virtues of Lord Shiva or Rudra); Mahavakya Upanishad, verse no. 6 (Brahm lives in the body as the Atma; Brahm is known as Hans), verse no. 10 (Brahm is the Supreme Being); Tripura Tapini Upanishad, Canto 5, verse no. 21 (Brahm is like the Akash element).]

३ /१ २ तच्छक्तिर्माया जडसामान्यात् ॥ ८६॥

3 /1 /2 tacchaktirmāyā jaḍasāmānyāt || 86||

(3/1/2) 'Maya' is the cosmic dynamic powers of the Supreme Being (also known as Brahm). The Lord employs this power known as Maya (which is the Lord's cosmic power that creates a veil of delusions) to create things from nothing, and then the Lord keeps the cycle of creation turning endlessly by again using this Maya to keep the creature trapped in it. [Hence, Maya not only deludes but also traps.]

This Maya, inspite of having a negative and gross connotation, is as much a part of Brahm, the Supreme Being, as the rest of the creation, and especially its inanimate and grosser aspects, because everything in existence, everything in creation, is a part of Brahm (refer verse no. 85). (86)

[Obviously, if everything is a manifestation of Brahm then Maya too is a manifestation of Brahm. Maya is the dynamism or the dynamic powers of Brahm that enables the latter to create this world—refer verse nos. 37-38, 42.

A remarkable point to note here is this: This creation is the product of 'Maya'—which means 'a veil of delusions'. To wit, this world, with its fascinating qualities, mind-boggling variations and magnificent charms has been created in the form of a delusion, and hence it is not true! If the world is a creation of delusion, and hence not true, how can its material charms and its very existence be true? Therefore, is it not foolish to pursue this world in the hope of having permanent happiness? Is it not stupid to expect eternity in this world which itself is transient and perishable?

So therefore, a wise and enlightened spiritual aspirant would not waste his time and life after 'this' world which has its existence in delusions, but would instead make effort to pursue 'that' entity which would give him true, real and eternal happiness. And that entity is the cosmic Consciousness personified as the Supreme Being or Brahm.

The only way to overcome the trap of Maya and find freedom from it is to have Bhakti for the Lord God. This fact is explicitly stated in Ram Charit Manas, Uttar Kand, (i) Chaupai line nos. 4-5 that precede Doha no. 44, and (ii) Chaupai line nos. 1-2 that precede Doha no. 45 where Lord Ram told the citizens of Ayodhya that: "A Jiva (living being) is trapped in the cycle of birth and death and continues to roam in it because of Maya which surrounds him on all sides and drives his deeds, circumstances, attitude, qualities and thoughts. So if you really wish to have heavenly happiness right here in this world and in this life, then you must practice the glorious virtue of Bhakti as it is a supremely liberating power that provides freedom from the evil effects of Maya."

Further we read in Ram Charit Manas, Uttar Kand, Chaupai line nos. 2-3 that precede Doha no. 117 that: "A Jiva (living being) is a fraction of Ishwar (the Supreme Being) who is a personified form of cosmic Consciousness, eternally pure and immaculate, and is innately a fount of bliss and beatitude. It is the same Jiva that gets tied in the snare of this cycle of transmigration and trapped in worldly miseries due to the negative impact of Maya just like an insect that is trapped by the spider's web. [Here, the Jiva is the 'insect', and the Maya is the 'spider's web'.]"

And how would a Jiva find deliverance from this dilemma? Ram Charit Manas, Uttar Kand, Chaupai line no. 4 that precedes Doha no. 119 gives the precise answer: "A Jiva can get freedom by worshipping and having devotion for Lord Ram, for then all auspiciousness would come to the Jiva even without his asking for them."

Srimad Bhagvad Geeta, 7/14, Lord Krishna says: "This fascinating power of mine that is known as Maya, the power that creates a veil of delusions, is astounding and most powerful. It consists of the three Gunas (the three qualities that combine to give shape to Nature; the mode in which creation exists) that are also at the root of this creation. This veil of Maya is extremely strong and powerful, and hence very difficult to break through. However, those who worship me resolutely are able to pierce through it very easily and cross its hurdles (to see the truth and find liberation and deliverance from the trap cast by Maya)."]

३ /१ /३ व्यापकत्वाद्व्याप्यानाम् ॥ ८७॥

3 /1 /3 vyāpakatvādvayāpyānām || 87||

(3/1/3) The elementary Truth of creation is that the Supreme Being, who is also known as Brahm, is immanent and all-pervading. He is immortal and immutable. He is omnipresent everywhere in this creation, both in its animate form as well as in its inanimate form. From this elementary Truth other things emerge. Hence, everything is a form of Brahm, and there is nothing other than this. (87)

[Refer to verse no. 85 herein above in this context. These verses resonate with the metaphysical and theological doctrine of the Upanishads as regards Brahm and the truth of existence. These verses clearly hint that a sagacious and erudite devotee must keep in mind that he must worship the Supreme Being alone if he wishes to derive real good from his spiritual efforts.]

३ /१ /४ न प्राणिबुद्धिभ्योऽसम्भवात् ॥ ८८॥

3 /1 /4 na prāṇibuddhibhyō'sambhavāt || 88||

(3/1/4) This huge and wondrous creation with its astounding diversity and multifarious forms that are most magnificent and exceedingly fascinating is not (na) a creation of an ordinary 'living being' (prāṇi) who may have used his intelligence (buddhi) to craft it. Verily indeed, it is not possible ('sambhavāt) for an ordinary 'living being' to use his mind and its creative abilities to create this universe that defies all explanations and is beyond imagination.

[Hence, it must be some 'superior being' who has done it. And who is that 'being'? He is the one who is known as the 'Supreme Being', the Lord God to whom the devotee offers his prayers.] (88)

[We have read that the Supreme Being is a personified form of cosmic Consciousness, and therefore he is the Supreme Atma or the Parmatma of this creation, or the supreme Self of this living creation. This picture is at the macro level of creation. At the micro level of creation we find that this same cosmic Consciousness resides in all the Jivas, the individual living beings, in this creation as their individual Atma or their true 'self'. Hence theoretically there is no difference between the Parmatma and the Jiva, or the Supreme Being and the oridinary living being.

We have also read that this cosmic Consciousness is the cause or the root of this creation; the creation has been created by this cosmic Consciousness—because only an entity that is living and conscious can do something, and not an entity that is inert and non-living. So it may be argued this wonderful creation may be a product of a 'Jiva' or an ordinary living being.

This verse addresses this question and settles all confusions in this regard. It says that though it is true that the consciousness is the same in the individual living being as well as the Supreme Being, yet there is a fundamental difference between the two. It is like the 'case of a father and his off spring—though both have the same gene yet the off spring has come from the father, and it is not the other way round. The individual living being is an image or a fraction of the cosmic 'whole' known as the Supreme Being, and it is not vice versa. The abilities of the living being has many limitations—such as that his physical body cannot be immortal, he cannot be present at more than one place at the same time, he is not immanent and all-pervading, he is not omniscient as he cannot know everything because of the vastness of knowledge that goes beyond his reach, and so on and so forth. These limitations do not apply to the Supreme Being as he has no physical body that may act as a barrier to the abilities of the cosmic Consciousness that the Supreme Being personifies. Hence, the inherent limitations that are put on the abilites of the Consciousness in the case of the ordinary living being do not apply to the Supreme Being at all.

Besides this point, when we examine this creation we find that is exceptionally complex and highly complicated in nature. It has a lot of ironies and paradoxes that confounds and boggles the mind. For instance, it has entities that are extremely small and sublime on the one hand, and most colossus and gross on the other hand. The diversity and variations in creation are baffling to the extreme, and only an Authority that is superior to others, that is supremely intelligent and resourceful, can first plan, and then execute and control this wondrous thing that is called creation. It surely requires special skills and expert craftsmanship to mould a structure like this creation is just by wishing it to be so.

To wit, this universe is not a creation of an ordinary living being, or even an ordinary god, but it is an expert craftsmanship that can be done only by an entity that has an extraordinary intelligence, imagination, skills, abilities, powers and authority to do so. And such an entity is none but the Supreme Being himself. Therefore, it is established that there is a 'Creator' who has created this universe, and that this 'Creator' is the Supreme Being who is the Lord God and the sole Authority in creation, supervising everything in his realm, from start to finish. This astounding creation that defies all imagination and understanding is surely not the product of any ordinary living being; it is surely not created by a Jiva, the individual creature of this mortal world.]

३ /१ /५ निर्मायोच्चावचं श्रुतीश्च निर्मिमीते पितृवत् ॥ ८९॥

3 /1 /5 nirmāyōccāvacaṁ śrutīśca nirmimītē pitr̥vat || 89||

(3/1/5) Having created the entire universe from its lowest to its highest form, or from its grossest to its subtlest form, the supreme Creator then created living beings from the most minutest of size to the ones of mammoth proportions who would populate this universe.

The Creator then deemed it necessary to create a body of knowledge in the form of the Vedas and other scriptures (śrutīśca) that would serve as guides to help the living beings, his 'off-springs', to know what is good for them and what is not in the same way that a worldly father teaches his sons and arranges for their best of education so that they can stand on their own feet, become prepared to face the harsh realities of the world with ease, and achieve great success and merit in life that would not only give glory to the concerned member of the family but to the whole family as well. (89)

[Here we note that the Supreme Being, the Parmatma, the Lord God, is also called the 'Father of creation'. Like any loving 'father' who goes out of his way to ensure that his sons live a comfortable and happy life when they grow up, worrying about their future right from the day they are born, the supreme 'Father' also makes sure that his own extended family, i.e. the vast creation which he has produced himself, lives happily and comfortably, is provided with all its needs, and its members not only attain glory for themselves but also for their family and their Father by living a life of righteousness, auspiciousness, probity, propriety and merit.

For this purpose the supreme Father, the Creator of this creation, produced a body of knowledge known as the Vedas (the scriptures). These scriptures help the living being to become enlightened about how to lead a life of merit, about the true purpose of life, about what is true and what is false in this world, about what is good and what is bad, and countless other things that are needed to be known. So a study of these scriptures prepares a living being to lead a life of merit and attain glory. On the other hand, neglecting the principles laid down in the scriptures would fill a person's life with misdeeds and evil that would ultimately lead to his downfall. It is like the case of a son who is admitted to a good school by his father in the hope that his son would acquire good education and shine in life. But it is actually upto the son to use this golden opportunity for his upliftment or waste it away by being in bad company at school and acquiring bad habits. What can the father do; how is he to be blamed for the ruined life of his son? The father surely wanted that his son becomes well educated and succeeds in life by teaching him good manners and his own vocation at home, and admitting him to the best school or college that he could locate. But if the son still gets spoilt by keeping bad company or not paying heed to his studies then he alone is to be blamed for ruining his own life. The father is filled with regrets, but since he loves his son most dearly he refrains from inflicting severe punishment on him. At some point of time the frustrated father would turn his attention away from his son who has become evil and spoilt, and would become focused on the other son who has lived upto his father's expectations, showering his love on the latter son. But in case the evil and spoilt son realises his mistake and decides to make amends and repent, the father would welcome him and bless him in his effort.

In a similar way, the supreme Father created everything of necessity in this world and made the living being heir to it; he created the Vedas so that his off-spring, the Jiva or the living being, is well taught about what is good for him. But some unfortunate Jiva spoils his own life by neglecting the teaching of the scriptures, while others follow the principles as taught by these scriptures and attain glory in life. At some point of time if the fallen and sinful Jiva regrets and decides to make amends by following the scriptures, the supreme Father welcomes him with open arms.

Another point to note is that a worldly father treats all his sons equally, and all have equal right over his assets, but still the son who loves his father more, who shows respect to him and is obedient to him, is dearer to the father than his other siblings. The father is more concerned about the welfare of son who loves him and is obedient to him as compared to the other sons who are disrespectful and wayward.

In a similar way, the supreme Father, the Lord God, has a soft corner in his heart for his true devotees who are totally dedicated to serving him selflessly, who are sincerely devoted to him, and who love him more than anybody or anything else in this world—i.e. the devotee who has 'Bhakti' is very dear to the Lord God. Then, like a worldly father who would go out of his way to help the son who loves him and is ever-ready to serve the father, the supreme Father, the Lord God, too goes out of his way to take care of his devotee who has Bhakti for him.]

३ /१ /६ मिश्रोपदेशान्नेति चेन्न स्वल्पत्वात् ॥ ९० ॥

3 /1 /6 miśrōpadēśānnēti cēnna svalpatvāt || 90||

(3/1/6) Sometimes it is argued that the Vedas are often too difficult to comprehend and their knowledge is very esoteric and complicated, so they cannot be said to be created by the Creator with the intention of giving knowledge to the common and ordinary Jiva (living being) because he would find it extremely difficult to decipher their contents. But it is not true because the Vedas are vast repositories of knowledge to suit all categories of the Jivas and to cater to all the levels of intelligence and wisdom they have.

To wit, though it is true that some of the knowledge contained in the Vedas are indeed too complex and esoteric, but such instances are limited and are intended for those Jivas who have high mental abilities. But the majority of the teaching of the Vedas is easy to understand and follow in practical life. Of course some basic level of intelligence and wisdom are necessary in this case too as it is with acquisition of any knowledge even in the secular world. (90)

[Usually it is believed that the Vedas, especially the part that contains knowledge of metaphysics and theology, are highly complex and incomprehensible. And the other part that deals with rituals is useless as it has no direct bearing for the enlightenment of a creature and his spiritual welfare. But this is also true in our secular world: all fields of learning, such as science, arts, commerce, philosophy, medicine, engineering, law, management, electronic technology etc., have varying levels of complexities in the school and college curriculum. All students are not of equal intelligence, and their aptitudes too vary from individual to individual. For instance, some students find mathematics beyond their abilities, while some simply enjoy this subject.

Again, all the basic subjects such as physics, chemistry, biological sciences (zoology, botany), mathematics, history, geography and languages are taught to all the students in school, whether they like it or not, and whether or not they are of any use to a student later in life. It is also the same case with the Vedas—all the knowledge contained in the Vedas is not equally useful to all, and a wise person would choose from the vast repository of knowledge that is made available to him only that part which suits him and fulfils his purpose of study.]

३ /१ /७ फलमस्माद्बादरायणो दृष्टत्वात् ॥ ९१ ॥

3 /1 /7 phalamasmādbādarāyaṇō dr̥ṣṭatvāt || 91||

(3/1/7) It is the Lord God who grants rewards or punishments for the deeds done by a creature. A similar thing is observed in this secular world too. (91)

[If the subject of a king does some good deed or service for the king, he is duly rewarded by the king. On the other hand if the person commits some crime or evil deed, the king would punish him. To wit, granting rewards or giving punishment is the prerogative of the king.

Similarly, it is the Lord God who gives reward and punishment to the Jiva according to the deed done by him.]

३ /१ /८ व्युत्क्रमादप्ययस्तथा दृष्टम् ॥ ९२॥

3 /1 /8 vyutkramādapyayastathā dṛṣṭam || 92||

(3/1/8) At the time of conclusion (of the cycle of creation, or the death of an individual creature), the elements that constitute this universe follow the reverse order in which they were created to finally merge with their primary source. This is also seen in this secular world. (92)

[The elements were created in a sequential order, from the subtlest to the grossest. The five fundamental elements of creation are sky, air, fire, water and earth. Out of them, the sky is the subtlest and the earth is the grossest, with the other elements in this series gradually increasing in grossness from air to fire to water. The sequence that was followed for the creation of these elements at the time of revelation of this universe is—sky, air, fire, water and earth in this order. All these five elements act as the basic building blocks for this creation. The creation is the sum total of these elements combining and interacting with each other in different ratios, permutations and combinations.

When the time of conclusion arrives, the elements are released and follow the reverse sequence of their formation: the earth dissolves into the water, the water into the fire, the fire into the air, the air into the sky. And finally the sky turns into the cosmic ether to form the cosmic void. When the new cycle of creation begins, this sequence of disintegration is reversed once again.

This sequence is easy to visualise. The 'earth' would disintegrate and sink into the ocean which consists of 'water'. To wit, the earth element is absorbed in the water element. This water would be evaporated by the heat of the sun, which means that the 'fire' would make the water vanish. To wit, the water element is absorbed by the fire element. The 'air' present in the atmosphere would blow out the fire with its strong gust, as is witnessed in storms where no fire can be kept alight. To wit, the fire element is absorbed by the air element. The 'sky' is fathomless and endless. We may experience a gust of wind on earth, but in outer space there is complete stillness. To wit, the air element is absorbed by the sky element. And then what happens to the 'sky' element. The sky element that constitutes this mortal world is absorbed in the endless void of the outer space filled with ether. This last frontier is eternal because it absorbs everything else and remains in existence till the time comes for the new cycle of creation to start. At that time, the elements that had collapsed earlier into the cosmic ether start to spread out in a sequence that is reverse of the one in which they had collapsed. To wit, first the sky comes into being, then comes the air that fills this sky, then this air blows softly to ignite the dormant cosmic fire, which in its turn provides warmth that helps life to spring up from its hibernating mode. The water element emerges to cool down the heat of the fire. Finally comes into existence the earth that would form a base for all the above elements.

How the grosser aspect of the earth disintegrates into its subtle aspect known as the 'earth element' will be clear by a simple example. An earthen pot represents the gross aspect of the earth as it is moulded from earth. When this pot breaks and its pieces crushed, its original shape vanishes and becomes indistinguishable from the earth and its soil on which it falls to become one with it. In this example we see that the grosser aspect of earth symbolised by the pot has disintegrated into the subtle form of the earth element when it falls on the ground and mixes with the soil to become indistinguishable from it.

A similar thing can be witnessed in the case of the water element. When we have water in a glass, this water has a form and observable attributes, and so it is the grosser form of the water element. But when this water is heated it evaporates and becomes invisible. Where has it gone? It has been converted into vapour and moisture that assumes so fine a form that we can't see it any more. The molecules of water that were in a gross form have now converted themselves into a subtle form. So we say that the grosser form of the water element has been transformed into its subtle form.

The fire that burns is visible and has certain characteristic features. But the same fire in the form of heat and warmth is not visible. The former aspect is the gross aspect of the fire element, and the latter is its subtle aspect.

The air that blows and is felt against our faces or the air that is filled with some kind of scent as from a flower or perfume is the grosser aspect of the air element, but the air that is still or the air that we breathe is its subtle form.

The sky above the earth seems to be of different hues of colour and filled with so many celestial bodies. This is the grosser aspect of the sky element. On the other hand, the space that fills the cosmos, or the space between the different internal organs of our own bodies which we can't see but which nevertheless is there is the subtle aspect of the sky element.]

----------*********----------

(7) SHANDILYA BHAKTI SUTRA

Aphorisms for Devotion to God and

The Principles of the Philosophy of Love for Him

[Roman Transliteration of Text, English Exposition, Elaborate Notes]

Chapter 3, Part 2:

Verse nos. 93-100

॥ शाण्डिल्य भक्ति सूत्रम् ॥

तृतीयोऽध्यायः

द्वितीयमाह्निकम्

|| śāṇḍilya bhakti sūtram ||

tr̥tīyō 'dhyāyaḥ

dvitīyamāhnikam

३ /२ /१ तदैक्यं नानात्वैकत्वमुपाधियोगहानादादित्यवत्
॥ ९३ ॥

3 /2 /1 tadaikyaṁ nānātvaikatvamupādhiyōgahānādādityavat

|| 93||

(3/2/1) 'That', i.e. the 'Supreme Being' (who is also known as Brahm, and who represents the cosmic Consciousness), is One and without a second (tadaikyaṁ). He is immutable, constant, eternal and without a parallel.

Inspite of this Truth that is absolutely irrefutable and unequivocal, the Supreme Being, or the Brahm, appears to be have countless forms and multifarious attributes because he has voluntarily assumed all these forms in order to reveal himself in the form of this creation (nānātvaikatvamupādhiyōgahāna). To wit, the apparent multiplicity in his otherwise One and immutable form is due to the fact that the entire creation, with its astounding array of variations and different forms of entities that baffle the mind, are all manifestations of the same divine entity.

It is like the case of one single 'sun' (āditya) appearing to be many in number if one sees its reflection in the water filled in a number of pots and pans. If these reflecting multiple reflecting surfaces are removed then one would realise that the truth about the 'sun' is that it is one and only one. (93)

[This verse basically teaches to see unity in diversity. Just like the different images of the sun seen in the water does not mean that there are more than one sun, the multifarious gross forms and astounding variations in virtues and attributes in which the cosmic Consciousness has revealed itself in this creation does not mean that its primary form is not pristine pure and has any kind of taint.

The Chandogya Upanishad, 3/14/1, says that: "All this is indeed Brahm, and nothing but Brahm."

The Katha Upanishad, 4/11 says: "There is no multiplicity here."

Srimad Bhagvad Geeta, 13/33, says: "Even as a single sun illuminates the entire world, the Atma that is pure consciousness, immutable and one too illuminates (gives meaning, life and consciousness to) this world."

Vishnu Puran, 2/16/22-23, says: "Even as the one unchangeable sky appears to have diferrent hues of colour such as grey or blue (due to dust, smoke, cloud, moisture and other impurities), so does the same pure and universal Consciousness known as the Atma appear to have different forms with multiple variations to a person who is deluded and ignorant. Whatever spiritual Truth there is in the world is known as the Atma, and there is nothing other than it."

It has been said earlier in verse nos. 85 and 87 of Shandilya Bhakti Sutra that the entire creation has come into existence from one single entity known as Brahm. It is Brahm that is revealed or manifested in the form of the entire creation. Put simply it means that all the units in this creation, the animate as well as the inanimate, the gross as well as the subtle, the minutest form as well as the most colossus one, are one or the other forms of Brahm itself. Verily indeed, there is nothing but Brahm; there is nothing in this creation that is not Brahm.

Brahm, i.e. the Supreme Being, is the personified form of cosmic Consciousness which is eternal, universal, without attributes, invisible, sublime and subtle. When this Consciousness reveals itself in the form of this creation it assumes certain characteristics that are unique to this creation, and also distinguish it from Brahm. Some of the characteristics of this creation that distinguish it from Brahm are the following: the creation is mortal, limited, with attributes, visible and gross, whereas Brahm is just the opposite of these.

The creation is of any value because its primary form known as Brahm represents the Absolute Truth. Obviously, without Brahm this entire creation would be meaningless and false.

And what or who is 'Brahm'? Brahm is the cosmic Consciousness that is at the root of this creation; it is the cosmic Consciousness that has created this living world. This is so obvious that it does not need any explanation—because only an entity that has intelligence, energy, dynamism and life would be able to do anything creative and constructive, for dead, inane and lifeless entities don't do anything at all, they can't create or do any constructive work.

There are two basic levels at which this cosmic Consciousness is understood. One is at the macrocosmic level, and the other is at the microcosmic level. At the macrocosmic level we recognise the universal Consciousness as 'Brahm' or the Supreme Being, while at the microcosmic level it is called a Jiva, the living being. This Brahm when it is viewed or understood or perceived at the sublime and subtle level of creation exhibits the characteristics of pure Consciousness—i.e. it is eternal, immutable, formless, without attributes, all-pervading, all-knowing etc. But when this same Brahm reveals itself in a grosser form that characterises this world, it also has to assume certain characters that are unique to this world—i.e. it is gross, mortal, subject to divisions, is perishable, with a form and attributes, is limited in scope, scale and reach, and so on and so forth.

So therefore, when Brahm (the cosmic Consciousness) reveals itself in the form of the Jiva (the living being) in this world, it appears to have lost its pristine form by assuming so many characteristics and attributes that are gross in nature and quite at variance from the sublime and subtle qualities and virtues of Brahm.

This situation leads to the mistaken belief that the Supreme Being has multiple forms known as Jivas, the living beings, in this world, and that they are separate entities, just like the many images of the single sun creates an illusion that there is more than one sun, and that each reflection of the sun has an independent truthful existence. If the water is stirred a bit then the image of the sun gets blurred or it may even vanish from sight, but does that mean there is no sun, or that the sun is affected in any way whatsoever?

So briefly, a wise and enlightened devotee sees his Lord God everywhere around him, in all individuals and things. So he never feels that the Lord is far away, for he knows that the nearest object to him represents his beloved Lord. This universal view of the Supreme Being marks the pinnacle of Bhakti; it is a signal that the devotee has reached that state of enlightenment where he has risen above the gross and the mundane to have a transcendental view the world, where he sees the entire world as a manifestation of his Lord God, and nothing else.

At this enlightened mental stage the devotee does not need to go to any 'heaven' where the Lord lives, because this so-called heaven is right here where he lives at present. This exalted state of mind marks the mature stage of Bhakti.]

३ /२ /२ पृथगिति चेन्न परेणासम्बन्धात् प्रकाशानाम् ॥ ९४ ॥

3 /2 /2 pṛthagiti cēnna parēṇāsambandhāt prakāśānām || 94||

(3/2/2) If it is said that since the mortal creature (the Jiva, the living being) has many attributes that are opposite to those of Brahm, the Supreme Being, so therefore the creature must be different from Brahm—then this argument is fallacious and misleading.

The reason is that this difference appears only at the superficial level, but if one looks a bit deeper he would discover the reality and the truth that the 'Consciousness' that lights the inner-self of the creature (i.e. which injects life into the gross body of the creature in the form of his Atma or soul) is the same Consciousness that lights up the entire creation in the form of the Parmatma or the supreme Atma known as Brahm. (94)

["Consciousness" represents life; without consciousness there is no life. All living beings have this Consciousness within their gross bodies. If they didn't have it they would be lifeless and dead. The individual living being represents this 'Consciousness' at the micro-level of creation. When we examine this creation from a broader and wider perspective, i.e. have a macro-level of understanding, we discover that it is the same Consciousness that pervades throughout this creation. At this level it is called the Parmatma, the Supreme Atma.

This Supreme Atma (known by different names such as Brahm, the Supreme Being, Parmatma etc.) is eternal, immutable and immanent because it represents the subtle and sublime form of pure Consciousness. On the other hand when this Consciousness reveals itself in a gross body of a creature it is called a Jiva, the living being.

Since the Jiva has a gross body, the Consciousness too appears to be gross. On the other hand, since Brahm is divine in nature, the Consciousness in this form too appears to be divine, sublime and subtle. But essentially they are the same.

An illustration would clear this concept. The same sun appears to have different levels of brilliance, different shapes, sizes and colour under different situations and times of the day. It may even lose its splendour altogether and get progressively reduced in size and shape during the solar eclipse. During a cloudy sky the sun may completely vanish from sight, or appear fleetingly and blurred. But does that mean that the primary form of the sun ever changes or is affected by the gross changes in its environment? The obvious answer is 'no'.

Another way to look at this example of the sun is this: The sun illuminates the world equally, but if there is a cloud or thick smoke in the sky then that part of the earth does not get sunlight. Does it mean that the sun is not shining or has become blurred, or that it has become partial or biased against certain parts of the world and has refused to give it light? Once again the answer is 'no'.

Similarly, the pristine pure Atma which is nothing but Consciousness remains unchanged and unaffected by the grossness of the world, both at the micro level of creation as well as at its macro level. But it appears to show diversity and variations due to many factors that are associated with this gross creation. If one becomes wise and enlightened then he would rise above the grossness of this mundane world to see and understand the truth and the reality of the Atma.]

३ /२ /३ न विकारिणस्तु करणविकारात् ॥ ९५॥

3 /2 /3 na vikāriṇastu karaṇavikārāt || 95||

(3/2/3) That Brahm, the Supreme Being, has no shortcomings, negativities and taints that are usually associated with this creation (na vikāriṇastu), though it is a fact that the creation is a manifestation of Brahm, and therefore whatever exists in this creation, including its negativities and taints, are deemed to have originated in Brahm as he is the cause of everything (karaṇavikārāt), making it look as if Brahm too is tainted and has negativities in him like his revelation known as creation.

This is a wrong and an erroneous surmise about the eclectic virtues of Brahm, and is contradictory to the actual facts. The fact is that Brahm is taintless and without any negativities of any kind. The reason is that Brahm represents pure Consciousness in its most divine, holy, sublime and subtle form. When this primarily pristine pure entity revealed itself in the form of this visible creation it automatically became grosser, because the product, the creation, is gross. To wit, Consciousness (or Brahm) appears to have lost its prisine purity, and instead become tainted by negativities that are so typical and so closely associated with this gross world. But grossness of the product, i.e. this creation, does not mean that the primary source of it, i.e. the Brahm, is gross too. (95)

[The reason why this creation, or this known world, with its taints, negativities and shortcomings does not reflect the true nature of its creator Brahm, the Supreme Being or the cosmic Consciousness, is that the creation is a product of the 'Maya Shakti' of Brahm. This Maya Shakti refers to the powers of Brahm to create delusions at a cosmic and universal level. Refer: verse nos. 86-88 herein above.

So therefore it follows that the creation, which is the product of the Maya Shakti, would definitely have virtues of its originator, which here is Maya Shakti, and it because of this fact too that the creation has grossness and many negative qualities that Brahm lacks though it is Brahm who is deemed to be the Supreme Authority who created everything.

To wit, even though Brahm is the Supreme Authority who is behind everything in existence, but the actual power that created this tainted and corrupted world is the Maya Shakti of Brahm, and not Brahm himself. It's like the case of an Emperor being held responsible and accused for any misdeeds done by his powerful ministers, knights or kings who have been empowered by the Emperor to govern his vast and extended empire. A person of low wisdom would accuse the Emperor for the many mischief created by others who act on his behalf, but an intelligent man of wisdom would realise the truth and would not blame the Sovereign for any evil for this man knows that the Emperor is an extremely holy person who can never be accused of any wrongdoings.

Likewise, wise and enlightened men never accuse Brahm of having taints, shortcomings and corruptions that dominate this world even though this creation has been created by Brahm because they know that it is the Maya Shakti that has spoilt everything.

So now, what is the solution? How would the Jiva, the living being who lives in this world and is invariably subjected to the negative impacts of the Maya Shakti that has produced so many spiritual problems for him, find freedom from its shackles and get rid of the torments caused by negativities, and get peace and happiness instead? The answer is to this grave spiritual problem of existence lies in the theme of this Book: it is 'Bhakti'. This is explicitly mentioned in the next verse no. 96 herein below.

To wit, if a person of wisdom develops devotion and love for the Lord God, if he turns away from this world which torments him and tries to drag him deeper into the whirlpool of miseries and troubles, and instead turn towards the Lord who is the great liberator and redeemer of all—then surely the person would overcome the negativities and taints associated with Maya and find deliverance from this world and its torments.

The intent of this verse is to convince the devotee that the Lord God he worships is pristine pure, holy and divine, and he should not be misled or go astray from his spiritual path by any confusions and doubts in this regard.]

३ /२ /४ अनन्यभक्त्या तदूबुद्धिर्बुद्धिलयादत्यन्तम् ॥ ९६ ॥

3 /2 /4 ananyabhaktyā tadūbuddhirbuddhilayādatyantam || 96||

(3/2/4) [This verse answers the great spiritual dilemma: how would one find freedom from the confusions and delusions that dominate this world, and attain peace, bliss and beatitude of an abiding nature?]

When one develops Paraa Bhakti for the Lord God (i.e. when one develops deep, true and unwavering devotion, love and affection for the Lord, when one completely surrenders himself to the Lord and worships him with faith and sincerity), one is able to overcome the distraction and confusion caused by the mind and its inherent tendency to doubt and be sceptic about everything.

It is only then that the spiritual aspirant finds eternal peace, bliss, felicity and beatitude for himself. It is only then that he finds freedom from all miseries and torments that cause so much consternation and perplexity for him. It is only then that he attains liberation and deliverance for himself, and emancipation and salvation for his soul. (96)

[The very first Upanishad of the Krishna Yajur Veda tradition is known as the 'Katha Upanishad'. In its Canto 2, Part 2, verse no. 13 we read: "He (the Supreme Being; Brahm) who is the chief amongst all wise and enlightened beings, who is the chief eternal being amongst all those who are deemed to be eternal, he who has revealed himself in the form of all living beings although he is One and without a second, he who gives all the living beings the reward according to their individual deeds though he himself is neutral and does not get involved in anything—verily indeed, eternal peace, bliss and beatitude are found by nobody else but only those persons who are self-realised, wise and enlightened enough to worship and visualise that Supreme Atma, the 'Parmatma', that represents cosmic Consciousness, right within their own self as their own Atma, which is also pure consciousness and an image of the Parmatma."

The importance of Bhakti has been emphasised in Srimad Bhagvad Geeta, 8/22 by Lord Krishna when he says: "That eternal unmanifest 'Purush', another name for the cosmic form of the Supreme Being, is the one in whom all living beings reside, and it is he who resides in all living beings (in the form of their Atma or pure conscious soul). He is attainable solely by Bhakti (devotion, love and affection for the Lord God).

Thus, a wise person should rise above the mundane and become 'self' realised. He must understand that of all the objects of veneration in this life, it is this 'Self', both at the microcosmic level of the individual creature as well as at the universal and the macrocosmic level of the entire creation, that is the most venerable. In all sooth and without gainsay, only a person who has understood this universal and irrefutable spiritual Truth and revels in the 'Self' would find eternal happiness and true joy in life, and nobody else.

And what is this 'Self'? It is the pure conscious Atma which is the true 'self' of all living beings at the micro level of this creation, and the Parmatma, the Supreme Atma that is known as the Supreme Being, at the macro level of this creation.

This Atma is a universal, eternal and pristine pure conscious entity. The rest of this creation is gross and perishable. So therefore, if a person pursues an entity that is itself perishable, i.e. if he pursues this gross world, he cannot expect to find eternity and peace as a reward; such a person is deluded inasmuch as he seeks eternity and bliss from an entity that is inherently mortal and a fount of miseries.

On the other hand, if a person is wise he would worship the

Atma which is eternal and blissful, and therefore the reward that comes to him is in likeness of his object of worship—i.e. he gets eternal bliss and happiness.]

३ /२ /५ आयुश्चिरमितरेषां तु हानिरनास्पदत्वात् ॥ ९७॥

3 /2 /5 āyuściramitarēṣāṁ tu hāniranāspadatvāt || 97||

(3/2/5) A self-realised and enlightened person who has attained Paraa Bhakti, i.e. who has developed the supreme form of devotion and love to the Lord God, is destined to liberation and deliverance from the cycle of birth and death in this mortal mundane world; he is destined to attain emancipation and salvation of his soul; he is destined to attain oneness with the Supreme Being as he is able to merge his Atma with the Parmatma, the Supreme Atma.

But he has to live in this world in a dispassionate and detached manner till the time all his past deeds and their consequences are dissipated. Since he has managed to control his mind (as stated in verse no. 96 herein above), no fresh deeds are deemed to be done by him that would create any new chain of consequences for him. So as a result, when he leaves his gross body at the time of his death, he finds final liberation for himself; he attains final deliverance from the cycle of transmigration. (97)

[This verse says that if a wise person develops the supreme form of Bhakti for the Lord God, he will be able to have peace and joy in this world itself. This wise devotee would not be subjected to the suffering from the countless torments, pains and miseries associated with life in this world from which his other friends and peers who do not have Bhakti suffer. So he leads a pleasurable life of joy and happiness spread all around him. This happens also because this wise devotee sees his Lord in every unit of creation as advised in verse nos. 85-93. He feels the same closeness with his beloved Lord God as he would find when his soul leaves the confines of the gross body to merge with the infinite Atma, the cosmic Consciousness.

Forsooth and without gainsay, this is, after all, the main objective of Bhakti.]

३ /२ /६ संसृतिरेषामभक्तिः स्यान्नाज्ञानात् कारणासिद्धेः ॥ ९८ ॥

3 /2 /6 saṁsr̥tirēṣāmabhaktiḥ syānnājñānāt kāraṇāsiddhēḥ || 98||

(3/2/6) A Jiva (the living being) is shakled to this world and feels miserable and tormented because he lacks the eclectic virtue of Bhakti (devotion, affection and love for Lord God) in him (saṁsr̥tirēṣāmabhaktiḥ). [The Jiva is trapped in this world due to the effects of Maya or delusions. Bhakti is the only remedy for this disease; Bhakti helps the Jiva to overcome the effects of Maya. Bhakti helps the Jiva to free himself from the fetters that tie his soul to the endless cycle of birth and death in this mortal world as it provides him the opportunity to attain God-realisation that grants eternal beatitude and felicity. Hence, till the time Bhakti develops in the heart of the Jiva he would remain trapped in the cycle of transmigration with its attendent miseries and torments.][1]

It is not correct to say that the Jiva is trapped in this world due to lack of Gyan (knowledge of all shades, philosophical, spiritual or empirical; awareness) because no living being, from the single-cell organism to the most advanced creature, is completely devoid of some level of knowledge and awareness, even if it is of a primary nature, for the simple reason that all living beings are 'conscious', and 'consciousness' is a personified form of the virtue of Gyan. Hence it is beyond doubt that lack of Gyan is not the primary cause of the Jiva's entrapment in this world (syānnājñānāt kāraṇāsiddhēḥ).[2] (98)

[[1]This verse essentially says that the chief cause of the creature getting trapped in the cycle of birth and death in this world is his lack of Bhakti (devotion for Lord God), and it is not lack of Gyan (knowledge).

This is because Maya or delusions causes the creature to think that the world, which is mortal and gross and full of miseries, is its true habitat, that real pleasure, joy and happiness is got from the material things of the world, that there is nothing beyond this life and world, that the world is true and worthy of attention, that success is measured by acquiring as much share of the material objects of this world as possible, and so on and so forth.

This fallacious and erroneous conception keeps the creature trapped endlessly in the cycle of birth and death because he would like to come back to this mortal world again and again at the end of his life.

It is said in the scriptures that Brahm, the Supreme Creator, has employed his cosmic powers of creating delusions, known as Maya Shakti, to keep the wheel of creation rolling endlessly till the time he wants to put a hold on it. To wit, the Lord is the controller and master of Maya. So therefore, if a certain Jiva is able to please the Lord God by having Bhakti for him, by surrendering before the Lord and praying that he be liberated from the miseries and torments caused by Maya, the merciful and compassionate Lord immediately orders his Maya not to disturb his devotee. The result is that this Jiva, the devotee of the Lord God, finds freedom from the clutches of Maya, which in turn means he is freed from its shackling effects to find eternal freedom from the cycle of birth and death in this mortal and gross world. The blessed Jiva's soul gets emancipation and salvation; he attains eternal peace, bliss, felicity and beatitude.

Earlier in verse no. 86 we have already read that this world has been created by Maya.

These facts—(a) that this creation has been created by the Lord using his Maya Shakti, (b) that Maya keeps the creature entangled in this world and its web of delusions, and (c) that it is Bhakti only that helps the Jiva to break free from the clutches of Maya, and thereby obtain freedom from all miseries and torments caused by the latter—are clearly reiterated at different places in Ram Charit Manas.

For instance, in Ram Charit Manas, Uttar Kand, Chaupai line no. 3 that precedes Doha no. 86, Lord Ram says: "My Maya has made it possible for this creation, along with all its creatures as well as its animate and inanimate aspects, to come into existence."

In Ram Charit Manas, Uttar Kand, Chaupai line nos. 2-3 that precedes Doha no. 89, we read that Kaagbhusund, the saintly crow, tells Garud, the celestial mount of Lord Vishnu, that: "I was blessed by Lord Ram with the glorious boon of Bhakti, and from that time Maya has had no effect upon me."

In Ram Charit Manas, Uttar Kand, Chaupai line nos. 4-5 that precede Doha no. 44, we read that: "The Jiva remains trapped and roams endlessly in the cycle of transmigration for countless generations due to the effect of Maya. This Maya surrounds the Jiva from all sides so much so that it drives and controls all his deeds, thoughts, nature, qualities, characters traits and circumstances."

In Ram Charit Manas, Uttar Kand, Chaupai line nos. 1-2 that precede Doha no. 45, we read that: "If you wish to have heavenly happiness and bliss right here in this world during your lifetime, then you must develop Bhakti for the Lord God. This is the best path shown by the Vedas and the Purans (ancient scriptures)."

In Ram Charit Manas, Uttar Kand, Chaupai line nos. 3-8 that precede Doha no. 116, we read that: "Maya and Bhakti are both like maids of the Lord God; they serve him and are obedient to him. But Bhakti is favourite of the Lord, whereas Maya is just like a court dancer. Hence, Maya is afraid to annoy Bhakti. So if a person wants to please the Lord he must first have Bhakti on his side; then Maya would be easy to overcome or subdue."

Another irrefutable fact that the Lord God cannot be attained by any method such as Yoga (meditation), Tapa (penance and austerity), Gyan (gnosis; acquisition of knowledge), Vairagya (renunciation, dispassion, detachment) etc., except by having love, affection and devotion for him, is also clearly mentioned in Ram Charit Manas, Uttar Kand, Chaupai line no. 1 that precedes Doha no. 62.

[2]Another important observation is that it is not the lack of Gyan that keeps the Jiva trapped in this world. All living beings have 'life' or 'consciousness' inside them, otherwise they would be dead in the first place. The presence of consciousness inside a Jiva, the living being, ensures that it has awareness, it can experience, it can learn and make decisions, no matter that they are very basic and rudimentary. Even a single-cell organism such as an amoeba or bacteria shows rudimentary awareness of its surroundings, and it responds to external stimuli to show that it can think and decide how to react to a given situation. If this is the case with the lowest of creatures in the hierarchy of creation, one would certainly deduce that a human being who is the most evolved of all the creatures does possess certain higher level of knowledge and awareness. This means that a human being can't claim that he does not know what he is doing and what are the consequences of his deeds; he cannot say that he has not learnt any lesson by seeing

how others are suffering from their misdeeds and evil actions; he cannot honestly say that he has found complete peace and bliss by remaining engaged in this world; and he cannot say that he has not realised that true happiness and peace is not to be found in this world but elsewhere, and that he is anxious to find out a way to break free from the endless cycle of miseries and torments in which he is trapped.

To wit, each single Jiva has some basic Gyan present in him, even if this Gyan is only rudimentary in nature, and not of high standard. So therefore, to say that Agyan, or lack of Gyan (knowledge of all shades, philosophical, spiritual or empirical; awareness), is at the root of the Jiva remaining trapped in this world and suffering from the miseries inflicted by it, will be a fallacious and erroneous proposition. The truth is that it is the lack of Bhakti that is at the root of the Jiva's predicaments and problems.

The remedy for the Jiva's spiritual ills and worldly problems is found in Bhakti—because it provides the Jiva with eternal peace, bliss and beatitude that no amount of Gyan or pursuance of any other path would ever do.

It is said in Vishnu Puran, 1/9/73, that a Jiva suffers from all sorts of wants, miseries, pain and grief only till the time he comes and surrenders himself before the Lord God, for the moment he does so all his torments vanish for good.

In this context, refer also to verse nos. 4-5 of this book.]

३ /२ /७ त्रीण्येषां नेत्राणि शब्दलिङ्गाक्षभेदाद्रुद्रवत् ॥ ९९॥

3 /2 /7 trīṇyēṣāṁ nētrāṇi śabdaliṅgākṣabhēdādrudravat || 99||

(3/2/7) To understand the underlying Truth of anything in this world, all Jivas have three sorts of 'eyes'—i.e. they have three tools, means or methods by which they can understand the Truth (just like the three eyes of Lord Shiva) (trīṇyēṣāṁ nētrāṇi).

These three 'eyes' (tools; means; methods) are the following: (i) The wise words of the scriptures that enlighten him about the Truth of anything (śabda); (ii) By inference or drawing a conclusion from available evidence or knowledge of anything; by deducing the Truth of something intelligently (liṅga); and (iii) By seeing the concerned thing in physical form to know about its Truth; by actually employing one's sense organs of perception to know about anything (prataksa).

These three tools or methods help the Jiva to 'see' the Truth and separate it from falsehood just like Lord Shiva (rudravat) who is able to see the difference between the Truth and falsehood (bhēdād). (99)

[Lord Shiva is reputed to have 'three eyes'. This is why he is also called 'Trinnetrum'—the Lord with three eyes. His two conventional eyes represent the view of the world during the waking state and the dreaming state of consciousness that are respectively known as the 'Jagrat' and the 'Swapna' states of existence. His third eye is the 'eye of wisdom' that symbolises the 'Turiya' state of consciousness that corresponds to the transcendental state where the pure 'consciousness' alone exists.

Similarly, a person has three ways to learn about the Truth of anything. One method is that he studies the scriptures and has faith in their words. The second method is that he makes intelligent deductions based on analysis of available knowledge. The third method is to actually see things for himself and become convinced about the Truth.

A wise person would employ all the three methods according to his aptitude and necessity. Ultimately he must understand the universal

Truth that real peace and happiness is found not in this gross mortal material world but in the spiritual realm; that if one wishes to attain eternal happiness and peace then it is only possible by pursuing the path of self-realisation and God-realisation because this path leads to the Jiva's liberation and deliverance from the cycle of birth and death, which in turn grants his soul eternity when it merges with the supreme Soul of this creation. This wisdom gives the Jiva a sense of bliss and happiness while he is still alive in this world, and at the time of death he finds eternal felicity and beatitude. To wit, 'heaven' becomes accessible to him right here in this world till he lives, and when he leaves his gross body he attains final deliverance, emancipation and salvation for himself.

Further, there are many prescribed methods to attain this spiritual goal—such as Yoga (meditation), Tapa (austerity and penance), Gyan (gnosis and knowledge, wisdom and enlightenment), Japa (repetition of holy Mantras), Dhyan (contemplation), Daan (charity), Yagya (sacrifices), and so on. But the best and the simplest method is the path of 'Bhakti'—the path of having devotion, love and affection for the Lord God.

Srimad Bhagvad Geeta, 14/11, says: "When the light of wisdom and enlightenment dawns on the horizon of a person, both at the level of his mind as well as at the level of his senses, then only can he see the Truth and realise its dominance everwhere."]

३ /२ /८ आविस्तिरोभावा विकाराः स्युः क्रियाफलसंयोगात् ॥ १००॥

3 /2 /8 āvistirōbhāvā vikārāḥ syuḥ kriyāphalasaṁyōgāt || 100||

(3/2/8) The concept of birth and death, or creation and destruction, is based on an error of understanding, a false perception of the reality, or a fallacious conception that the Jiva, who has not realised the 'Truth', has. [The Jiva who has not understood the Truth about his own 'self'—that this 'self' is not the gross body but pure Consciousness known as the Atma or the soul, and that this 'Consciousness' is an eternal, immutable and universal entity. Hence there is no question of its taking a birth and dying. This Truth applies both at the macro level of creation as well as at the micro level.]

A wise Jiva would understand that the true cause of this Atma taking birth and dying to take a re-birth once again lies in the Theory of Karma which says, inter alia, that if one gets involved in doing deeds in this world then he is bound by its consequences, and this chain continues endlessly as the creature goes on doing one deed after another in the hope of fulfilling all his desires which themselves are endless. Hence, once the Jiva allows himself to get involved in worldly deeds, he has fallen in a trap from which it is well neigh impossible to extricate oneself unless one is wise enough to see the 'Truth'. (100)

[The meaning is very clear. A wise person is one who realises that his true freedom lies in breaking the cycle of Karma by remaining detached from his deeds and their rewards. How is this possible in the physical world that relies on deeds to keep moving? The answer is that the wise person would offer all his deeds to the Lord God and think that he is just obeying the Lord's command. He is deemed to be serving the Lord selflessly, and therefore inspite of doing deeds he is deemed to be un-involved in them just like a faithful and obedient servant who carries out the orders of his master is not deemed to be the owner of the fruits or rewards that come as a result of anything done by him on the behalf of his master.

In this context, refer to verse nos. 64, 58, 75 and 91 also.

In short, a wise person takes the shelter of the supreme form of Bhakti as described at different places in this book Shandilya Bhakti Sutra in order to fulfil his spiritual aspirations. This is the Truth he must understand.]

समाप्तश्च तृतीयोऽध्यायः ॥ ३॥

इति श्रीशाण्डिल्यमहर्षिप्रणीतभक्तिसूत्रम्

samāptaśca tṛtīyō 'dhyāyaḥ || 3||

iti śrīśāṇḍilyamaharṣipraṇītabhaktisūtram

Thus ends Chapter 3 of Shandilya Bhakti Sutra expounded by the illustrious, learned and enlightened sage Shandilya.

----------*******----------

ABOUT THE AUTHOR

Ajai Kumar Chhawchharia left home when he was approximately 29 years of age due to an inner call of his heart that told him to devote his life in the service of his beloved Lord God, Sri Ram. Worldly attractions did not enchant him at all. So, he didn't marry, and after his father's death he came and settled permanently in Ayodhya, the holy town in India associated with Lord Ram.

Presently he works as an honorary manager of a world famous Kanak Bhavan Temple at Ayodhya, and spends his time writing in English so that the world can access the wonderful nectar of metaphysical, spiritual and devotional philosophy that is contained in Indian scriptures for which they are so renowned.

His English Books published separately by a reputed publisher of India, the details of whom can be had by contacting the author on his email given below, include: (i) The series on '108 Upanishads' in five volumes having eighteen parts, (ii) Veda Vyas' 'Adhyatma Ramayan' in two parts, (iii) 'Devi Puran Ramayan', (iv) Valmiki's 'Adbhut Ramayan', and (v) 'Biography of Lord Ram' based on Tulsidas' books.

Genre of Writing: Spiritualism, Philosophy, Metaphysics, Religious, Devotional and Theological.

The author's Books are available for order online both in 'e-book' format and 'paper-back book' format at

(a) www.amazon.com ; (b) www.pothi.com (in 'paper-back book' version), and (c) www.draft2digital.com (in 'e-book' version).

List of Books that are currently available as mentioned above :-

(A) (1) The Chariot of God: Dharma Rath; (2) OM and Naad; (3) YOGA—Its Practice and Philosophy according to the Upanishads; (4) Ram Geeta; (5) The Revelation of Creation—as envisioned in the Upanishads; (6) The Pentagon of Creation: As Expounded in the Upanishads; (7) The Triumvirate of Creation; (8) Maya: The Whirlpool of Delusions in Creation; (9) Surdas-Ram Charitawali; (10-a) The legend of Lord Shiva: Book 1 'Lord Shiva's marriage with Parvati'; (10-b) Book 2 'Lord Shiva's Sacred Hymns'; (10-c) Book 3 'Shiva's different names & their significance, Shiva Puran, Upanishads'; (11) the Mahavakyas of the Upanishads; (13) Lord Ram's marriage with Sita (based on Tulsidas' books "Ram Charit Manas", "Janki Mangal", "Ram Lala Nahachu" & "Geetawali", and sage Veda Vyas' book "Adhyatma Ramayan"; (14) "Anthology of Sacred Hymns, Stotras & Mantras of Lord Ram"; (15) "Vairagya Shatkam" of king-sage Bhartrihari; (16) An Anthology of the Sanyas Upanishads-Parts 1 and 2; (17) "Kaag-Bhusund Ramayan" or the "Aadi Ramayan" based on Tulsidas' Ram Charit Manas; (18) The Legendary Glory of Hanuman; (19) "Narad Bhakti Sutra"—Aphorisms for Devotion for God and the Principles of Love for the Lord; (20) "Shandilya Bhakti Sutra"—Aphorisms for Devotion for God and the Principles of Love for the Lord according to the illustrious sage Shandilya; (21) "Bhakti Sutra Mala"—A Garland of Spiritual Wisdom in the form of an Anthology of Aphorisms pertaining to Bhakti or devotion, love and affection for Lord God.

(B) Goswami Tulsidas Series: (1) Book 1- 'Dohawali'; (2) Book 2- 'Parvati Mangal'; (3) Book 3- 'Kavitawali'; (4) Book 4- 'Janki Mangal'; (5) Book 5- 'Ram Lala Nahachu'; (6) Book 6- 'Geetawali Ramayan'; (7) Book 7-

'Vairagya Sandipani'; (8) Book 8- 'Vinai Patrika'.

The rest of the Books are in various stages of production, and would be made available on-line at the above websites as and when they are ready.

Contact details of Ajai Kumar Chhawchharia—

Postal address:-36-A, Rajghat Colony, Parikrama Marg, P.O.—Ayodhya, Pin—224123, Distt. Faizabad, U.P. India.

Phone:—(India) +919451290400; +919935613060.

Email of Author: (1) ajaichhawchharia@gmail.com

(2) ajaikumarbooks@gmail.com

Facebook : www.facebook.com/ajaikumarchhawchharia8

Linkedin: www.linkedin.com/AjaiKumarChhawchharia

Goodreads:
https://www.goodreads.com/author/show/991710.Ajai_Kumar_Chhawchharia

52894969R00148

Made in the USA
Columbia, SC
08 March 2019